LEFT FACE

LEFT FACE

Soldier Unions
and
Resistance Movements
in Modern Armies

DAVID CORTRIGHT

AND

MAX WATTS

Contributions in Military Studies, Number 107

GREENWOOD PRESS
New York • Westport, Connecticut • London

Library of Congress Cataloging-in-Publication Data

Cortright, David.
    Left face : soldier unions and resistance movements in modern
armies / David Cortright and Max Watts.
        p.   cm.—(Contributions in military studies, ISSN 0883-6884
; no. 107)
    Includes bibliographical references and index.
    ISBN 0-313-27626-9 (alk. paper)
    1. Military unions—History—20th century.   2. Armed Forces—
Management—History—20th century.   I. Watts, Max.   II. Title.
III. Series.
UH740.C67   1991
331.89′041355′00904—dc20   90-46702

British Library Cataloguing in Publication Data is available.

Library of Congress Catalog Card Number: 90-46702
ISBN: 0-313-27626-9
ISSN: 0883-6884

First published in 1991

Greenwood Press, 88 Post Road West, Westport, CT 06881
An imprint of Greenwood Publishing Group, Inc.

Printed in the United States of America

The paper used in this book complies with the
Permanent Paper Standard issued by the National
Information Standards Organization (Z39.48-1984).

10 9 8 7 6 5 4 3 2 1

The "forgotten" fifth verse of "The Internationale":

> Les rois nous saoûlaient de fumès.
> Paix entre nous, guerre aux tyrans!
> Appliquons la grève aux armées,
> Crosse en l'air et rompons les rangs!
> S'ils s'obstinent, ces cannibales,
> A faire de nous des héros,
> Ils sauront bientôt que nos balles
> son pour nos propres généraux.

from *Les Boeufs Voient Rouge*, April 1975

Contents

Preface

Dear reader, we ask your indulgence for the peculiar nature of the volume before you. Apart from its unusual subject matter, soldier resistance, the book suffers the odd circumstance of being both history and a report on current events. *Left Face* was written over a period of more than fifteen years and was constantly interrupted by the activist obligations of the two authors: David Cortright to the demanding duties of Executive Director of SANE during the 1980s in the United States, and Max Watts to the founding and nurturing of the independent left-wing daily newspaper *Die Tageszeitung* in West Germany.

The book began from our participation in soldier movements in the 1960s and 1970s and continued through periodic observations into the 1980s and 1990s. Much of the manuscript was written in the 1970s and later reworked into historical perspective, although updates were continuously added right up to 1990.

Our sources and documentation are also unusual. The bulk of the information comes from low-ranking soldiers in the form of interviews and direct observation. We rely on scholarly journals and official reports, but most of our documentation is through the words and experience of soldiers in more than a dozen countries. Over the past twenty years we conducted more than a hundred interviews and group discussions with low-ranking soldiers, both conscripts and volunteers, in the U.S., Dutch, French, German (West and East), Italian, Swiss, Australian, British, Swedish, Danish, Finnish, Norwegian, Austrian, Polish, Belgian, Spanish, Portuguese, and Chilean armed forces. It is from this rich resource that the story of *Left Face* is told.

We were motivated to begin our inquiry in the early 1970s by the striking realization that the resistance then occurring in the U.S. military, which we and others assumed to be soley due to the Vietnam War, was in fact similar to resistance trends in other armies. We hypothesized at the time that this rebelliousness among soldiers, conscripts and volunteers, was connected to a broader social phenomenon: the spread of antiauthoritarian or postmaterialist values among youth in the world's most affluent countries. We rated the level of capital accumulation in these countries (by the admittedly crude measure of GNP per capita) and noted that GI resistance appears only in countries near the top. (See Table 1.1, Chapter 1).

We urge the reader not to take our theoretical framework too strictly. We mean it only as an approximation of an explantion, by no means certain. We agree with Alain Touraine from his study of student movements, *Post Industrial Society*:

These new movements do not come into being with the clarity that historical and sociological analysis will one day give them. They are formed in a period of rapid change, and do not, as events, have only one specific meaning. (pp. 66-67)

Nonetheless, the threshold concept has shown considerable predictive value. Spain and Greece, where no GI movements existed when we began the book, were just below the initial threshold line. Within a few years, however, evidence of soldier resistance emerged in both countries. In the 1970s we had speculated on the likely development of soldier resistance in Eastern Europe, also just below the initial threshold. Sure enough, by the late 1980s, twenty years after the West's "1968," a democratic revolution swept through the region and soldier resistance and military union movements appeared in the European socialist countries, in particular in East Germany and the Soviet Union.

Ultimately this is a book about peace, about a process within the military that could be considered bottom-up disarmament. When armies are more democratic and are challenged from within by trade unions and soldier resistance, their capacity for unpopular missions is diminished. When this occurs in all armies, none is at a disadvantage and the prospects for peace are enhanced all around.

We turn now to the soldiers themselves and their many struggles for greater freedom and dignity.

LEFT FACE

1

Soldiers Organize: An Overview

Amid knapsacks and army field jackets, in a musty auditorium strewn with pamphlets and newspapers, more than a hundred soldiers and recent veterans gathered in Amsterdam in November 1974 for the first International Soldiers' Congress. They trekked to Holland from nine European countries and the United States to exchange experiences in their common work for peace and justice inside the army. From the United States came Specialist Fifth Class Tom Doran, a short-haired paratrooper from Fort Bragg, North Carolina. A group of U.S. GIs also arrived from the garrison at Hanau, West Germany--accompanied by the longest-haired lieutenant in the army, Matthew Carroll. From France came a young draftee freshly released from the stockade for alleged subversion. In the West German delegation was a clean-cut panzergrenadiere conscript, clandestinely in Amsterdam, officially home on sick leave.

The congress was hosted with great efficiency by the Dutch soldiers' group, BVD (The League of Conscripts), who provided, among other amenities, a makeshift but effective translation service into four languages. The three-day gathering concluded with a huge, spirited rally in a modern arena across the street from the Utrecht headquarters of the VVDM (the Dutch Conscripts' Union), at the time the largest draftee organization in the world.

The Amsterdam congress showed soldiers and their civilian supporters the similarity of problems within different armies. Even more striking were the parallels discovered among the soldier movements of these armies. Soldiers from one country found that the struggles they were carrying on at home matched those of soldiers from other nations. The soldiers' movement had found common ground across many different countries and political circumstances.

Soldiers Rising

For most Americans the very existence of soldier protest comes as a complete surprise. Yet the soldiers' movement is very much in evidence in many countries. It first appeared not as an organized political movement but as a string of individual, spontaneous protests. Beginning in the mid- to late 1960s, the armies of Western Europe and the United States witnessed a steady increase, first in conscientious objection, then in desertion and unauthorized absence, and soon in organized protests and demonstrations. These diverse signs of soldier discontent rapidly coalesced into genuine social movements, sometimes with an infusion of support from civilian groups.[1]

The oldest and best organized soldiers' movement is the Dutch. Conscript committees first appeared in Holland in the mid-1960s. In July 1966, following a three-day uprising by Amsterdam's politicized hippies, the Provos, a group of soldiers formed what was to become the first permanent conscripts' union in history, The Union of Military Conscripts or VVDM. VVDM grew rapidly in its early years and by 1970 boasted 30,000 members, an amazing 70 percent of all conscripts. The union has had a long and inventive tradition of mass action, often employing provocative, even sardonic methods of protest. To resist what they considered the demeaning custom of saluting, for example, VVDM organized a "national saluting day" during which conscripts saluted everyone--each other, civilians and, yes, even officers. To dramatize poor conditions in the barracks, they mounted a "sleep out" in which dozens of soldiers spent the night on the lawn in sleeping bags. To protest short hair, conscripts refused haircuts and went to jail. Through more than two decades of continuous action the Dutch conscripts have won major changes in the condition of service, including the right to wear their hair any length they choose, and are among the highest paid soldiers in the world. We will have much more to say about the Dutch in Chapter 7.

Scandinavia has also witnessed considerable soldier organizing. This is especially so in Sweden, a nation that, contrary to popular impression, has a very large (per capita) army. Opposition began in the late 1960s with isolated, spontaneous protests. Within a few years it acquired a high degree of organization and mass support through the Draftees' Working Group, VAG. In the early 1970s thousands of soldiers engaged in protest campaigns and demonstrations. In 1972, for instance, approximately 1,000 soldiers in camps all over Sweden staged a collective sick-call strike. As in the Netherlands, these actions resulted in important victories, including the abolition of restrictions on leave and a huge increase in pay and separation bonuses. Conscript organizing has also emerged in Norway, Finland, and Denmark, as we shall examine in Chapter 8.

In Germany, the armed forces have faced only limited conscript organizing (although a large officer-directed Bundeswehr Verband, or Army Association, has existed for more than three decades). However, the Federal Republic has witnessed an unprecedented level of conscientious objection. The number of objectors began rising in the late 1960s from a previous level of 5,000 a year to 30,000 a year in the early 1970s, to more than 60,000 a year in the late 1980s.[2] Pacifist movements in Germany are among the strongest in the world. Rank-and-file soldier committees have also appeared, and there has been considerable interest in soldier groups affiliating with civilian unions. (The German military will be examined in Chapter 9.)

Important soldier organizing also arose in the 1970s in the French, Italian, and Spanish armed forces. In contrast to Holland and Sweden (where conscript movements have been officially recognized, if not sanctioned), soldier resistance in the Latin countries has been met with widespread repression. This has forced soldier movements to assume semiclandestine forms.

In France, early sporadic conscript organizing coalesced in the spring of 1974 around the so-called *L'Appel des Cent*. This "Call of the One Hundred" was initiated shortly before the 1974 presidential elections and was eventually signed by some 5,000 servicemen. During the campaign, 200 artillerymen marched through the southern provincial town of Draguignan to protest the arrest of petition signers. The resulting publicity and trial of three of the Draguignan soldiers in Marseilles brought national attention to the soldiers movement and sparked additional protests elsewhere. Soldier committees and GI newspapers began to sprout everywhere, with almost 100 groups active by the end of 1975. In November of that year several of these committees stunned an already shaken military establishment by announcing the formation of a "Syndicat des Soldats," a Soldiers' Union. This attempt to form a union was immediately denounced in hysterical speeches by the prime minister and even the president, and the organizers were arrested and thrown out of the army. After this incident the French soldiers movement shrank and went back underground, where it continues to this day (see Chapter 11).

In Italy a highly politicized soldiers' movement developed after 1970. It has included protests by draftees as well as Air Force sergeants. The two movements are interrelated and have attracted wide followings. In one joint effort in late 1975, over 10,000 soldiers and NCOs demonstrated. Interestingly, the powerful Italian Communist Party has never supported these soldiers, preferring to cultivate friendships with hopefully "republican" (liberal) generals. A substantial soldiers' movement also developed in Spain in the mid- to late 1970s. Like their counterparts in France, though, the Spanish conscripts faced severe repression, and their attempts to organize a soldiers' union were suppressed. (See Chapters 12 and 13.)

Other armies have also experienced resistance and organized opposition, including Switzerland, Austria, Belgium, to a lesser extent Britain and Australia, and, more recently, South Africa and Israel. In 1989 and 1990 such tendencies began to appear among soldiers in Eastern Europe as well. In all, soldiers movements have occurred in more than twenty countries.

The United States has also experienced soldier resistance. The GI movement of the Vietnam era was one of the most important soldier movements of any country in recent years, and was certainly the most extensive in American history. As described in detail in Cortright's *Soldiers in Revolt*, the disintegration of morale and discipline among low-ranking GIs during the latter stages of the Indochina war was a major factor in bringing that conflict to an end.

Since the all-volunteer force and the end of the Indochina war, organized protest in the U.S. military has largely disappeared. Little public evidence of dissent exists, and only a handful of struggling GI newspapers still appear. Nonetheless, widespread disciplinary conflict and morale problems have persisted. As we shall examine in Chapter 2, AWOL and desertion rates remained unusually high into the 1970s, while discharge and attrition rates soared to record heights. Occasional organized protests also appeared, including minor mutinies aboard ships in 1975 and a union petition of 2,000 GIs in 1977. Although less extensive than before, GI resistance continued into the all-volunteer force.

The New Soldier

In the United States, as in all the countries we have observed, the role of the soldier has undergone fundamental changes unrelated to specific wars or political events. The soldier movements of recent years are less a reaction to specific events than a reflection of fundamental changes in the attitude of youth toward the military. Today's soldiers think and behave differently than their predecessors. They are more skeptical of authority and more frequently act in opposition to military leadership. We view this soldier resistance as a general social phenomenon, part of what was called the "new left" in the 1960s or was sometimes referred to as a "counterculture," or "adversary culture." In more recent times social theorists refer to "new social movements" or to postmaterialist values. However it is described, the underlying phenomenon is the same--a challenge to society's hierarchical institutions, most particularly the armed forces.

Some will object, of course, that our analysis is overdrawn. They claim that such soldier resistance is nothing new, that similar events occurred before, for example in 1917-1919, or in 1945, and in any case that "it is now over." We disagree. Today's movements are not the same as the spasmodic, short-lived revolts that occurred during and after earlier wars. Soldier resistance today is a more permanent, peacetime development that is transforming the very nature of military service.

Even the establishment Trilateral Commission has lamented the "near collapse of the traditional authority structure" in the military. In its 1975 report *The Crisis of Democracy*, the commission observed that "the army, at least in its role as training school for organizational discipline and symbol and embodiment of patriotic values, has lost its moral and psychological appeal."[3] Traditional values of unquestioning obedience no longer dominate within the ranks.

These traits are not always overtly political, but they can spell trouble for highly structured institutions such as the armed forces. Armies are highly vulnerable to antiauthoritarian movements, far more so than universities or even factories. Media reports tend to give a contrary impression: There was more fuss in 1968 about the occupation of Columbia University led by Mark Rudd than about the month-long takeover of LBJ (Long Binh Jail) in Vietnam by imprisoned GIs.

Youth revolts may attract greater attention in Berkeley or the Sorbonne than in Mannheim or Fort Bragg, but the latter are far more threatening to the social order. Armies are the ultimate defenders of state power and authority. They are, as the Prussian kings inscribed on their cannon, the "ultimo ratio regis", the court of last resort. As long as society remains divided into classes, that is, into distinct social groups with sharply different access to wealth and ownership, governments will face a continuing need for the force of the military. But governments will also face a troubling contradiction: The armies that defend the interests of the rich and powerful take the vast majority of their soldiers from the poor and working classes. In order to ensure that privates will march, act, and if necessary kill and be killed for the interests of the ruling classes, armies must, in the last resort, be rigid and authoritarian. There are narrow limits to the degree of permissiveness allowable within such armies. It was perfectly possible for the red flag to fly from the ASTA (Student Union) of the University of Heidelberg for four years, but when it was hoisted over the U.S. Army's Turley Barracks in neighboring Mannheim for ten minutes it created a major furor. The very logic of the army's purpose required its immediate removal.

The repressiveness of military life is of course nothing new. What has changed is that soldiers are now less willing to tolerate the traditional restrictions and have started to do something about it. Previously a sullen if grumbling mass at the bottom of the military pyramid, soldiers have begun to stir. Even as enlisted life has improved in recent years (as it undeniably has throughout Europe and in the United States, in large part because of soldier struggles) GIs continue to fight for better conditions. Despite pay raises and a relative easing of discipline, armies have been unable to placate the now-restive soldiers. The classical model of unquestioning obedience and rigid hierarchy has begun to erode. This shift has enormous potential significance for the future purpose and role of the armed forces.

The Threshold Theory of Military Resistance

An important aspect of the phenomenon we are observing is the remarkable similarity of resistance events in the armies of more than a dozen countries. The levels of activity vary within these armies, but the basic forms and character of the resistance are strikingly similar. All of the nations where this resistance has emerged are highly capitalized. Resistance has developed only in the most highly industrialized nations, and only after a certain time--let us call it point "T"--in the late 1960s and early 1970s. None of the countries below a certain level of capital accumulation has exhibited the kind of independent enlisted resistance evident in the more industrialized societies. GI newspapers, for example, are confined solely to the recent experience of the most highly capitalized nations. They did not exist in previous historical periods,* and they do not exist in the developing nations.

A direct relationship seems to exist between the degree of capital accumulation and the tendency toward enlisted resistance. This can best be illustrated by drawing up a table that ranks the nations of the world according to some measure of capital accumulation. If we use the admittedly limited standard of gross national product per capita, we find the following listing of the most developed nations (the nations experiencing GI resistance marked by an asterisk):

---

*Rare exceptions were such publications as *The Flame*, edited by John Reed in Moscow in 1918-19 for distribution among American and British troops fighting the Bolsheviks in Murmansk and Archangel. The paper was produced for GIs, though, not by GIs.

Table 1.1
GNP Per Capita Ranking, Population per Soldier,
and Resistance in the Army[4]

Rank Country	GNP per Capita	Population Per Soldier	Form of Resistance
1 Kuwait	11491	95	No: OPEC country.
*2 Switzerland	7632	154	Yes: Active soldier committees and GI papers.
3 United Arab Emirates	7442	18	No: OPEC country.
*4 Sweden	6808	113	Yes: Considerable conscript activism; strong movement for unionism in the 1970s (see Ch. 8).
*5 USA	6666	97	Yes: GI movement, continuing problems in volunteer force (see Ch. 2).
6 Canada	6221	271	No: Volunteer force with high population per soldier ratio, but "manning crisis" recruitment problems (see Ch. 5).
*7 West Germany	6201	127	Yes: Widespread pacifism with some soldier organizing (Ch. 9).
8 Iceland	6186	–	No Military.
9 Luxembourg	6085	355	No: No known resistance; very high population per soldier ratio; very small military.
*10 Denmark	5964	137	Yes: National government-sponsored conscript organization spurred by leftist conscientious objector and soldier groups (Ch. 8).
*11 Norway	5767	114	Yes: National conscripts organization with some left-wing tendencies (Ch. 8).
*12 Belgium	5603	109	Yes: Small independent union of Flemish conscripts. Unionization of NCOs and junior officers.
?13 Australia	5420	193	? High population/soldier ratio. Strong draft resistance during Vietnam War; attempts at NCO/officer union formation (Ch. 5).
*14 Netherlands	5138	119	Yes: Large soldiers' movement and strong soldier unions (Ch. 7).

Table 1.1 (continued)

Rank Country	GNP per Capita	Population Per Soldier	Form of Resistance
15 Libya	5089	73	No: OPEC country.
*16 France	5059	105	Yes: Widespread soldier committees, newspapers in the 1970s. (Ch. 11). Right-wing officer revolts in earlier years.
17 Qatar	4933	45	No: OPEC country.
*18 Finland	4652	130	Yes: Conscript union (Ch. 8).
*19 Austria	4413	204	Yes: Periodic soldier resistance. High population to soldier ratio; small army.
20 New Zealand	4354	233	No: High population per soldier ratio; volunteer military.
21 Japan	4107	471	No: Little resistance. Very high population per soldier ratio, the highest of any developed country.
22 Saudi Arabia	3889	141	No: OPEC country.
*23 Israel	3869	23	Yes: Relatively late development of resistance influenced by "national mission" of military (Ch. 1).
*24 East Germany	3598	117	Yes: Early indications of unrest in the ranks. Soldier activism as part of the 1989 democratic uprising (Ch. 10).
25 United Kingdom	3419	158	No: Very little internal opposition, but considerable recruitment difficulty. High population to soldier ratio (Ch. 5).
*26 Czechoslovakia	3343	73	Yes: Indications of soldier organizing during the 1989 democratic uprising. Czechoslovak draftees now organized in the "Union of Youth in Uniform", SVM.
*27 USSR	2789	72	Yes: Growing draft resistance and unrest among conscripts, especially in the Baltics. Formation of an officer-led union in the 1980s (Ch. 10).

Table 1.1 (continued)

Rank Country	GNP per Capita	Population Per Soldier	Form of Resistance
˙28 Italy	2632	132	Yes: Widespread soldier organizing in 1970s. Many committees and papers among conscripts and Air Force NCOs (Ch. 12).
˙29 Spain	2388	124	Yes: Soldier committees and union movement in 1970s. Some (separate) resistance among captains. (Ch. 13).
30 Bahrain	2342	237	No: OPEC country.
˙31 Hungary	2330	102	Yes: Growing concern for conscientious objection and soldier rights as part of recent democratic renewal.
?32 Poland	2283	111	? Early Solidarity sympathies among soldiers; growing movement for conscientious objection to the draft.
33 Singapore	2273	257	No
?34 Ireland	2209	257	? Some individual protests. High population to soldier ratio; small volunteer army. Soldiers' union founded in 1990.
˙35 Greece	2184	56	Yes: Recent development of soldiers' movement.

Threshold level of GNP/Capita below which no independent rank-and-file resistance has yet been observed. Note: "Exceptions" of Portugal (rank 42) and South Africa (rank 48) discussed in chapters 1 and 14.

Rank Country	GNP per Capita	Population Per Soldier	Form of Resistance
?36 Romania	2054	123	? Officers rebellion against Ceausescu dictatorship. No evidence of independent soldier organizing.
37 Venezuela	2038	282	No: OPEC country.
38 Gabon	2002	257	No: OPEC country.
39 Trinidad and Tobago	1949	966	No: OPEC country.

Table 1.1 (continued)

Rank Country	GNP per Capita	Population Per Soldier	Form of Resistance
40 Oman	1878	78	No: OPEC country.
?41 Bulgaria	1844	57	? No evidence of soldiers joining 1989 protests.
*42 Portugal	1693	39	Yes: Effective "Armed Forces Movement" of left-wing officers (captains, majors) and NCOs; subsequent development of rank-and-file GI resistance (Ch. 14).
43 Lebanon	1401	173	No independent soldier resistance.
?44 Yugoslavia	1330	92	? Little soldier resistance as such, but recent agitation among students, youth, in northern, developed republics against "professionalization of the military" in favor of maintaining draft.
45 Argentina	1330	189	No rank-and-file soldier resistance; rank-and-file left-wing veterans organizations; right-wing generals.
46 Iran	1318	142	No known soldier resistance; air force NCOs and officer cadets supported anti-Shah revolution (Ch. 16).
47 Cyprus	1281	167	No
*48 South Africa	1272	507	Yes: Some resistance among white soldiers; GNP/Capita figures inapplicable, as based on total population (Ch. 1).

* GNP data from 1974; values expressed in 1974 prices and converted to dollars at 1974 exchange rates. Our table also includes data for population per soldier. This is added to measure the degree of mass participation in the military. A low population per soldier ratio, such as that of Sweden, indicates a large per capita armed force, what sociologists term a "mass army." Those nations without a mass army, e.g., with a population per soldier ratio above say 150, seem to be less affected by resistance behavior than those below. This is an important factor for explaining some of the exceptions to the general rule, as we shall note below.

The connection between a certain threshold of capital accumulation and resistance within the lower ranks is clear. Nearly all the nations at the top of our table have witnessed resistance inside the army. If we draw a line under the top thirty-five or so nations, and arbitrarily define all those above this threshold as highly capitalized, we find GI resistance only in these societies. Most of the nations above this line have experienced some form of GI-initiated resistance; few of the nations below it have been so affected.

Some readers will immediately ask: "What about Portugal?" Portugal, number forty-two in the table, is below our threshold level, but it witnessed a major military resistance movement in the mid-1970s, which did include, in its latter phases, an important enlisted soldiers' revolt. However, the Portuguese example does not fall exactly into the category of GI-initiated resistance. The originators of the Portuguese military movement were not enlisted men, but officers, mostly captains and majors of the MFA, the Armed Forces Movement. An independent enlisted resistance did appear, the SUV (Soldiers United Will Win), but it lasted only a few months and came only after rapid and intensive political upheaval throughout the entire country. The Portuguese case is a model not so much of soldier-led resistance but of an entirely separate phenomenon: the rise of leftward officer movements in the less capitalized countries.

The Portuguese situation is like that in a number of other countries, all of them below the capital accumulation threshold, in which groups of officers are breaking with traditional right-wing military politics. Leftward and nationalist tendencies among officers have led to the overthrow of established conservative regimes in several countries, including Ethiopia, Libya, Egypt, Iran and Peru. The recent nationalist uprising against the Ceausescu regime in Romania was a similar case of reformist officers helping to overthrow an unpopular and corrupt dictatorship.

It is essential to emphasize that this is a phenomenon separate from the independent soldier resistance described earlier. There is no indication of any sustained progressive officers' movement in the highly capitalized nations. In these countries the continuation of right-wing political leanings among officers remains the norm. The reader need reflect only on the origins of the French Fifth Republic, or observe the reactionary tendencies among certain British, Italian, or U.S. generals, to see the continuing right-wing leanings of the officer corps in these societies.

Two other related phenomena we have observed in countries near or below the threshold are the development of left-leaning non-commissioned officer (NCO) movements, and the tendency in these countries for the NCOs of the more technical services, the air force and the navy, to show greater independence from the (normally reactionary) command structure. Sometimes this NCO resistance occurs in countries where there is an active GI movement (such as Italy; see Chapter 12). However, there have been well-documented cases of NCO resistance in countries well below the threshold, where the army privates still follow the most repressive orders. A month before Chile's generals putsched bloodily against the Allende government, navy NCOs in Valparaiso attempted to frustrate the coup. In Iran the Shah was toppled when air force cadets and NCOs in Teheran joined and armed the civilian demonstrators. Neither Iran (GNP/capita rank of 46) nor Chile (GNP/capita rank of 58) can be considered highly capitalized. In neither country was there any sustained rank-and-file GI resistance: Chilean and Iranian infantrymen obeyed their generals' orders and continued to fire at their civilian brothers and sisters despite mass upheaval (see Chapters 15 and 16).

Generalizing from these observations of soldier and officer movements worldwide, we have drawn up a set of hypotheses about military resistance:

1. Independent left-wing movements among low-ranking soldiers and conscripts appear only in nations above a certain level of capital accumulation.
2. Left-wing military movements in nations below a certain level of capital accumulation occur among officers and NCOs.
3. An inverse correlation seems to exist between the rank of left-leaning soldier and officer resisters and the degree of capital accumulation of the country concerned.

Our primary formula, that the armies of highly capitalized nations develop enlisted resistance, is the fundamental thesis of this book. Our second hypothesis on the nature of left-wing officer movements is also important but is treated only briefly (in Chapters 14, 15, 16, and 17). We concentrate here on the heretofore neglected movements of enlisted people in the highly capitalized countries.

Our first hypothesis does not imply that capital accumulation is the sole factor in the development of soldier resistance, still less that resistance somehow automatically arises at a certain level of industrialization. Capital accumulation is a necessary condition for enlisted resistance but is not a sufficient one.

We also do not mean to imply that the level of capital accumulation is directly related to the intensity of resistance. It is not necessarily true, for example, that Holland or the United States will have greater soldier resistance than less-developed Italy. The process seems to work in a more general manner. Once a nation has reached a certain plateau or threshold of development, altered soldier behavior becomes possible; however, the intensity of the resistance then seems to depend primarily on other factors, including national political conditions and military policies. Resistance does not develop until a certain level of capitalization has occurred, but its success or intensity cannot be subsequently linked to the degree of capital accumulation.

In these highly capitalized nations, the process seems to be one of a "tipping effect." At a certain point, behavior patterns suddenly alter, creating a qualitative change after a quantitative buildup. After a period of accumulated development, quantity is transformed into quality, resulting in an apparently drastic change. At time "T" these changes affect a sufficiently large proportion of society's youth to alter attitudes toward the military. The result is a change in behavior and the emergence of soldier resistance.

The Exceptions

While it is true that enlisted resistance occurs only in societies that are highly capitalized, not all highly capitalized nations necessarily experience resistance. Indeed several of the most developed nations in the world have witnessed only very limited resistance. These include Britain, Japan, Canada, Australia, and New Zealand. These exceptions do not contradict our formulation, but they do add important qualifications.

The key exception is that GI resistance does not occur in volunteer armies with a low soldier-to-population ratio, that is, where there is no "mass army" effect. In this class of exceptions are the volunteer armies with a population-per-soldier ratio above 150.

Japan, for example, is a very highly capitalized society, and after World War II it developed a strong sense of antimilitarism. It might be expected to show GI resistance. But its Self Defense Force is a relatively small volunteer force with a population-per-soldier ratio of 471. It has seen very little internal opposition (although a few examples of soldier protest have been recorded, including a statement opposing SDF deployment to Okinawa by soldiers in 1972).[5] The volunteer armies of Canada, Australia, and New Zealand likewise have witnessed no sustained soldier movements. Once an army slips below a certain size in relation to the general population, it becomes more immune to the upheavals and changes that affect that society. It is no longer a mass army, and hence is more isolated from societal change.

The Highly Motivated?

When we initially began our studies in the early 1970s, there were two other countries that seemed to be exceptions to the rule--South Africa and Israel. (South Africa ranks only 48th in the GNP/capita table, but the standard of living for the "white only" population is comparable to that of Europe or North America.) In both countries the dominating populations, whites in South Africa, Jews in Israel, live in highly capitalized societies and serve in mass armies. Yet in neither country did we see any evidence of soldier resistance.

We assumed at the time that GI movements would not develop in these countries because of motivation, because of the soldiers' "belief in the mission." Whatever one might think of that mission, it had the support of the dominant classes. The soldiers would remain loyal because of the perceived threat to their self interest from local enemies.

Contrary to our expectations, however, GI resistance has emerged in both countries. In Israel, officer-reservists helped found the "Peace Now" movement. Hundreds of conscript officers and soldiers have marched in Peace Now demonstrations and have participated in antiwar campaigns. During the 1982 invasion of Lebanon, another lower-ranks organization was created, "Yesh Gvul" ("There Is a Limit" or "There Is a Frontier"). The members of Yesh Gvul asserted that they would participate in a legitimate defense of Israel but that they could not sanction the use of the army beyond the nation's boundaries. Many lower-ranking soldiers joined this effort, protesting the occupation of Lebanon and urging Israeli withdrawal. In the wake of the massacre at the Saba and Shatilla camp in Beirut, opposition to the Lebanon invasion became widespread both in society and in the army. A letter asking to be excused from service in Lebanon was eventually signed by more than 3,000 soldiers and reserve officers. More than 150 soldiers were jailed for actually refusing to serve.[6]

Yesh Gvul again became a center of opposition to military policy during the Palestinian Intifada. The Israeli army's often brutal suppression of rock-throwing Palestinian youths in the occupied territories convulsed the entire country and sapped the spirit and moral conscience of the army. In 1988 applications for religious-objector status in the Israeli army reached 17,000, an all-time high.[7] Growing numbers of conscript-reservists and regular soldiers joined Yesh Gvul in questioning the army's role and demanding an end to the occupation. By 1989 more than 600 army reservists had signed a public declaration stating they would not serve in the territories. Despite a growing crackdown against these military "refuseniks" (and a harsh new policy of indefinite imprisonment announced by the Israel Defense Force in March 1989), more than seventy soldiers have gone to jail rather than participate in the suppression of the Intifada.[8]

"Motivation" per se seems no longer sufficient to keep rank-and-file soldiers "in line," especially when the "cause" is unjust and increasingly unpopular. White South Africans are no exception.

No Longer Alone

Bill Anderson was a middle-class, English-speaking white South African boy. He was opposed to apartheid. When he was fifteen he had once asked the black maid to sit down and have tea with him. Flustered and unaccustomed to such gestures of kindness, she refused. Two years later Anderson went with her to the two-room hut where she lived with her six children. He was shocked and revolted. But he was not interested in politics, and when he got his call-up papers, he went.[9]

On his first day in the army Anderson was told to sign some papers. He said: "I'd like to read them first." The sergeant said: "Sign. Now." Anderson asked "Why?" The sergeant knocked him down, as thirty other new recruits, "National Servicemen," watched in stunned silence. Afterwards Anderson was ordered to carry a thirty kilogram sandbag everywhere for a week to teach him discipline, and to not ask why.

In late 1975 Anderson was sent to Angola, in the 6th South African Infantry. His unit was stationed near the Namibia-Angola border, on the Cunene River. As Anderson described it: "We saw little action, although from time to time we shot a 'terrie' (a terrorist), or a cattle rustler." Anderson also witnessed and was disgusted by atrocities. "A PF [permanent force, regular army] sergeant made a dust-cover for his jeep's gear shift from a dead black man's scrotum."

That year the South African Army was defeated in central Angola, when Angolan and Cuban troops blocked their advance on Luanda.[10] The soldiers were told that this was because the promised U.S. assistance had failed to arrive.* They withdrew back into Namibia.

In Namibia Anderson's battalion fought against SWAPO, the Southwest African People's Organization. That meant rounding up civilians suspected of supporting the guerrillas and interrogating them. In Onondanga, Anderson had a tent near the battalion headquarters. He was both lucky and unlucky. Many privates had no tents. But Anderson had trouble sleeping. The headquarters were used to interrogate prisoners, who screamed all night. Anderson was upset and wrote letters to civilian friends, to his pastor, to his family. They replied: "Don't exaggerate. Don't worry." In 1976 Anderson finished his first term of service and went home, disgusted. He told what he had seen, but few seemed interested. After a few months he was called back to duty for further military service. He took a plane to London, instead. Deserted.

Private Anderson wanted to forget all about the army and apartheid, to put it all behind him. He was a civilian now, he thought. One Sunday he went to Hyde Park corner to listen to the speakers. A brown man, Indian

---

*See story of Larry Johnson, Chapter 2.

probably, was lambasting the South African government. When two young men, Boers, began to heckle the speaker, Anderson lost control. "I went wild. Started yelling at them, in Afrikaans. They beat me up. Some British blacks came by and chased them off." An Englishman there asked Anderson what he had said. He told him about Angola, the scrotum, the nights of torture. "Would he repeat this publicly?" "Yes." Private Anderson's story was published in the *Guardian*: Later he gave testimony at the United Nations in New York.[11]

At home Anderson was considered a traitor. But soon he found he was but one of many; other South Africans had also fled the army and the draft. They formed a group in London called COSAWR, the Committee of South African War Resistance, and it grew steadily.

In 1975 when Anderson protested atrocities in the infantry, he felt utterly alone. Within a few years, though, other soldiers and draftees began to have the same doubts about the army and its mission. In 1978 the first South African GI newspaper, *Omkeer* (Afrikaans for "About Face"), appeared.[12] Inside the country an End-Conscription Campaign, ECC, developed. Within the army incidents of mass protest occurred. In September 1985, forty-five soldiers of the elite 1st Parachute Battalion based in Bloemfontein collectively went AWOL. Later forty came back. At first they were charged with mutiny, but the charges were reduced to AWOL, and they were sentenced to ninety days "DB," detention barracks.[13]

By 1985 pastors were no longer telling the conscripts not to worry. When the ECC organized a three-week fast to get the "troops out of the townships," some twenty national servicemen came to St. George's Cathedral in Capetown.[14] They complained about the army and spoke out about what they were sent to do: to kill blacks in the townships.

By 1988 resistance in South Africa had reached the point where 143 white draft-age men publicly declared their intention to refuse military service. The dramatic announcement came in press conferences in four South African cities and followed a court decision in which David Bruce, another white draft resister, had been sentenced to a maximum of six years in prison for refusing military training. Said Bruce and the other South African resisters, "We could not bring ourselves to serve an army upholding a racist system by violence".[15]

In the U.S. Army, during the Vietnam War years, resistance passed through a number of distinct phases. Initially there were individual heroes, protesters who stood up and said: "I will not go." They went to jail. Then they began to desert, go AWOL. By 1967-1968, the emphasis shifted to more collective forms of protest. Soldiers began to stay right there inside the army and "do their thing" by organizing from within. Of course the same social process does not pass exactly from one country and period to another, but the similarities are there. Only time will tell if white South African GIs contribute to their country's liberation from apartheid. Already many would-be oppressors are rethinking their role.

Why?

The root causes of resistance and its links to social developments are explored in detail in Chapter 19. For now the simplest way to describe the process is in terms of the young person's living standard. For many soldiers of today's highly capitalized societies, entry into the enlisted ranks represents a drop in the quality of life, a step down from a previous civilian life of relative convenience and affluence. This was much less true for earlier generations. It is still less true in undercapitalized countries such as Brazil today. In the poor countries military service for the young peasant, whose alternative might be an urban shantytown, still represents a step up in status and socio-economic well-being.

In the highly capitalized nations the situation is different. As capital accumulates and the overall standard of living rises, the previous compensations of military life--the fact that army service sometimes meant better food, clothes and sanitation--no longer apply. As urbanization has proceeded, the percentage of recruits from poor rural areas has declined. A very large proportion of soldiers now come from the urban working class, where their prior existence was freer and more pleasant than life in the barracks.

This is not to deny that in the volunteer forces of the United States and Britain entry into the military may represent an improvement in salary and economic well-being for many recruits, particularly for nonwhites. Military service sometimes pays better than available civilian jobs, and indeed is often the only employment at hand. "Economic conscription" is an increasingly important aspect of military service, one that tends to dampen the resistance impulse, at least at first. Moreover, military establishments have reacted to unrest in the ranks with sweeping reforms, raising pay and eliminating some of the most blatant irritants. The relative success of the volunteer force in the United States and Britain confirms that such reforms can weaken overt opposition.

The relationship between youth and military service is also affected when the civilian standard of living stagnates or declines due to economic recession and the general slowdown in capitalist development. Soldiers will be less likely to challenge the military if they face economic uncertainty and unemployment on the outside. Both of these factors--army reforms and greater economic insecurity--can account for a relative decline in the GI resistance movement.

Despite these factors, however, entry into the military still represents a step down for most young people. Even where on a strictly cash basis the army may offer an improvement over previous circumstances, the overall quality of military life is still inferior to that of civilian society. An absence of personal freedom, the frustration of one's instinct of workmanship, the suppression of individualism and initiative--these and other factors add to the material inadequacy of military life and contribute to an overall sense of lowered status and deprivation.

Soldiers may be satisfied for a time with reforms or may be chastened by economic difficulties on the outside, but they are unlikely to remain content for long. As many a sergeant has complained, they quickly return to their "ungrateful" ways. Even in a period of economic uncertainty, young people in highly capitalized society remain skeptical of authority and hierarchy. The result is a continuing tendency toward resistance within the lower ranks of the military.

2

After Vietnam: Resistance Continues

Vietnam and the Roots of Resistance

The seeds to understanding the U.S. military today can be found in the upheaval that swept the ranks during the Vietnam War. We will not attempt to recount here the massive resistance that racked the armed forces during that period. *Soldiers in Revolt* and other books tell the story in great detail, documenting a GI movement of unprecedented dimensions.[1] Few would deny that enlisted opposition rose to massive proportions by the early 1970s or that it played an important role in helping to end the war. Even top military leaders, while publicly denying the fact, knew full well the depth of GI resistance.

One of the most interesting retrospectives of the Vietnam era is a two-volume study of soldier dissent prepared for army commanders in 1970 and 1971 by the Research Analysis Corporation, a Virginia-based think-tank that frequently served army needs.[2] The two reports, *Determination of the Potential for Dissidence in the U.S. Army* and *Future Impact of Dissident Elements Within the Army*, were not available when *Soldiers in Revolt* was written. They provide hitherto unavailable insight into the startling dimensions of GI resistance, depicting a movement even more widespread than those of us involved at the time thought possible. The study provides important data not only on the scale of the GI movement but also on the socioeconomic characteristics of those involved. It also gives valuable clues for assessing the potential for continuing opposition within the volunteer force.

The study documents the pervasiveness of resistance through a survey of 844 soldiers at five major army bases in the continental United States. The GIs were asked about their involvement in various forms of protest. The Research Analysis Corporation's sociologists classified protest under two separate headings, "dissidence" and "disobedience." Under "dissidence" they grouped attendance at a coffeehouse, publication of a GI newspaper, and participation in a demonstration. Under "disobedience" they placed insubordination, refusing orders, individual sabotage, and the like. This separation conforms to what GIs and their supporters, without benefit of sociology degrees, long ago established as the distinction between the GI movement and GI resistance. The first category involves more verbal and formal forms of opposition, while the second implies a more physical and immediate response. Dissidence is often created, as we shall see below, by so-called "middle-class intellectuals" and is aimed at the higher ranks: colonels, generals, and even the commander-in-chief. The resister or "disobedient," on the other hand, strikes out at a more immediate target: the first sergeant or company commander.

The survey finds that during the height of the GI movement one out of every four enlisted men participated in dissident activities, with an equal percentage engaging in acts of disobedience. The combined results show a startling 47 percent of low-ranking soldiers engaging in some form of dissent or disobedience, with 32 percent involved in such acts more than once.[3] If frequent drug use is added as another form of resistance, the combined percentage of soldiers involved in disobedience, dissidence, or drug use comes to an incredible 55 percent.[4] The army's own investigation thus shows that half of all soldiers during the 1970-1971 period were involved in resistance activity--a truly remarkable and unprecedented level of disaffection.

Interestingly, the report notes that levels of dissent and disobedience were highest in Grade E-5, among those nearing the end of their first term of service. While 25 percent of those in Grades E-1 to E-4 engaged in dissent at least once, the percentage among first-term E-5s was 38 percent.[5] These E-5s were almost certainly three-year volunteers, since few draftees with a two-year term made it past the rank of E-4. The army's study thus seems to confirm what GI activists have long noted. Contrary to popular impression, soldier opposition was far more concentrated among volunteers than among draftees.

Another form of resistance, probably excluded from the Research Analysis Corporation study by definition, was desertion. By fiscal year 1971, desertions (defined by the military as unauthorized absence of over thirty days) had reached a servicewide yearly total of 98,000; AWOLs (short-term absence of less than thirty days) were running at three times this figure. The overall desertion rate in the army at the time of the study was 7 percent. Clearly, unrest within the army during the latter part of the Vietnam era reached epidemic proportions.

The study's conclusions about the social origins of resisters are also important. The study shows that "dissidents" and "disobedients" have different social backgrounds, the former being more middle-class, the latter being more working-class. Analyzing personnel records of over 1,000 dissenters (gleaned from files of the army's Counterintelligence Analysis Detachment, CIAD), the report portrays the dissenter group as follows:

- over half were volunteers (although many were draft-induced volunteers);
- they were more likely to come from the Pacific states and from the Eastern and North-central regions;
- they were more likely to have been to college than most GIs;
- they scored significantly above the average on Army Classification Battery Tests. (While they had very high scores on Verbal Reasoning, they were slightly below average in mechanics categories such as Automotive Information.) Dissenters clearly tended to be well-educated and to come from suburban, middle-class backgrounds.[6]

While dissenters were found to be above average in terms of class and educational achievement, those involved in disobedience tended to have less-advantaged origins. The educational levels and socioeconomic backgrounds of those inclined toward direct resistance matched those of the average volunteer soldier. The army study summarized this comparison as follows:

It may well be that the better educated do not engage in direct confrontations with individual superiors from whom they would presumably receive punishment, but they rather confine their dissidence to coffeehouse and protest meeting attendance, contributions to underground newspapers and other covert or nonpunishable activities. This supports what we learned through the interviews where the NCO's said it was not the college-types, but rather the ill-educated, undisciplined individual who caused them most of their troubles.[7]

This differentiation between two types of opposition is extremely important for understanding the changing nature of resistance in the volunteer force. As we shall observe in Chapter 5, the social composition of the all-volunteer force is now significantly different from that of the Vietnam-era military and has changed in directions that would make disobedience forms of resistance more prevalent. With the enlisted ranks now almost totally lacking the college-educated, suburban-reared white men who sparked the overt manifestations of the GI movement, the "dissident" component of resistance has declined. The army's study would thus seem to offer a gloomy forecast for the possible continuation of the GI movement.

If we focus on disobedience and insubordination, however, we find an entirely different prospectus. The changing socioeconomic base of the volunteer force actually reinforces the tendency toward direct resistance. As the percentage of poor and less-educated recruits increases, levels of insubordination and disciplinary conflict should be expected to remain high, and perhaps to rise. As we shall see below, this is exactly what happened.

The 1971 study also notes that an end to the Vietnam War might induce soldiers to focus more on conditions of service and on the army's treatment of individuals. Soldiers were asked to identify which army practices cause the greatest unrest. By far the most frequently cited problem was "harassment of the troops and lack of personal freedom and dignity." The next most frequently cited complaint was "unnecessary make-work duties and practices," followed by "personal appearance standards--hair regulations." Issues such as the draft or low pay, conditions that could be ameliorated through the volunteer force, rated low among GI complaints.[8] Soldiers were much more interested in basic issues of dignity and individual rights. This prediction conforms perfectly with actual developments in the post-Vietnam military. Since the volunteer force has not resolved the basic grievances cited above, it is no surprise that complaints about personal freedom and service conditions continue.

"For the Convenience of the Government"

The army's study of Vietnam-era resistance provides a useful guide to understanding present-day unrest within the ranks. As predicted, articulate forms of dissent such as GI papers and organized demonstrations have disappeared. College-educated recruits make up a much smaller percentage of today's volunteers than during the Vietnam period, and they have much less influence than before. Their particular manner of expressing resistance has thus diminished. This does not mean that resistance per se has ended, however. Soldier complaints about harassment and a lack of personal dignity have persisted, creating serious internal conflict and a widespread receptivity to unionization. The GI movement may be dormant, but resistance continues.

Unauthorized absence and desertion in the immediate post-Vietnam period remained unusually high. In 1975, four years after its withdrawal from Indochina, the Marine Corps had an AWOL rate of 300 per 1,000, 30 percent of the entire force, by far the highest rate in the Corp's history and nearly double the rate during the Vietnam period.[9] In the navy, unauthorized absence rates climbed steadily after Vietnam, reaching a record high of 83 per 1,000 in 1979.[10]

While absence rates declined in the 1980s, incidents of disciplinary discharge increased dramatically. One of the strongest indications of continuing unrest within the volunteer force is the extraordinarily high discharge rate. Discharges that were less-than-fully-honorable rose sharply at the end of the Vietnam era and continued rising into the 1980s, reaching their highest levels in recent history, nearly four times greater than in the 1960s. The 1976 servicewide "bad discharge" rate was nearly 14 percent, meaning that one out of seven discharges was less than fully honorable (80,000 in all)--a startling sign of disciplinary unrest (see chart 2.1).

Chart 2.1
Less-Than-Fully-Honorable Discharge Rates
All Services: 1970-1976

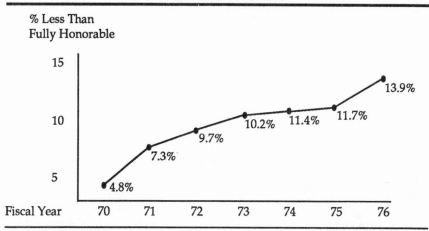

Source: Office of Asst. Secretary of Defense for Manpower & Reserve Affairs, OASD (M+RA) (MPP)

These rates jumped even higher in 1982-1983. In all the services, less-than-fully-honorable discharges rose sharply, to a startling 34 percent in the navy and 26 percent in the army (1984 figures).[11] The apparent reason for this jump was the addition of a new category of so-called "uncharacterized" discharges. These are now given out in the thousands to new recruits because of "entry-level performance." In other words, the armed forces are discharging a high percentage of trainees in their early days of service, in the hope of avoiding trouble later (see table 2.1).

These numbers are not merely statistics. They have very real human consequences. As numerous studies have shown, a bad discharge can cause severe economic and social difficulty for the person thus stigmatized.[12] Even the general discharge (the least punitive of the four less-than-honorable discharge categories) can mean employment problems. Soaring military discharge rates thus tell not only of serious disciplinary conflict within the ranks but also of widespread hardship for separating veterans. It is a bitter and tragic irony that so many young people who join the volunteer army for personal advancement receive a bad discharge and thus may end up in a worse economic condition than when they enlisted.

Table 2.1
Less-Than-Fully-Honorable Discharge Rates
Army, Navy, and Marine Corps
1977-1986

Fiscal Year	Army	Navy	Marine Corps
1977	16.8%	18 %	N A
1978	28.7%	15.4%	18.4%
1979	14.3%	12.1%	13.1%
1980	N A	11.1%	13.3%
1981	16.5%	13.8%	17.5%
1982	19.5%	19.8%	21 %
1983	22 %	32.1%	29 %
1984	26.6%	33.7%	29 %
1985	22 %	20.6%	24.3%
1986	N A	22.6%	22.8%

These numbers do not tell the whole story of discharges in the all-volunteer force. The armed forces have resorted with increasing frequency to so-called expeditious or "attrition" discharges. These are more streamlined administrative actions that allow a commander to separate the soldier rapidly, often with an honorable discharge. With the advent of the volunteer force, these attrition discharges have become widespread (see chart 2.2).[13] Expeditious discharges have become the command's most effective tool for eliminating troublemakers and thus reducing internal opposition. Soldiers who show the slightest sign of causing trouble are quickly separated. Overall, a third of all recruits entering the volunteer force have been kicked out prior to completion of their normal enlistment. Many of these separations are classified under such headings as "unsatisfactory performance," "discharge in lieu of court martial," "misconduct," and even "defective attitude" and "apathy."

These figures indicate that the services continue to face internal problems, but that they deal with them through the simple expedient of mass discharges. As long as recession-induced queues persist at recruitment offices, commanders will have free license to separate any and all who cause difficulty.

The discharge system is very important for understanding resistance in the U.S. volunteer force. No other army in the West seems to have anything comparable. It is the unique product of a successful volunteer recruitment system operating in a period of limited opportunity for masses of young people. Given widespread economic insecurity and a glut of potential recruits, the military can "afford" to discharge a large percentage of those who join.   The whole system is dependent on youth unemployment and

Chart 2.2
Percent Attrition Among Non-prior Service
Total Accessions, All DOD

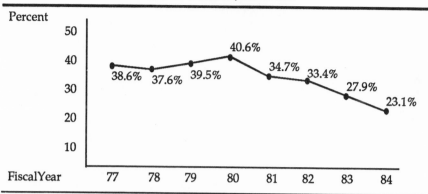

Source: Defense Manpower Data Center, Arlington, Va.

economic conscription, but as long as such conditions prevail, administrative discharges remain a vital means of minimizing internal unrest. Discharge policies are an important part of the U.S. all-volunteer force and play a key role in shaping GI resistance.

The Movement Continues: Stormy Seas

In the first part of this chapter we distinguished between movement and resistance, what military sociologists term "dissent and disobedience." There is no question that individual resistance, disobedience, has continued. Organized dissent, what others term the movement, on the other hand has been far less visible. While U.S. soldiers today may be less inclined to publish newspapers than in the past, they are still capable of fighting for their interests and will organize in an ad hoc manner when the pressures of unmet grievances require it. While the focus of this dissent has shifted from questions of war and peace to seemingly more mundane matters such as working conditions and personal freedom, the intensity and potential impact of such dissent remain powerful.

One of the most striking features of the post-Vietnam GI movement was the concentration of dissent within the navy. An important reason for this development was the increased demand placed on navy men and machines by present military strategy. The policies developed in the wake of Vietnam, first known as the Nixon doctrine, call for the U.S. government to eschew intervention by large land armies and opt instead for greater reliance on carrier-based airpower. The use of ground forces has been deemphasized, while the navy has been brought to the fore, called upon to assume front-line duty as the policeman of U.S. interests. Not only has the navy's mission broadened, but its geographic area of responsibility has also extended, with naval fleets reaching regularly for the first time into the Indian Ocean, and carrier task forces stationed abroad (home-ported) in the harbors of foreign allies. The additional military burden imposed by these new requirements has created special hardships and stretched an already overworked fleet to the limits of its endurance. The result was an unprecedented wave of peacetime resistance. In the years after the Indochina war, the navy witnessed more than a dozen incidents of mass protest.

One of these "mutinies" (so-called by conservative military commentator, Colonel Robert Heinl) occurred in San Diego in August 1975, when sixty sailors from the engineering section of the destroyer U.S.S. *Sterett* walked off their ship to protest oppressive working conditions. One of several California-based ships that witnessed quasi-mutinies during this period, the *Sterett* had been the scene of months of disputes between the engineers and their supervisors over job safety and improper equipment. The crew boasted its own "underground" newspaper, appropriately titled the *Sterett Free Press*. In addition to the usual enlisted opposition to harassment and excessive military discipline, the sailors claimed that they could not properly perform their work assignments due to poor leadership and inadequate gear.[14]

The worsening climate on the *Sterett* came to a head on August 5 when the harried engineers were restricted for failing an equipment inspection. The crew members claimed that the machinery could not meet the standards demanded by their superiors and that they were being harassed. Frustrated at an inability to air their grievances or obtain a rational response from the command, the men opted for a radical show of mass protest. They angrily defied the order to remain on ship and went ashore to a nearby dock. When the crewmen vowed that they would not return until the ship's captain met with them, the shaken command agreed to hear the engineers' complaints at a lengthy and boisterous meeting in the ship's mess deck. The walk-off proved to be a major success. As a result of the action restrictions on the engineers were lifted and the ship's sailing date was delayed for several days for needed equipment repairs.

Similar campaigns against poor living and working conditions occurred earlier in 1974 on two other San Diego-based ships. On the U.S.S. *Chicago* sailors edited a paper entitled *Pig Boat Blues* and launched a petition drive against harassment and frequent drug busts. On the U.S.S. *Agerholm*, disgusted crewmen put out several issues of a newsletter entitled *Scaggie Aggie Review*.[15]

In several of the protest campaigns of the mid-1970s sailors were joined by their wives to demand improved safety and health conditions. In 1976 the death of a crewman from the U.S.S. *Bryce Canyon* prompted a major demonstration of sailors and their civilian supporters at Pearl Harbor's Nimitz Gate in Hawaii. In 1974 wives and girlfriends of crewmen from the aircraft carrier U.S.S. *Coral Sea* formed a group called Save American Vessels, SAV, and staged a series of protests against the aging ship's unsafe conditions. In November of that year 1,500 crewmen and their wives signed a petition urging that the ship not be deployed to the West Pacific. Despite the protest the *Coral Sea* sailed on December 2 as scheduled. The departure was not without incident, however. As the huge carrier pulled out, women from SAV unfurled a banner to the applause and clenched fists of enlisted men on the flight deck. It read: "Good luck on your captain's suicide mission."[16]

"Mutiny" on the Midway

One of the most disconcerting questions for civilian leftists trying to understand soldier movements is "what do the resisters want?" The civilians often expect servicemen to have an opinion on issues that are not their problem at the time. Soldiers and sailors are not initially interested in abstract notions of imperialism or theories of social justice. They resist not according to preset plans but in relation to incidents and conditions in their daily lives. Theirs is not a program or a theory but a simple demand, "Don't tread on me." The difficulty for civilians is seeing how this impulse is important, and how it can sometimes have weighty political implications.

An illustrative case within the navy was that of the U.S.S. *Midway* during the summer of 1974. It showed how an initial protest over simple issues of harassment can set into motion a chain of events that eventually challenged the entire military system. In this case a conflict over brutality in the brig soon encompassed issues of U.S. intervention, and eventually leaped into a public furor over the deployment of nuclear weapons.[17]

The *Midway* "mutiny" at the Yokosuka Naval Base near Tokyo was one of the largest mass actions of the post-Vietnam era. It was sparked by the usual problems of harassment, intolerable working conditions and, in the case of the ship's large black population, racial discrimination. The event that precipitated the mid-June uprising was the beating of black crewmen held in the ship's brig. Black and Puerto Rican crewmen responded to the beating angrily, and they were joined by a small contingent of white sailors. On June 14, as the huge carrier was about to embark from its Japanese home port, some eighty sailors left the ship and refused to sail. Although in violation of navy law for missing ship's movement, several of the resisters held a press conference to condemn the navy for its insensitivity to their needs. In their press conference and subsequent public meetings, the resisters also raised the important political demand of an end to home porting and a return of the Midway to the United States. This demand was no doubt partly motivated by a desire to return home to wives and friends, but it was also based on a conscious understanding of and opposition to interventionism.

Although the navy ignored the demands of the *Midway* crew and quickly pressed court-martial charges against approximately thirty resisters, navy authorities were unable to keep the flames of the *Midway* mutiny from flaring again, this time touching off an international diplomatic furor. During the trial of one of the resisters, Michael Hammond, civilian defense attorneys raised an explosive political issue. As a way of challenging the legality of the circumstances in which Hammond was charged, civilian defense attorney Chris Coates raised that most unmentionable of subjects-- the presence of nuclear weapons on the carrier. Crewmen knew, although the Japanese public was not informed, that the Midway regularly carries nuclear weapons while in Yokosuka's waters, in direct violation of status of forces agreements between the United States and Japan. When Coates asked his question, the military judge immediately silenced him and cleared the court. The issue was too hot to be handled in public.

Although the navy denied the appeal and convicted Hammond for his actions, word of possible nuclear weapons on board the *Midway* got out to the local population and to the world press. The unassuming sailor became a hero. Thousands of Japanese citizens marched for his freedom and demanded clarification from the U.S. government on the status of nuclear weapons on navy ships. Articles about the issue also appeared in the U.S. press, and inquiries were made by members of the U.S. Congress. The incident added fuel to an already serious controversy about U.S. nuclear weapons in Japan and sparked a major diplomatic controversy. Out of an innocuous court-martial proceeding against seaman Michael Hammond thus emerged an international dispute over U.S. nuclear weapons policy.[18]

For those who believe that all this is in the past, the behavior of U.S. navy personnel in Australia may be of interest. In the mid-1980s both seaborne and land-based Aussies, protesting against the visits of American nuclear-armed vessels, have been pleasantly surprised by the frequent though low-key support they receive from U.S. sailors. In Sydney and Melbourne sailors have often visited harbor-side protest camps; though fearful of being identified by officers, they have offered encouragement and support.[19] On several occasions they have been observed on deck raising a clinched fist salute to protesters on the "Peace Squadron" boats sailing below. Contacts between Australian antinuclear protesters and U.S. sailors are becoming frequent and friendly.

Let It Grow

One of the most widespread grievances among U.S. enlisted volunteers in the post-Vietnam era was the military haircut policy. On the surface a seemingly innocuous distraction, the length of a soldier's hair, like any of the points of struggle mentioned above, can produce unanticipated but far-reaching political controversy. Of course GIs have always complained about short hair, but in the volunteer army the issue has occasionally become political and has produced surprising examples of mass dissidence.

An early example of protest was the case of Dan Pruitt, an air force sergeant from Alabama stationed at Alconbury Air Force Base in England. When Pruitt refused a haircut in early 1974, over 800 airmen signed petitions supporting his stand.[20] The Pruitt case sparked a number of additional haircut incidents among soldiers stationed in other parts of Europe, particularly Germany. The most important of these were the cases of Lou Stokes, a Sp/4 who refused orders for a haircut, and Daria Smith, a black enlisted woman stationed with Stokes at Mannheim who refused to remove her Afro wig. During the lengthy legal proceedings against Stokes in 1974, local soldiers expressed strong support for his stand. The trial also provided an opportunity for an unusual display of solidarity from the long-haired conscripts of Holland. The Dutch soldiers came as witnesses to prove that long hair does not interfere with one's ability to perform military functions. They also came with hundreds of signatures on petitions of support for Stokes and helped organize an international soldier demonstration in front of Funari Barracks in Mannheim, where the trial was being staged. The Dutch conscripts marched, with full-flowing hair, through the local barracks grounds, to the cheers of American soldiers. The commanding colonel's reaction to his NATO allies: "Get those fucking hippies out of my barracks."[21]

Although the army ultimately convicted Stokes and sentenced him to four months' imprisonment, the groundswell of opposition to haircut regulations among U.S. soldiers in Germany continued to expand. Even before the conclusion of the Stokes case, another example of haircut resistance was brewing in the Pioneer barracks at Hanau, centered around that rarest of phenomena, an officer who joined his men, in this case Lieutenant Matthew Carroll. Apart from illustrating the intensity of feeling about haircut regulations, the Carroll case showed why officers have played such a minimal role in the GI movement and how any officer who too strongly identifies with his men will be eliminated from military service.[22]

Carroll had possessed all the qualifications that might have made him into a highly successful career officer. A corps commander while at Texas A&M, he was an outstanding young officer in his first assignment near the East German border with an ADM (an atomic demolition unit, assigned to place atomic land mines in the path of any invading Russians.) Carroll did a good job in this unit and as part of his reward was sent to the Race Relations Institute at Patrick Air Force Base in Florida, where he was taught how to understand the problems of his men. (Carroll was exceptional among Anglo Texans because, despite local prejudices, he had married a Mexican-American woman, Hilda. He was obviously well qualified for his new assignment.) Upon returning to his unit in Hanau, Carroll became one of the most successful instructors in the army's race relations program.

Not only did he teach, he also learned. One of the first things he learned was that the major problem bothering both black and white soldiers was the army's rigid haircut policy. As he began to identify with his men, Carroll too started wearing his hair longer. At first he did not openly challenge the army, preferring instead to mat his hair down with a homemade concoction of sugar water to keep it within regulations. Only in the evenings, after showering and washing his hair, did he allow his full-flowing locks to wave freely. Before long, of course, his officer "peers" became outraged and his superiors ordered him to get a haircut. Carroll considered such directives an infringement on his rights as a free U.S. citizen, rights that he was extolling daily in his race-relations classes. Forced into a bind, Carroll came to the radical conclusion that even in uniform he should be allowed to look like a human being. He decided to take his stand: He would no longer cut his hair.

Carroll received little or no understanding from his fellow officers, but among lower-ranking enlisted men he became a hero. Nearly 100 GIs attempted to crowd into his Pioneer barracks apartment one evening to express their solidarity; almost 1,000 signed petitions supporting him and the right of all soldiers to wear long hair. When Carroll attempted to testify at a session of the Lou Stokes trial, the cup ran over and his officer "colleagues" brought him before a general court-martial for refusing a direct order to cut his hair. During Carroll's trial, the convening authorities were caught violating their own rules of court procedure, so the army bowed out gracefully by allowing Carroll to resign with an honorable discharge. The lieutenant kept his hair and the GI Bill, and the army lost a "troublemaker" who also happened to be a top-rate officer.

We will close our saga of the haircut struggles with a look at perhaps the most dramatic case, that of the "Berlin Brothers." Once again, an innocuous-seeming spat over hair and grooming standards mushroomed into a major confrontation, resulting in a quasi-mutiny and causing severe turmoil in the highly sensitive U.S. garrison in West Berlin. It is hard to determine, as in many of these cases, exactly when the Berlin Brothers decided that their hair and head were their own property, but by fall 1974 eight soldiers had decided to face whatever the army had to throw at them and had rejected repeated orders to shave and get a haircut. The important aspect of this case was not merely that the soldiers collectively refused orders to shear their hair, but that they also organized a mass campaign among their fellow soldiers to support this resistance.

The Berlin Brothers had several advantages. One was the existence in Berlin of one of the oldest and best-established GI newspapers, *Forward*, which allowed them to present their case to fellow soldiers. The other was their location in the heart of a large city, where they were able, with the help of civilian supporters at *Forward*, to contact U.S. media and present their case to the entire United States and most of Germany. As the case developed in October and November and the resisters became increasingly militant in their denial of army authority, approximately 1,200 area soldiers, more than a third of the entire U.S. enlisted force in Berlin, signed petitions backing the stand of the Berlin Brothers.[23]

As in other haircut battles, the controversy soon spread beyond the elementary issue of hair. In this instance the spark of larger revolt was army racism. When the local command tried to break the unity of the soldiers by singling out a black resister for punitive transfer, the struggle escalated dramatically. The soldiers saw the army's punishment of Sp/4 Rufus Thompson as an attempt to break the black and white solidarity that had developed around the case. On the morning of November 25, twenty-two men of C Battery, 94th Artillery, refused to report for duty and staged a day-long sit-down strike.[24] The resisters issued a list of demands calling for an overhaul of military regulations and an end to command attempts to divide their group. Reflecting their deepening hostility to army authority, they also adopted the radical position that enlisted people should have the right to approve the selection of officers.

Faced with the presence of CBS television reporters, who hovered all day near the site of the strike and pressed with embarrassing questions, the army reacted in a rather confused manner, at first even promising the strikers that their demands would be "taken into consideration." Only after the strike was voluntarily broken off and media attention was diverted elsewhere did the army react in its usual one-sided manner. The soldiers were separated and dispersed and in some cases were punitively discharged. The demands of the resisters and the grievances that started the dispute were ignored. Most of the original eight protesters were tried in late 1974 and early 1975 and were sentenced to jail terms of several months. The Berlin haircut battle was lost, but the GIs silent war against short hair, occasionally bursting into cacophonous rebellion, has continued.

A Vacuum of Motivation

The reaction of many civilians to these haircut campaigns, or to the other struggles we have described, is often "so what?" How can the length of a soldier's hair have any political significance? They consider such reform efforts unimportant. This thinking ignores key underlying themes within the haircut struggle and indeed misses the whole point of GI resistance. For activists such as Matthew Carroll and Dan Pruitt, opposition to military haircut standards went far beyond mere matters of personal appearance. Haircuts have become a rallying cry for the thinking soldier—a key symbol of the desire to assert control over one's head and the thoughts within it. The struggle becomes, in effect, a crusade for independence and personal freedom—a demand to think for one's self.

The issue also relates to the role of the army in civilian society. The haircut became the principal reminder of the soldier's separation from society, a point that many haircut resisters found deeply troubling. Pruitt, for example, specifically warned of possible military use against civilians, decrying command attempts to "keep people in the service separated and segregated from the public." In Pruitt's words: "They force us to look different and try to make us different. We are not. This is more true at home, where we may be engaged in domestic wars against our brothers and sisters."[25]

Some will ask: "Why won't the army let these soldiers grow their hair longer? Why won't they compromise?" The military sees, quite correctly in this case, that any concession obtained through struggle endangers the basic premise of absolute discipline and control. The officers will think: "If they get away with it on the hair issue, what's to stop them from raising other challenges?" Democracy and accommodation are fine in theory, but in an army that may be called upon to fight unpopular wars of intervention, the command must maintain total control over its soldiers.

The army's fears seem in part well founded, for the underlying motivation of haircut and other reform struggles is often a striving for greater independence from command authority. At the very least such campaigns suggest a "vacuum of motivation," an indifference to the supposed pre-eminence of the military mission. The protesters from the *Coral Sea*, for example, were told that SAV's campaign for a delay in the ship's sailing was impossible because no other carrier was available to take the *Coral Sea's* place on station in the Pacific. The arguments made sense in terms of the navy's mission, but the women and their men were thoroughly unimpressed. To them the safety of the crew was more important than the orders of the command. Such attitudes are anathema to military absolutism.

Larry Johnson and the "Non-war" in Angola

Larry Johnson was a Harlem Black, a brother off the block. He became addicted to heroin when he was twelve, but at eighteen, after his brother crippled himself in a drug-induced suicide attempt, he went cold-turkey, curing himself of the habit. To avoid a relapse and "get away from it all" he joined the army. By the winter of 1973 he was nineteen years old, a Pfc, a clerk in army administration in Strasburg Barracks, a small isolated army post in the hills above the West German country town of Idar Oberstein.[26]

One day as he was paging through an issue of the hardly radical black monthly, *Ebony*, Johnson's attention was drawn to a picture of some white soldiers laughingly holding up severed human heads. The soldiers were Portuguese and the heads were those of Africans, allegedly FRELIMO guerrillas fighting for the independence of their country, Mozambique. Johnson read the accompanying article carefully and learned that the Portuguese, in their decade-long war to retain their African colonies, were heavily dependent on military support from their NATO partners, including Italy, West Germany and the United States.

Private Johnson was a member of the company's Human Relations Council, a recent army innovation intended to smooth racial tensions. He felt that American involvement in an antiblack war in Africa was a matter for discussion within the council. Council leader and company commander, Captain Green, disagreed, diplomatically suggesting that Johnson investigate further, no doubt hoping that this would end the matter. But Larry Johnson was not just an average brother off the block after all. Determined and self-disciplined, bespectacled and well read, his friends and fellow GIs called him "The Professor." Although on an isolated army post in Germany, "Professor" Johnson was able to uncover documentation showing not only that the United States was supporting the Portuguese war financially but also that the U.S. army in Fort Bragg and the navy on the Puerto Rican island of Culebra were training Portuguese officers (the same officers, Johnson contended, who had conducted massacres in African villages).

When Johnson proposed a unit-wide discussion of his findings, Captain Green countered with, "Write to your Senator."

"Yessir," replied Johnson. "Will you sign the letter too?"

"I couldn't do that," replied Captain Green. (He thought it might hurt his career.)

"But sir, you agree with me."

"Yes, but I can't sign such a letter."

"Sir, I can no longer respect you."

Green, embarrassed, ended the conversation.

After viewing a film about Martin Luther King on April 1, Johnson decided to act. On the next day he went to work in the personnel office wearing his civilian clothes; he sat down at his desk, his arms crossed, a one-man sit-down strike. His explanation: "I couldn't wear the uniform, nor work for an army that supports Portuguese atrocities against our brothers in Africa."

Johnson refused direct orders to put on his uniform or to start working. Restricted to his room, "Professor" Johnson started classes on the U.S. role in Africa. Dozens of black and white GIs began to attend. Attempts to lock him up in the army's mental hospital in Landstuhl (a method of repression perhaps learned from close study of the Soviet Union) failed when a military psychiatrist refused to confirm a diagnosis of "maniac delusions." Charged on seven counts of disobedience and "failure to repair," Johnson was transferred to another unit in Kaiserslautern. The transfer turned out to be a major tactical error, for in the much larger post at Kaiserslautern Johnson found widespread support and was soon put in touch with the Lawyers Military Defense Committee (LMDC), which provided legal defense in his June court martial.*

As part of his defense effort, LDMC Attorney Howard DeNike sought the help of Italian priest Cesare Bertulli, who had been superior of forty-one White Fathers, a Catholic order working in Mozambique for twenty-five years until he had been expelled in 1971 for protesting Portuguese atrocities against the Africans. Bertulli testified as a character witness for Johnson in the "mitigation" final stages of his military trial, prior to sentencing. (Johnson had been found guilty on half a dozen counts.) Although the judge attempted persistently to block his testimony, Bertulli, a skillful dialectician, was able to confirm Larry Johnson's charges of Portuguese massacres and atrocities in Mozambique and to explain NATO complicity in the Portuguese war effort. He also pointed out that the war in Mozambique would grind to an immediate halt were Portugal to be deprived of NATO and U.S. assistance. The jury, deeply impressed, gave Private Johnson an unexpectedly light one-month jail sentence.

In principle, Larry Johnson's imprisonment and subsequent discharge should have ended this episode. However, dozens of GIs attended the trial, and the GI papers *Forward* (in West Berlin), *FighT bAck* (in Heidelberg) and *FTA With Pride* (in Mainz-Wiesbaden) gave the case extensive coverage. Moreover, during his imprisonment in the Mannheim stockade, "Professor" Johnson continued to give classes on Africa to his fellow inmates, most of whom returned to units spread throughout West Germany. Hundreds, probably thousands, of "ill-educated" U.S. GIs thus learned for the first time of their government's involvement in Mozambique, Angola, and Guinea-Bissau.

---

*Founded during the Vietnam War to provide legal assistance to GIs victimized by racial discrimination or punished for the exercise of their First Amendment rights, the Lawyers Military Defense Committee maintained an office in Heidelberg until the mid-1970s.

History is not an exact quantitative science, and when its protagonists are nineteen-year old privates, documentation is much harder to obtain than in the case of memoir-writing generals. The records that have been made are unfortunately unavailable, since the files of Military Intelligence are not open to historians. In the case of Pfc. Larry Johnson, however, the authors can testify that the potential for resistance that he embodied contributed much to the liberation of his black brothers in Mozambique and Angola.

Some years later we were able to discuss this period with both Portuguese officers and soldiers, and with South African soldiers who had been stationed in Angola. The Portuguese told us that by the time of the Johnson trial, in mid-1973, their then-fascist government was desperately attempting to play its last card: direct U.S. military intervention against the "Marxist revolutionaries" in Africa. When this "anticommunist assistance" failed to materialize, the Portuguese officers realized that the decade-long counterrevolutionary struggle to retain their colonies was lost. In April 1974 they stopped fighting in Africa and turned against their own dictatorship; Mozambique, Angola, and Guinea-Bissau became independent.

As the Portuguese armies left, however, the fledgling governments of the ex-colonies came under attack from new enemies. In particular, the MPLA administration in Angola, the biggest of the former colonies, soon faced a double threat: a CIA-led mercenary invasion from Zaire in the northeast, and, in November 1975, a massive invasion by the South African army, driving 1,000 kilometers north from its bases in Namibia toward the Angolan capital of Luanda.[27] The Angolans, backed by Cubans rushed in to help them, defeated both the CIA mercenaries and the South African army. Private Bill Anderson, then with the 6th South African Infantry in Southern Angola, said to the authors: "We were told, to explain such an incredible defeat by black Communists and Cubans, that the Americans had promised to come in but that they had broken their promise and left us in the lurch."[28]

CIA officer John Stockwell, in charge of the northern operation, has fully described the invasion from Zaire in this book, *In Search of Enemies*. But so far there has been little publicity concerning the aborted "contingency" plans for assisting the South African army in Angola. And who would dream of connecting Angola with GI resistance in the 509th Airborne in Vicenza, Italy?

Soldiers from this unit had long been active in the GI movement and when the unit was stationed in Mainz-Gonsenheim, not too far from Kaiserslautern, they published the paper *FTA With Pride*, one of the most successful GI papers in West Germany. In November 1975, with the unit now transferred to northern Italy, rumors spread among the soldiers that the 509th's two reinforced battalions, some 3,500 men, would soon be sent to Africa. As in many of the "dirty work" front-line units, some 40 percent of the soldiers involved were black, and their attitude toward this potential engagement was well expressed by a young soldier during a rap session with one of the authors: "If we go to Africa--sure I'll shoot--at anything with a white face." Thanks to the help of an American woman activist, commuting from Florence, the soldiers were able to publish several issues of a GI paper: *Getting the News*. One of the feature stories in the paper was the case of Larry Johnson.

As rumors of an African deployment persisted, about 200 soldiers collectively refused orders to go on an airborne training exercise, fearing that they might end up jumping into the skies over Angola. Their protest ended only after they were specifically promised that they would be sent to Wildflecken, Germany, as indeed they were.

The South Africans fought, and lost, alone.

Obviously a major factor then preventing American intervention on the side of Portugal, and later South Africa, was the still-fresh Vietnam experience. But a second factor preventing such interventions was, and is, the likelihood of widespread resistance within the ranks of the U.S. military. With nonwhites making up a third of the combat units and a tenth of the aircraft carrier crews that might be used in such operations, U.S. military forces face severe constraints in intervening against black nationalism. The Larry Johnsons of the world, unmentioned in the history books, must be taken into account by Pentagon planners.

For Pfc. Larry Johnson, retired, there was a pleasant epilogue: White soldiers in the 527th Military Intelligence Battalion, in Kaiserslautern, who read that the judge in the Johnson case had decreed there were no wire taps involved in the trial, suddenly decided it was time to tell the truth. As they described it, they were "tired of being pigs." They blew the whistle on an army spying operation code-named "Penguin Monk," which included tapping the phone of the Lawyers Military Defense Committee (LMDC) defending Pfc. Johnson. The verdict against Johnson was annulled, and six years later Johnson received $15,000 as part of a compromise settlement of a suit filed by the LMDC and the ACLU (American Civil Liberties Union).[29]

Military Intelligence: A Contradiction in Terms

John Michael (Mike) McDougal had joined the army because of love, drugs, and the Arabic language. He had left college and gone to Morocco to study Arabic. While there he fell in love with Danielle, a "pied-noir" Frenchwoman born in the ex-colony. When Danielle ended the romance, Mike returned to Texas and tried to drown his sorrows in drugs. One day he woke up sick and realized he was on his way to a fatal overdose. Like

Larry Johnson from Harlem, he joined the army to break his habits, and he did.[30]

By this time, 1972, the draft was winding down and college students willing to volunteer could write their own ticket. McDougal wanted to study and use Arabic in the army. When they asked him to join Military Intelligence, he said OK, as long as he had a chance to develop his language skills. He had no prior knowledge of or objection to Military Intelligence. McDougal studied Arabic for nine months at the Fort Bliss language school in Texas. Then he was sent, to his surprise and annoyance, to West Germany.

In 1972 there had been trouble at the Olympics in Munich. Palestinians had taken Israeli athletes captive and had killed several of them. The U.S. army's Military Intelligence units, part of the anti-Palestinian team, found to their dismay that although their electronic wizardry could pick up conversations hundreds of meters away, no one understood what was being said. The "terrorists" were speaking in Arabic. It was most mortifying, particularly since Munich was the home of the 66th MI group, Military Intelligence headquarters in Europe. Although the Palestinian incident was already over, Arabic specialists were now sent to each of the group's three battalions. McDougal got the 527th in K-town, Kaiserslautern.

When there were no Arabs to spy on, Mike was put to work keeping tabs on "anti-army activists." During the trial of Larry Johnson, LMDC lawyer Howard DeNike brought White Father Cesare Bertulli to the stand to confirm that the U.S. army was helping the Portuguese kill black Africans in their murderous colonial war. In preliminary court proceedings the army's trial counsel seemed remarkably well informed concerning this witness. The prosecutor stated that "even an 18-year residence in Mozambique" was no reason to admit the priest to the witness stand. This was curious, since "18 years" had been mentioned in DeNike's initial conversations with Bertulli, although the priest later corrected the lawyer and reported that his stay in Mozambique had actually been 25 years. Where did the army hear 18 years? Could they be tapping the phones? DeNike wanted this cleared up; Judge Green (no relation to the captain commanding Johnson's company) asked the trial counsel, who denied the charge and pooh-poohed the very possibility of any phone taps. Such taps, as the lawyers knew, would infringe upon the defendant's right to a fair trial and contravene the 6th Amendment of the U.S. Constitution. When DeNike persisted, Judge Green cut him off. "You heard! There are no taps! Get on with your case!"

One of the authors covered the trial for *The Overseas Weekly*. He headlined a rather cynical story: "No Phone Taps, Judge says. He should know." Mike McDougal, now a well-noted Spec/4, read *The Overseas Weekly* story while filing transcripts of the very same tapped phone conversations! Suddenly his world was turned upside down. He realized, as he later told one of the authors, "I'm spying, not on Arab terrorists but on people just like myself." When Larry Johnson went to jail, McDougal decided to act. He brought the transcripts, proof of the phone taps, to the Lawyers Military Defense Council, the authors, and to the press.

A first story based on McDougal's revelations ran in the alternative "Liberation News Service" LNS, in mid-July. No reaction from the army. Then, on July 28, 1973, the *New York Times* and CBS headlined the story. The Armed Forces Network, AFN radio, featured it on the 6:00 P.M. news.

It soon became apparent that much of the material released by McDougal pointed to illegal activities on the part of military intelligence, illegal both under American and German laws. Military intelligence quickly sent a high-powered investigating team to Kaiserslautern not to investigate the wrongdoing but to track down the leakers. McDougal was appointed driver of the investigators' team and watched their work with great interest. They combed through the 527th from the top to the bottom. When, eventually, he, a lowly Spec/4, was also routinely questioned, he stated immediately that he had nothing to say in the absence of his lawyer. Despite some pushing around he said nothing further to the investigators, but that evening CBS news carried a prerecorded interview: "When I joined the army, I swore to uphold the Constitution. What we are doing here is unconstitutional. I asked my commanding officer whether it was illegal, he said it would be in the States, but over here it was OK. I tried to go through channels, but got nowhere. So I informed the lawyers defending other GIs that their phones were tapped, and gave them some proof."

McDougal was restricted to his unit and given a job stringing barbed wire around the barracks. He found this work healthier than late-night filing, and was able to talk to the press over the fence he was building. He was told that charges would be brought against him, but after four months all charges were suddenly dropped without any explanation. McDougal was subsequently transferred to an infantry unit in Mannheim.

By mid-August 1973 soldiers all over Germany were going public, revealing army spying operations against GIs, civilians, and even U.S. Democratic Party organizations in Germany. Watergate in the Federal Republic! In West Berlin, military intelligence had deemed not only the GI paper *Forward* and its civilian supporters subversive, but had extended its surveillance to "Americans for McGovern" and the "Berlin Democratic Club." Although initial intelligence reports revealed that "nothing subversive" was going on among the McGovernites, army officers insisted on maintaining the surveillance, sending their spies into the organization, and continuing wiretaps and letter-reading. When copies of this material found their way to the U.S. Senate, Democratic leaders in Washington were not amused.

The Lawyers Military Defense Committee offered its services when about twenty of the "targets" decided to file a suit in Washington Federal Court. The defendants charged that their civil rights had been violated. The army defended itself in Washington by first saying it had never done any of "these things," then by admitting past sins but promising it was not doing "it" anymore. This defense was quickly compromised by the discovery of a new spy, a GI working in the LMDC office in Heidelberg as a trainee, who was caught photocopying files for his superiors. "I was told to find out what you knew, where you know it from." Eventually the army stated that this spying had not "harmed" the targets, that it was practically for their own good.

In 1980, after seven years of litigation, the army ran up the white flag and offered an out-of-court settlement: they would pay 30 percent of the damages claimed. The plaintiffs accepted and received a total of $150,000 split by about twenty people, with Larry Johnson receiving $15,000. The army also promised not to do "it" again and turned over some 50,000 pages, a part of the files collected on them, to the plaintiffs.

McDougal, who had finished his term of service happily in the infantry, "healthier than in MI", never got the promotion to Spec/5 that he had been promised just before he did his duty to the U.S. Constitution. But Danielle, who had come to Europe in the meantime, approved heartily of his actions and married him when he left the army. They both worked for a while in Cairo, where Mike got a better chance to use his Arabic than in Kaiserslautern.

Clouds Over the Nukes

Drugs are an accepted, permanent feature of enlisted life in the U.S. armed forces. Their link to politics, though, is often unclear. Leftists have often seen drugs as a hindrance to resistance; in the early days of the GI movement some groups made a conscious decision not to work with soldiers who used drugs because they might be "unreliable." Such attitudes reflected a complete misunderstanding of the nature of GI resistance, and usually had to be quickly abandoned, since any mass action was sure to attract a large number of "dopers." Drug use may not be a conscious political act--far from it--but its consequences, like those of the haircut struggles, can have a political result.

The questions of drug use and hair length have an important political similarity: both directly concern a large percentage, probably the majority, of enlisted members in the U.S. military, and to some extent the armies of other highly capitalized nations. In terms of resistance, however, there is a big difference. Hair struggles are intermittent and are initiated by the GIs themselves. Drug conflicts are permanent, and it is command-initiated action--"busts"--that bring latent hostilities to the fore and often create a politically charged conflict situation.

One of the areas where the drug problem remains severe and where it frequently bursts into battle is among soldiers assigned the responsibility of storing, transporting and if necessary using America's arsenal of 4,000-5,000 tactical nuclear weapons in Europe. Although regulations require strict prohibitions against drug use near nuclear facilities, it is precisely in these units where drugs seem to be most prevalent. Time and again we have been told by soldiers in Pershing missile units, by Military Police (MPs) guarding nuclear weapons depots, and by air force Security Police protecting nuclear bomber flight lines that: "You can't guard these things without being stoned."

Typical is the story of the 144th MP unit assigned to guard one of the largest collections of nuclear warheads in the world--the 9th Ordnance Exclusion Area near Miesau, West Germany. Forty-five of the approximately 120 enlisted men in the unit were removed from duty in November 1974 after a large number of soldiers were caught smoking hash while on guard duty at the Miesau nuclear depot. The men were caught when a phone call to guard tower 6 produced a reply from a stoned soldier who actually thought he was in tower 1 (in fact, tower 1 was empty since everyone had gone to tower 6 to share in a bowl of hash.)[31]

While most of the GIs in Europe use and prefer hash to harder drugs (in the States marijuana is the more available form of cannabis), some units, like the Munitions Maintenance Squad of Atomic and Hydrogen Bomb Loaders at Bitburg Air Force Base, were heavy users of heroin. Indeed, the MMS unit, along with the local Security Police, had by 1975 taken over the heroin trade from Amsterdam to the Eifel area of northwest West Germany, pushing not only among airmen and their families at the isolated U.S. air bases at Bitburg, Spangdahlem, Hahn, and elsewhere, but also among the local German civilian population.[32] One of the constant causes of friction between German authorities and U.S. military officials is the large amount of hard drugs entering West Germany that are transported or controlled by elements of the U.S. forces.

We cannot do more than touch on the many cases of drug-related political dispute. We will explore here only one case, that of the 74th Field Artillery Detachment (FAD), stationed at Schwabstadl, twenty kilometers south of Augsburg in southern Bavaria. The 74th FAD was a small unit of around 250 U.S. soldiers assigned with West German airmen to guard the warheads and launching pad of ground-to-ground Pershing I missiles. The fifty-kiloton warheads of the Pershing I were targeted at cities in Eastern Europe. The case of the 74th FAD shows again how an initial series of very minor events can quickly extend to a larger political dispute over U.S.

nuclear policy, in this case resulting in a GI petition against deployment of the neutron bomb. A minor drug bust and complaints over harassment and lax security sparked a movement that seriously challenged the assumptions of U.S. nuclear policy.

The case began in fall 1977 as a plea for civilian assistance from several low-ranking enlisted men stationed in the unit. One of the authors received a letter (unsolicited and quite unexpected) from a young soldier who called himself Rufus, a vocal and articulate high school graduate. Rufus was asking for help to fight the army over a recent off-base bust, where he had been found with a bowl of hash. Rufus had long complained about army conditions, but he was pushed to take action when he was busted for what he considered a trivial offense. He was, after all, only a minor drug user compared to many others in his unit. Angered at this minor injustice and authentically worried about the lack of security in the unit, Rufus and others decided to do something to expose local conditions. It was an interesting mixture of "Why me?" and a real concern about a highly sensitive situation that was quite different from what he had been led to expect.

The original complaint from Rufus and others cited rampant drug use within the unit (far more intensive than that for which Rufus had been busted). Soldiers guarding the launching pad and warheads were so stoned that they could not properly function on duty. Serious security lapses resulted from soldiers going berserk, either through drugs or sheer boredom, and directly threatening their superior officers or the rockets themselves. The soldiers pointed to several examples where GIs had threatened to fire their rifles into the warheads. (Although such an act would not produce a nuclear explosion, it might set off a conventional explosion that would spread radioactivity over a wide area.) The initial complaint concluded with a blistering attack on the local command and its total insensitivity to the needs of the men or the security of the weapon site.

Such problems are not confined to the 74th FAD; they occur often in atomic weapons units. One example of lax security is the common practice of disconnecting perimeter trip wires designed to warn guards of possible penetration of the compound. Since most of the alerts from these trip wires are caused by rabbits rather than invading Russians, soldiers find the task of constantly going out to check them a major headache. When they are more interested in getting stoned, they simply disconnect the wires.

An interesting sidelight concerns Army Regulation 50-5, which applies specifically to atomic units and which requires the immediate removal from duty of anyone caught using drugs. It is a perfect example of a law that cannot be enforced. As the GIs in these units joke, if the regulation were applied strictly, atomic weapons in Europe would have to be abandoned.

To return to Schwabstadl, shortly after sending their letter, the protesters within the 74th FAD met and held a series of discussions with soldier and veteran organizers from the Heidelberg GI newspaper, *FighT bAck*. Through an airing of their grievances and deeper examination of the underlying tensions in the unit, the FAD soldiers began to think more seriously about their mission. Their encounters with the military activists in the Heidelberg area sparked a reevaluation of their mission and of the whole policy of employing tactical nuclear weapons in Europe. They became particularly concerned about the proposals at that time to deploy people-killing, property-saving neutron bombs in Europe. Where they had thought previously only of drugs and local problems of harassment and security, the soldiers now began to look at the larger political purpose of the weapons deployed in their unit.

Out of these discussions arose the idea of a petition against the neutron bomb, an action that was seen as the best current way of opposing U.S. nuclear weapons policies in Europe. The signature effort began within the 74th FAD, but before the petitions could get out they were confiscated by local commanders. Military intelligence forces descended on the unit, and Rufus and other spokesmen were suddenly silenced through threats and transfers.

While nothing more was heard from the 74th FAD, the idea of the neutron-bomb petition quickly caught fire elsewhere, particularly in units stationed near the Heidelberg area. Several hundred signatures were obtained in local barracks, even inside the Mannheim stockade. Although the original issues had long since been forgotten and the FAD protesters silenced, the petition that they initiated continued to circulate and gather signatures. The appeal also eventually spread to bases in the United States, where it was circulated by enlisted activists at Fort Meade, Maryland, and the Philadelphia Naval Yard.

By spring 1978 this soldier petition effort became linked with the civilian antineutron bomb campaigns sponsored by SANE and other national peace organizations. Civilians and active-duty citizen-soldiers joined together for a protest demonstration against the neutron bomb during the NATO ministers' meeting in Washington on May 30 and 31. While more than 100 civilians picketed outside the U.S. State Department, several active-duty servicemen presented the names of over 400 GIs to representatives of Congress who had come to accept the petitions. The soldier petition was sharply worded and powerful:

We the undersigned soldiers are opposed to deployment of the neutron bomb. A weapon which preserves property while destroying people may be good for those who own property, but not for those of us who have only our lives to give. We are against a weapon which makes war more likely.

The neutron bomb petition was an important symbolic sign of the potential for resistance within the volunteer force. Although the national news media chose to ignore the demonstration and petition, the assembled heads of state no doubt got the message. While ministers and generals of the NATO alliance met inside the State Department, the enlisted people on whom they must ultimately rely were gathering on the streets outside with civilian peace activists.[33]

The neutron bomb campaign was a sign of the continuing potential for opposition in the ranks, and a warning to the assembled military leaders: Policies may be decided by presidents and generals but in the last analysis they must by carried out by GIs. Just as with the case of Larry Johnson and others opposed to U.S. intervention in Africa, the movement against the neutron bomb showed that the ranks of the military no longer march in lock-step, that when soldiers realize the implications of their mission they will sometimes say "No!"

The "Nonunionization" of the U.S. Military

As U.S. soldiers and veterans (including one of the authors) returned to the United States after the Amsterdam Soldiers' Congress of November 1974, they were mesmerized by visions of the Dutch Conscripts' Union--long-haired soldiers holding political meetings in the barracks, thousands of conscripts marching behind union banners for more pay and personal freedom. The example of the Dutch brothers--their striding sense of power and confidence, their many freedoms won through struggle--had an exhilarating, intoxicating effect. As the airliner touched down on U.S. soil, however, sober reality quickly dispelled this initial flush of optimism. The eclipse of activism in the U.S. military, the wholesale discharge of militant GIs, the closing of organizing projects--all made the thought of unionizing the U.S. military seem like a pipedream.

Little could anyone suspect that within a year the notion of a soldiers' union in the U.S. military would indeed be a very live and credible option. Still less did anyone expect that the impetus for unionization would come from the conservative AFL-CIO union, the American Federation of Government Employees, which announced in summer 1975 that it was considering an organizing drive among soldiers. Few activists would have believed that such a radical proposal could emanate from that union in particular. With nearly half of its 280,000 members among the military's civilian employees, the AFGE was and still is openly tolerated by the army and often seemed indistinguishable from the army itself. Many GIs doubted that such a union could become the agency for the radical transformation of soldier life that they had witnessed in the barracks of Holland.

Typical of the reaction that greeted AFGE's announcement of interest in organizing the military was the hesitancy and disbelief of American GI activists in Heidelberg. When the editors of the GI paper *FighT bAck*--recently discharged SP/5s Craig Muma and Ed Taylor--discovered, almost by chance, that an AFGE local office existed in nearby Frankfurt, they were greatly surprised. Where had the union been, they asked, during the numerous GI struggles that had occurred in that area over the last eight years? When contact with the local was established, they were even more astounded: It turned out that the union president, Chester Cole, had been a major in the U.S. army. Although the major was very sensitive about his officer past, insisting that "not every officer is a lifer," and emphasizing that the union would welcome GIs, the soldiers were not convinced. Although the *FighT bAck* organizers recognized the benefits of establishing contact with the AFGE, and were in fact at that time circulating a petition in support of unionization, they could not overcome their instinctive distrust of higher officers. Their hesitancy reflected the inability of soldiers and unions to join together and presaged the fundamental conflict between the aims of GI activists and those of the union leadership.

Early Precedents

The concept of unionism had always been part of the U.S. GI movement. One of the very first soldier organizations was the American Servicemen's Union (ASU), founded in 1968. The ASU was able to reach hundreds of thousands of GIs but was unable to weld them into an effective, permanent organization. After achieving a membership of perhaps 15,000 in 1970, the ASU collapsed and by 1973 had all but disappeared. (The ASU was for lower enlistees and draftees only; all "lifers"--senior sergeants and officers--were excluded).[1]

While a number of enlisted campaigns in the post-Vietnam era focused on work conditions and pay, most were confined to a single ship or unit and rarely spread to other servicemembers similarly situated. In 1974, however, a union-style struggle arose in the navy that cut across geographic lines and affected an entire occupational group. This was the VRB/OUT campaign, an effort by nuclear and electronics technicians and their wives to recover Variable Reenlistment Bonuses. At issue were payments of up to $6,000 promised to the technicians in exchange for six-year reenlistments. In 1974 the bonuses were abruptly canceled by the government, but the sailors were told they had to remain on duty. The enlisted men and their wives were outraged and demanded "VRB or Out." Chapters of VRB/OUT appeared in San Francisco, Long Beach, and San Diego, California; Newport News, Virginia; Charleston, South Carolina; and Honolulu, Hawaii. They filed a major law suit and in some cases picketed navy and government buildings. By 1975 the number of plaintiffs reached 900. Two years later the sailors eventually won a favorable judgment in the Supreme Court, but by then many had already been discharged.[2]

The VRB effort resembled a labor campaign, but the local chapters never considered forming a permanent union. The groups never made contact with AFGE either, for by the time the federation arrived on the scene in 1975, the active phase of the VRB struggle had ended. For its part, AFGE never intervened in the ongoing legal struggle, which continued all during its two-year involvement with the military, and never made the slightest effort to support the sailors' demands.

The Improbable AFGE

The AFGE's absence from the earlier GI movement can perhaps be explained by the overtly political, antiwar (initially deemed "antipatriotic") nature of that struggle. The union's lack of interest in the trade-union campaigns of later years, however, seems more inexplicable. Efforts such as the VRB/OUT struggle were very close to conventional "bread and butter" unionism. In retrospect, the failure of AFGE or any other union to link up with the VRB technicians foretold the basic problems to come--the incompatibility of GI resistance and establishment unionism. This is a contradiction that has arisen not only in the United States, but also in Germany, France, and elsewhere. The independent, often spontaneous style of modern soldier resistance seems as discomforting to union officials as it does to company commanders. Given this dilemma, the mystery is not so much that the AFGE failed to carry through its organizing drive, but rather that it even ventured to try in the first place.

AFGE is an unlikely agent of radical activity. In more than fifty years of organizing government and military employees, the union has shown little sign of labor militance or antigovernment protest. To the contrary, it was founded in the 1930s as a professional association of high-ranking civil servants, and it long maintained a docile, almost "company union" posture. The union has traditionally had a promilitary political outlook. In 1972, for example, the national union expelled three locals in the Washington, D.C., area for passing anti-Vietnam war resolutions. More than a thousand members--many of them supporters of a caucus organization known as Federal Employees for Peace--were barred from the union. The national union President at the time, John Griner, seemed more concerned with supporting commander-in-chief Richard Nixon--ostensibly his management adversary--than in preserving his own membership.

Although the union's positions have been sometimes right-wing, it would be inaccurate to portray the federation as uniformly reactionary. The static picture of a conservative company union does not fit. The federation experienced considerable growth and change in the 1960s. At an earlier period it would not have been necessary to expel any AFGE locals, since left-wing or antiwar tendencies rarely even existed. By the early 1970s, however, long-term trends were at work that were changing the character of this largest of federal employee unions. Indeed, the impetus for AFGE's proposal to organize the military can be traced in part to deeply rooted developments not only within the federal union but also within public employee unions in general.

The Rise of Public Sector Unionism

As a whole, the U.S. labor movement has stagnated for several decades (since the anticommunist purges of the late 1940s). Membership as a percentage of the workforce at first remained about constant, and in recent decades has steadily declined; few major advances have been registered. The important exception to this trend has been the phenomenal growth of public-sector unionism. The American Federation of State, County, and Municipal Employees (AFSCME), the Service Employees International Union (SEIU), the teachers' unions (the American Federation of Teachers and the National Education Association), as well as AFGE--all have shown growth in recent decades. This trend reflects one of the most important fundamental tendencies of modern society, namely, the growth of the state sector, through an expansion of military expenditure (the warfare state) and social services (the welfare state). As government work rolls have swelled, union membership has increased. Not only is there a larger pool of government employees but also an increasing percentage of these employees are now joining unions, as the prestige of the once-privileged government worker has declined. Part of this development has been the spread of unionization to sectors previously immune to labor tendencies, particularly police forces. Union membership has expanded among all government workers, especially among those at the state and local level.

For AFGE in particular, major growth occurred during the 1960s. In the decade between 1960 and 1970, AFGE membership more than tripled, jumping from approximately 80,000 to nearly 300,000. The major reason for this expansion, apart from the above-mentioned swelling of the federal bureaucracy, was Executive Order 10988, signed by President Kennedy in January 1962. Part of a preelection pledge designed to gain labor support, the order officially authorized federal employee unionism and laid down basic ground rules for labor management within the government. It was essentially an enabling act, paving the way for an immediate expansion of unionism within the federal government. AFGE, until then a somnolent fraternal association of government professionals, quickly surged forward as a potent force within the government. As union membership soared, the social base of the union changed. The middle- and upper-level bureaucrats who once dominated the federation were now joined by large numbers of blue-collar and clerical workers. The racial, sexual, and age composition of the union altered during this period, producing a younger union membership with a larger percentage of blacks and women.

Along with this strengthening of the union came a trend toward more assertive, authentic trade unionism. Traditionally, public employees have been treated as second-class citizens in terms of trade-union rights: They were denied, and indeed often did not request, the powers of regular industrial unions, most importantly, the right to strike. As unionism expanded among government workers, however, the barriers to full-fledged unionism began to give way. Government employees increasingly demanded the same privileges and powers enjoyed by their industrial co-workers.

Within AFGE this trend had been expressed by minor but significant gestures towards greater militance. In 1970 the union voted to change the name of its chapters from *lodges* to *locals*, and, more significantly, voted to lift the clause barring strikes from its constitution. Demonstrations and picket lines have now become commonplace, as have union drives on behalf of political candidates. At the 1976 convention in Las Vegas AFGE delegates voted to authorize their leaders to call strikes; they also for the first time approved the building of a strike fund and cheered a proposal to initiate a "work to rule" or job slow-down campaign. Although AFGE remained fairly conservative and timid, the federation was advancing.

The Weapon in the Holster

Apart from these long-term, more general trends, the roots of AFGE's interest in the military can be traced to more immediate policy concerns. Perhaps the most basic was the link between civilian and military pay in the government--the so-called "comparability" principle established in 1971. Under this system, any percentage salary increase won by civilian federal employees is automatically extended to military servicemembers. To many AFGE members, paying dues for union activities that they hoped would increase their salaries, it seemed that soldiers were getting a "free ride," reaping the benefits of pay increases without contributing to the union. Some began to argue that soldiers should, so to speak, pay their way. This feeling materialized concretely for the first time in 1974 when the AFGE leadership under then-President Clyde Webber--who had recently replaced the late Vietnam War supporter John Griner--issued an appeal to active-duty servicemembers to support the union's drive for higher wages. The union's message: "Help us and you'll benefit, too." Fifty thousand leaflets were distributed to GIs in what was probably the first time that any establishment union actively sought the cooperation of servicemembers. According to AFGE, the soldiers reacted positively and contributed numerous letters to Congress urging a pay increase.[3]

This novel appeal to the barracks was given urgency by a second factor--the steady erosion of federal employees' pay under the latter years of the Nixon Administration. According to AFGE analyses, government wage increases throughout the early and mid-1970s failed to keep pace with inflation and amounted to a relative reduction in pay. As union leaders sought means of countering this trend and increasing their bargaining power, the possibility of organizing in the military came to be seen as a means of strengthening their political clout. While many union members honestly wanted to bring GIs into the union, some of the union bureaucrats considered the entire matter a form of potential blackmail against the government, a means of pressuring management to concede higher wage increases. Several federation officers characterized the GI organizing plan as a "weapon in the holster."

Perhaps the most basic compulsion for an interest in military organizing, a factor quite in contradiction to the notion of a holstered but never-to-be-used weapon, was survival. Many saw military organizing as a means of renewing the federation's growth. Although union membership increased by 300 percent during the 1960s, this growth had peaked at 320,000 in 1972, and after that, membership began to decline. As a result, the union's treasury began to slide into the red. The search for new members led to the all-volunteer force. The lure of 2 million unorganized soldiers was a powerful attraction to growth-conscious union leaders eager to replenish the union's treasury and expand their power.

While some union officials may have been interested in merely enriching the treasury or bluffing the government, other AFGE leaders, particularly national vice-presidents Al Kaplan (from Chicago) and Virgil Miller (from Minneapolis) sincerely wanted GIs in the union and had sound political reasons for doing so. These leaders and the union activists who supported them hoped that an infusion of low-ranking soldiers would breathe new life and vigor into an otherwise stodgy, ossified organization. Some also consciously recognized that soldiers, as they have in the past, might be used as strikebreakers against government employees and that bringing GIs into the union would help to prevent or at least complicate such action in the future. Another political consideration was the feeling that unionization, by linking soldiers to the civilian labor movement, would help maintain civilian control over a professional military and check the tendency of a volunteer force toward social isolation. Finally, there were many, particularly those who had been GIs themselves recently, who genuinely thought that the union could offer badly needed protection and services to GIs.

Obviously, this welter of conflicting argument, all emanating from a single organization, reflected a confused and uncertain approach. Indeed, AFGE never developed a coherent, well-conceived plan. The union's motivations mixed an honest concern for oppressed GIs, some enlightened analysis of the role of armies in society, a self-interested desire to use servicemembers to benefit present members, and a somewhat heavy-handed attempt at bluff. This incongruous combination was reflected in the behavior of the top leadership--a compound of honest militancy, confusion, and ultimately, cowardice.

The Fateful Confusion

Although the military establishment maintains perhaps a dozen or more intelligence agencies and the FBI has a long history of ferreting out radical plots within unions, the first news of AFGE's plans came not from the intelligence services but from a most unlikely harbinger of subversion, the *Wall Street Journal*. The story of AFGE's interest in the military and of their decision to begin planning for soldier membership landed like a bombshell on the *Journal's* pages on June 27, 1975, sending shockwaves through the military establishment and Congress and touching off a fire storm of outcry and recrimination.[4] Shrieks of "sheer horror" rang from the Pentagon, while military commanders reeled in wounded disbelief. Congressional military absolutists such as Senators John Tower and Strom Thurmond vowed a fight to the death against this mutinous plot. Professional military groups, including the Fleet Reserve Association, the Reserve Officer Association, and the Association of the United States Army, reacted as if the armed services were about to be dissolved. From all sides, even from liberals, came a veritable torrent of criticism and abuse. Everyone was against it, with the exception of the ordinary GI, whose voice remained unheard.

The AFGE leadership, shocked and no doubt frightened by the intensity of this early opposition, soon began the first of many verbal retreats. Union officials attempted to play down the issue and deprecate its importance. In one of the first official statements on the subject in August 1975, President Clyde Webber tried to assure the Defense Manpower Commission that AFGE was "simply studying the possibility" and conspicuously avoided even the mention of unionizing the military. Webber talked only of pay and comparability, ending his testimony with a revealing glimpse of the union's philosophy towards management: "We have found the mood of management has mellowed . . . Our role in the scheme of things has grown to the point where we are now really helping management . . ."[5] As in so many of AFGE's public pronouncements on soldier organizing, the whole exercise was an attempt to skirt the issue.

While these and other disclaimers were no doubt designed primarily to parry criticism, they also reflected genuine and deep-rooted misunderstanding within the union. Perhaps the most glaring confusion was the view that the armed forces are a social unity, that officers and men share common interests. This classless myopia led them to believe that officers, NCOs and low-ranking enlisted GIs could abide together harmoniously in the same union. By concentrating excessively on pay, the union tended to see all servicemembers in terms of the same, across-the-board percentage wage increase. They failed to recognize that money is not a sufficient inducement for GIs to stick their necks out and join a union. Without a class analysis of the military, the union officials and staff constantly confused the needs of officers and GIs. A planning paper prepared in June 1976, for example, talked in one place of "professional representation" (proposing to "improve the status and prestige of a military career") and in another of "grievance representation" (emphasizing such problems as disciplinary and discharge proceedings). The fact that these "all things to all men" proposals were aimed at very different social groups that were locked in often bitter daily conflict at the unit level never seemed to dawn on the union leaders.

This confusion between officers and the enlisted men ultimately came down to an unstated but obvious preference for organizing NCOs and officers. The union's constant reference to "professionalism" and its emphasis on retirement benefits and pensions clearly implied a partiality towards careerists. One reason for this orientation may have been the belief that the higher paid and more permanent NCOs and officers would be more "profitable" to the union than low-ranking, frequently transitory GIs. The more basic explanation, however, is the simple fact that most of AFGE's leaders and staff feel more comfortable with officers and NCOs than with GIs. Few of AFGE's national vice-presidents or leading staff officials served in the military as ordinary GIs, none in the post-"T" Vietnam-era military. Only Chicago area vice-president Al Kaplan, who was a private in the Marine Corps in the early 1960s, and who was once almost court-martialed for slugging a sergeant, had recent experience as a GI. Whereas other union officials talked of pay and retirement at a June 1976 meeting, Kaplan argued for unionism by pointing to the deaths of Marine Corps recruits during training.

An important factor in explaining this officer bias of the AFGE leadership is their class position: The economic and social status of union officials is closer to that of field-grade officers, majors and colonels, than to privates and Sp/4s. It is a long way from the air-conditioned, Musak-ed offices of the AFGE national headquarters to the dusty, noisy barracks of Fort Bragg.

The irony, and ultimately folly, of this preference for officers and NCOs was that the union was trying to organize in precisely those strata of the military where it was least wanted. The GIs, who make up the bulk of the military and who would have welcomed unionization, were ignored. Although, as we shall see below, the military's own surveys showed that support for unionization was greatest at the bottom and almost nil at the top, AFGE was unable to alter its self-defeating biases. That this was not merely an accident but rather a deeply rooted characteristic of unions in modern society is evident in the fact that similar attitudes prevail among union leaders in such countries as France and West Germany.

Fear and Loathing in Las Vegas

Given the confusion of the AFGE's approach to military organizing and the growing stridency of its critics in Congress and elsewhere, it was perhaps a minor miracle that the issue ever went beyond the point of mere discussion. Yet by September 1976, following heated debate within the federation's National Executive Council, the question of military organizing was formally brought before the union's 25th biannual convention in Las Vegas. The actual proposition before the 2,000 delegates, many of them younger than the leadership, with a substantial proportion of nonwhites and women, was not whether to begin an actual organizing drive but the more limited question of whether the membership clause in the constitution should be changed to allow servicemembers into the union. The leaders consciously played down the basic issues of unionization and military organizing. One of the most radical political steps imaginable was being presented as a minor amendment to the bylaws.[6]

The manner in which the AFGE leadership put the question on the floor showed their condescending attitude toward the delegates and their desire to push the issue through without debate. When the vote came up on the third day in the midst of a heavy calendar of other business, national vice-president Virgil Miller blithely mumbled into the microphone: "Well, here's another noncontroversial topic, organizing the military." The delegates, many of whom felt very strongly about the issue and were ready to do battle, booed and hissed; they could not believe their ears. The fatigue and exhaustion that had till then befogged the convention's proceedings gave way to heated excitement. An anxious tension swept the hall, as dozens of delegates rushed to the floor microphones for debate.

The first three or four speakers blasted the proposal, arguing fanatically about conflicts of interest and imminent mass mutinies. The next few speakers, including a young Vietnam veteran, spoke up in favor of the idea, arguing that GIs needed protection and emphasizing that the resolution would not commit the union to an organizing drive. In response to a question from the floor, newly elected president Ken Blaylock stated that the resolution would merely change the wording of the Constitution and was only a first tentative step toward organizing the military. Despite these assurances, the next speaker rose to castigate the plan and complain about overextending union resources. At this point an increasingly impatient Blaylock intervened in the debate on a point of personal privilege, as he called it, and launched into a long and impassioned speech in favor of the resolution. Having only a few hours before won a stunning victory as union president on a platform calling for greater militancy within the union, Blaylock chastised the delegates for not endorsing the programs necessary to back up his new pledge of aggressiveness. He hammered home on the "weapon in the holster" theme, claiming that this step was necessary to give AFGE greater bargaining power. (No mention was made of the needs of soldiers.) Blaylock ended his plea on a feverish pitch with a rousing appeal for unity and strength. His last words were drowned in a chorus of applause and cheers.

The next speaker at the floor microphone happened to be national vice-president Al Kaplan, perhaps the strongest supporter of the resolution. With the roar of the crowd still ringing in the hall, Kaplan and his aides huddled quickly and decided to call the question. In the midst of this euphoric and highly charged atmosphere created by Blaylock's appeal, the motion to cut off debate carried overwhelmingly. Without hesitation Blaylock then called for a voice vote on the resolution itself. It too passed convincingly. Stunned delegates looked at each other in amazement. Against all predictions, the military organizing resolution had passed.

A frequent charge leveled against Communists in the heyday of the old left was that their ends and means were incompatible. While they fought for worthy ends, such as an egalitarian, classless society, they were charged with using contrary means to achieve these goals and, in the process, of deforming the desired end. Such arguments are directly relevant to AFGE's convention, and indeed to their entire approach to military organizing. The goal of a military union may have been desirable (at least to low-ranking GIs), but the means of achieving this end were ultimately counterproductive. Railroading the resolution through the convention without providing delegates a chance to debate fully or understand the issue was typical of the union's top-down approach and its avoidance of the mobilization of members and GIs that alone could have brought success. Inappropriate means prevented the desired end.

The False Start

Despite the limited intentions of AFGE's leaders, the decision of the Las Vegas convention created a sensation in the ranks and touched off a flurry of pro-union activity. News of the convention's action, carried in *Stars and Stripes*, *Army Times*, and other military newspapers, created the impression that actual unionization might begin at any moment and emboldened some soldiers to step forward. At several bases, including Fort Devins, Massachusetts; Fort Benjamin Harrison, Indiana; and McGuire Air Force Base, New Jersey, groups of servicemembers approached existing AFGE locals to explore possible affiliation. (In all three instances the AFGE national office prevented the locals from organizing soldiers.) Overseas, where AFGE was almost nonexistent, rank-and-file soldiers began to build new pro-union soldier committees in the hope of becoming actual union locals at a later date. In addition, most of the existing GI organizing projects began to work openly for unionization.

As 1976 drew to a close, momentum seemed to be building for the beginnings of unionization in the military. Within the AFGE, however, vacillation continued. Some leaders, particularly vice-president Kaplan, urged an immediate organizing drive, while others, including President Blaylock, argued for delay and caution. A crucial juncture in this internal debate, probably the turning point in the union's aborted attempt to unionize the military, came in December 1976 at a meeting of the union's National Executive Council. With support growing in the barracks and thousands of membership inquiries pouring in from the ranks, the union leaders were gathering to decide on the machinery for an actual union drive. Momentum was building for soldier unionization, and the assembled leaders were being asked to take a major step in that direction.

In the midst of debate on the issue, however, the union leaders were given a sudden and unexpected taste of the controversy their decisions could create. On the morning of December 9, as they were about to vote on hiring a staff to prepare for military organizing, the leaders were greeted with a front-page headline in the *Washington Post*: "Campaign is Set by AFGE Union to Enlist Military."[7] The article, reprinted from its subsidiary, the *Trenton Times*, the day before, incorrectly claimed that AFGE Local 1778 at Fort Dix was "recruiting all over the base" and falsely linked the union to the Enlisted Peoples Organizing Committee, (EPOC), a rank-and-file support group, and with the Quaker-sponsored Friends Military Counseling Group. The impression created was that pacifists and radicals were organizing GIs for AFGE on Fort Dix and McGuire Air Force Base. Through either deliberate obfuscation or very shoddy journalism, the article attributed EPOC's demand for "the right to resist illegal orders" to AFGE.

Faced with this wildly distorted publicity, with phones ringing off the hook and reporters calling for information, the vice-presidents plunged into paralysis. Rather than facing up to the issue and proceeding with their plans, they tabled the motion at hand and hastily moved on to other business. By postponing any decision until March, the union dissipated the growing momentum for unionization and allowed the mounting opposition within Congress and the Pentagon to assert itself.

Right-Wing Counterattacks

All during the preceding months, as AFGE and soldiers discussed and debated military unionizing, the hawks in Congress and the military establishment, led by their aging standard-bearer, Lieutenant General of the Reserves Strom Thurmond, prepared the counterattack. Right-wing political forces launched several campaigns, including a so-called poll mailed to millions of citizens by Americans Against Union Control of Government (the public-employee wing of the National Right to Work Committee), and a major lobbying effort by the Reserve Officers Association and several other military associations. The main focus of this opposition was Thurmond's bill to outlaw military organizing, S. 3079, 94th Congress, 2d session. (When introducing the bill in the *Congressional Record* in March 1976, Thurmond reprinted an article by one of the authors as a dire warning to Congress of the dangers that could result from unionizing the military.)[8] Thurmond's bill, and similar measures introduced in the House of Representatives, contained sweeping prohibitions against not only unionization but practically all forms of military organizing and counseling. Despite its dubious constitutionality, Thurmond's bill received a sympathetic hearing before the Senate Armed Services Committee in March and July 1977 and breezed through the Senate on a 72-3 vote in September of that year. The bill subsequently passed the House of Representatives as well. The Department of Defense implemented the bill even before it was passed in an October 1977 directive, 1354.1, prohibiting all forms of "collective job-related action" within the ranks and banning union solicitation on base.

Although the DoD directive and parts of the Thurmond bill were aimed primarily at active-duty soldiers, their greatest impact was probably felt within the union rather than in the military. The chilling effects of the directive and of the bill were very real and powerful (the directive prohibited GIs from even "speech-making" in favor of a union), but they probably added little to the draconian restrictions already in place. Having been told since the first day of basic training that they were in the army to defend democracy rather than to practice it, soldiers were probably puzzled to learn that they had any rights left to be withdrawn. It must be remembered that GI organizing has always been a perilous enterprise. In some ways the Thurmond bill could even be seen as a moderation of military repression. The law imprisons organizers for only five years, whereas in 1969 the twenty-seven "mutineers" of the Presidio stockade in San Francisco, whose "crime" had been to sit down and sing "We Shall Overcome" as a protest against the shooting death of a fellow prisoner, received initial sentences of fifteen years or more.[9]

The right-wing counterattack had its strongest effect within AFGE. The leaders hardly feared imminent jail sentences; their more immediate concern was with the political fallout of this antiunion drive. The senators who rushed over themselves to join Thurmond in condemning military organizing were often the very same legislators needed by AFGE to win pay raises. (The Comparability Pay System permits federal unions to override presidential wage recommendations through a vote of the Senate.) Unlike most unions, much of AFGE's membership and political support is in the South and Southwest, where the largest military bases are located. Over the years the federation has acquired a unique working relationship with otherwise antilabor, reactionary Southern senators. The controversy over the Thurmond bill split AFGE from its Senate allies and in the union's view jeopardized other legislative objectives, most importantly a bill that would establish formal collective bargaining for federal employees. This growing criticism of AFGE created enormous pressure to abandon the military organizing project and further contributed to the deepening sense of paralysis within the union.

A Democratic Demise

From the time of the national convention and even before, a compromise proposal of those opposed to or at least unsure of the military organizing efforts was to submit the question to an unprecedented referendum of the union membership. Such a democratic method for determining long-range union policy is extremely rare in the labor movement. Unfortunately in this case, its main effect was to avoid immediate action and introduce additional delay in a campaign where timing was of fundamental importance. Indeed the vote was a gigantic cop-out, a means of gracefully withdrawing from an unwanted brink of confrontation. The decision to run a referendum was less a sudden attack of ultrademocracy within the union leadership than an attempt to avoid taking a stand on an increasingly difficult and potentially damaging proposition.

Some of the leaders, enamored of the weapon-in-the-holster approach, had never wanted to begin an organizing drive in the first place and were no doubt glad to get off the hook. Others, who might have genuinely wanted soldier members, were probably having second thoughts and misgivings about the proposal because of the vicious political blasts unleashed against the union. In any case, the leadership's unwillingness to support the measure assured its defeat. The national office did not campaign for a yes vote and made only minimal attempts to discuss the issues involved. When the question "Should the national office commence military organizing?" went out to the locals in summer 1977, its defeat was already a foregone conclusion. Given the enormous political pressures against military organizing, the leadership's unwillingness to explain fully the issues or campaign for the referendum amounted to tacit acceptance of its defeat and abandonment of the military organizing project.

The result of the union vote, actually a winner-take-all referendum of its 1,566 locals, was a resounding defeat. Locals representing 151,582 members voted no while locals representing 38,764 voted yes, four to one against.[10] The margin of the referendum's defeat shocked even its supporters (who had expected to lose but not so devastatingly) and indicated how sharply the union membership had turned against the proposal. Since the beginning, many members had been less than enthusiastic about the issue, but certainly far more than 20 percent of them had supported soldier organizing a year earlier in Las Vegas. Their minds were changed by the growing dint of criticism and right-wing reaction and by the leadership's confusion and misdirection. The manner in which the project was handled alienated the members, contributing to an already widespread sense of uneasiness about the union hierarchy.

Not all no votes were against soldier organizing per se. To a significant degree the vote was an expression of distrust toward the national leadership and frustration at the weakness of the existing civilian organization. "How can we go out and help GIs when we can't even organize in our own agencies?" was a common reaction among rank-and-file members we met. It is of interest that during the dozen or so local AFGE meetings on the referendum the authors attended, no one disputed the right and the need of soldiers to organize. They questioned instead whether AFGE would be the right vehicle (as we shall see, many soldiers had similar misgivings) or whether this would be the right moment to mount such a mammoth undertaking. In any case, few questioned Blaylock's September 1977 statement announcing the vote: "AFGE will not be acting to organize military personnel now nor at any time in the foreseeable future."[11]

The Unheard Soldier

It is easy to say with hindsight that AFGE's military organizing project was doomed from the outset. The federation was considering perhaps the most revolutionary departure in the history of U.S. labor, certainly the most radical since the formation of the CIO, without coherent direction and without a clear understanding of what it was attempting. Union leaders often viewed the project in a cavalier, almost flippant, manner, and seemed impervious to the political tempest their proposal had created. Indeed some within the union, including several of the leaders responsible for directing the effort, probably never intended to organize the military in the first place and were raising the issue solely as a bluff to the federal government. Assuming that others were serious in their intentions, however (as many within the union most certainly were), how could the effort have been handled differently? What specific steps would have been necessary to ensure a successful organizing drive?

While we have no crystal ball with which to second-guess history, we focus on one fundamental error: an unwillingness to address the interests or needs of the largest pool of potential union members, the lower-enlisted ranks. Our reading of AFGE's two-year experience and of the successes and failures of military unionism in Europe suggest that only an immediate mobilization of rank-and-file enlisted soldiers could have produced a rapid and successful organizing drive.

Throughout the debate on military organizing, AFGE and others talked a great deal of the lessons to be gleaned from the military unions of Europe. (Indeed the federation sent one of the authors to conduct a special study of these unions.) Despite their interest, however, AFGE seemed unable to draw the appropriate conclusions from this experience. The lessons of the German model, for example, should have showed AFGE the folly of competing with military associations for the favor of NCOs and officers. The German OeTV (a public employee union similar to AFGE) had in ten years managed to organize only 1 percent of the German army's NCOs and officers, most of whom prefer instead the giant armed forces association, the Bundeswehr Verband. The OeTV's unwillingness to accept rank-and-file draftees, the equivalent to U.S. first-term soldiers, has consigned its military organizing efforts to insignificance.

The lessons of the VVDM in Holland, meanwhile, show that low-ranking soldiers can be effectively organized, but that this process requires mobilization and mass participation by the soldiers themselves. The popularity and success of the Dutch conscripts' union derived not only from its ability to improve the soldier's daily life but also from its policy of constantly involving the rank-and-file in union activity. The European experience provides ample support for a union strategy based on the mobilization of first-termers.

We need not rely on European armies for proof of rank-and-file interest in unionization: The evidence of widespread support among U.S. volunteers is overwhelming. During its two-year campaign, for example, the AFGE national headquarters reported receiving over 10,000 unsolicited letters and petitions from active-duty service members, many from soldiers in grades E-4, E-5, and E-6, that is, first-termers and middle-grade sergeants.[12] Ken Blaylock told the Senate Armed Forces Committee, "We have had all kinds of requests . . . that we go ahead and organize."[13]

Testament to a strong interest in unionization also came from the military establishment. Even the staunchest opponents of unionization were forced to admit that support for the concept had reached "alarming" levels. For example, Robert Nolan, executive director of the Fleet Reserve Association, admitted to Representative Samuel Stratton of New York that "the support I found for the concept of a military union amongst the junior personnel is absolutely astounding." Admiral James Watkins, Chief of Navy Personnel, made the same point in greater detail to the Senate Armed Services Committee in summer 1977:

Information available to me from a variety of sources . . . convinces me that the mounting interest in unions among enlisted and officer members alike is significant. I first noticed the beginnings of this interest in late 1975, saw it increase noticeably in intensity during 1976, and level off at nearly constant amplitude so far during 1977 . . . Validation of the union threat in the Navy is corroborated by a broad range of Navy sources, including . . . the flood of letters from our people to various Navy officials . . . [and] data taken from nearly every Command in the Navy. . .An existing survey taken of entering Navy recruits over the past three years indicates a significant movement toward favoring military unions . . . As many as 30 percent of Navy personnel might join a union if one were available today. I would expect this percentage to run higher among enlisted members and lower among officers.[14]

The most important point is that this support for unionization was concentrated primarily within the lower ranks. Although Blaylock and others within AFGE constantly confused this issue, claiming that union sentiment was greatest among "career types," all available evidence points to the opposite conclusion: Support for unionization is inversely related to rank. As in any work force, those at the bottom of the pyramid have the greatest need and desire for unionization. This is confirmed most reliably in a series of scientific surveys conducted within the armed forces themselves during 1976 and 1977. Although the studies were conducted by career officers or NCOs, the results showed substantial union support.

Perhaps the most significant and scientifically rigorous of these studies was the Manley-McNichols report, conducted at the Air Force Institute of Technology, at Wright-Patterson Air force Base in Ohio during April 1976.[15] Based on 938 completed questionnaires (520 from officers and 418 from enlisted airmen), the study disclosed what its authors considered surprising union sentiment within the lower ranks. When asked to respond to "I would join a union," 37 percent of enlisted airmen agreed, 30 percent were opposed, and 33 percent were undecided. Among officers the comparable percentages were 16 percent in favor, 63 percent against, and 21 percent undecided. These findings were confirmed by other surveys showing similar results. One study, conducted at Seymour Johnson Air Force Base in North Carolina, questioned 207 enlisted people and 76 officers. When asked, "Are you in favor of the creation of a labor union within the U.S. Air

Force?" 44 percent of the airmen said yes, 32 percent said no, and 24 percent were undecided. Among officers, only 17 percent were in favor, 68 percent were opposed, and 14 percent were undecided.[16]

A less scientific survey conducted by the Citizen Soldier organization in New York showed similar results.[17] In responses to questionnaires sent to military subscribers of *Playboy* and *Penthouse* magazines, Citizen Soldier found strong support for unionization among enlisted men, especially junior NCOs, with officers overwhelmingly opposed. The responses of 327 returned surveys to the question "I agree that service people need a union" were: 52 percent of enlistees said yes, while only 13 percent said no (among junior NCOs the positive response was 61 percent). By contrast, 57 percent of the officers were opposed, with only 16 percent favorable. Interestingly, the navy command purposely did not conduct an official fleet survey because, according to Admiral Watkins: "Such an action would probably not be in the navy's best interest and [would] merely serve to fan the unionization fires."[18]

These military surveys, combined with the flood of inquiries received by AFGE, demonstrate what could fairly be described as mass support for unionization within the lower ranks. The armed forces witnessed an enormous groundswell of union sentiment during 1975-1977, with hundreds of thousands of rank-and-file servicemembers literally waiting to be organized. A union drive in fall 1976 probably would have produced immediate, overwhelming success. As Blaylock told the Armed Services Committee: "I could have expanded the membership of this Federation by 50,000, I am sure, if I opened this thing up after September."[19] The point, of course, is that he did not. The union refused to open its doors to the GIs clamoring for admission. The flames of unionism, ignited by AFGE's initial announcements, were allowed to flicker and die.

Soldiers Organize: The Enlisted Peoples Organizing Committee

Although AFGE never replied to the soldiers who wrote to them, and indeed even ordered locals at Fort Dix, Fort Devins, and elsewhere to turn away GI applicants, grass-roots union activity flared up on bases and ships throughout the military in 1976 and 1977. Despite constant command repression, soldiers spontaneously attempted to organize local efforts in support of what they thought would be the unionization of the military. The full extent of this activity will probably never be known. Not even the various military intelligence services can have a full picture, for local commanders often suppress information about internal dissent that they feel will reflect badly on their record. Our information is limited, therefore, to those few occasions when the tip of the iceberg surfaced and union supporters in the ranks made contact with civilian supporters.

Although Strom Thurmond and others tried frequently to link the political left to unionization of the military, in fact the venture failed to attract any significant activist participation, not from the Old Left (such as the Communist Party), and not even from New Left groups that had been involved in the GI movement only a few years before. The only concerted civilian involvement in unionization issues during these years came from a handful of miniscule GI support groups staffed on a volunteer basis by recently discharged soldiers and veterans. One of these efforts was the Enlisted Peoples Organizing Committee (EPOC), a Washington-based group of active-duty soldiers and civilians that launched a pro-union petition drive. The committee, which included one of the authors, was perhaps the first soldier support group to back the AFGE initiative and mobilize enlisted participation. Despite EPOC's extremely limited resources (its total budget for two years during this period was $3,000, less than a month's salary for an AFGE officer), its petition drive sparked soldier activity on dozens of ships and bases and produced one of the few visible expressions of GI support for unionization.

The petition was designed to demonstrate union sentiment and focus attention on the kind of activist, rank-and-file organization wanted by GIs. The document read:

Enlisted people need a union. We the undersigned feel it is necessary to exercise our right to organize. We want a democratic union that will:
• Work for an overall change in the military legal system and provide legal assistance;
• Work for such basic labor rights as overtime compensation and job safety, and establish a workable grievance procedure to solve unit-level problems;
• Guarantee that enlistment contracts, pay, and benefits aren't changed to our detriment;
• Fight against racist and sexist supervisors and policies;
• Protect and extend our Constitutional rights, especially freedom of speech and association and the right to privacy.
The right to organize a union belongs to all citizens. We urge Congress to reject any attempt to limit this right.[20]

Launched in summer 1976 with the help of several other GI support groups, the petition gained a substantial following in the United States and overseas. In May 1977, 1,900 signatures were submitted to Congress in a Washington, D.C. press conference. Petitions came from hundreds of sailors aboard the U.S.S. *Coral Sea* and other Pacific ships, 200 servicemembers from the Washington, D.C. area, 300 soldiers and airmen from Fort Bragg and Pope Air Force Base in North Carolina, 500 soldiers from bases in Germany, and hundreds of others from such diverse locations as Iwakuni,

Japan, and Juneau, Alaska. (Petitions bearing hundreds of additional names were lost, stolen, or destroyed by commanders all over the military who, despite legal guarantees to the contrary, often take a very restrictive view of the soldier's right to petition Congress.) Several active-duty soldiers were on hand to present the petition in 1977, including a Fort Belvoir (Virginia) GI who appeared with a mask over his face.[21]

The "Insane" Fulda Soldiers

The perils of circulating such a petition and an appreciation of its impact at the local level can be seen from the 1976 experiences of the Fulda Soldiers' Committee.[22] Fulda is a medium-sized town at the eastern-most limit of West Germany, right up against the "Iron Curtain." Stationed there in Downs Barracks was the first squadron of the U.S. 11th Armored Cavalry regiment, a reinforced reconnaissance unit assigned to guard over 300 kilometers of the west/east border. The 11th ACR is one of the most "front-line" units in the entire U.S. army, constantly out on field duty "facing the enemy." When one of the authors visited there in 1976, we received a certificate claiming we had been to the "frontiers of communism."

The Fulda Soldiers' Committee began in summer 1976 when members of the first squadron, together with local German youths ("street people" they were called), put out a bilingual leaflet protesting "off-limits" policies against GIs at local discos and the destruction of the local countryside by U.S. tanks on maneuvers. (Such bilingual leaflets have appeared in West Germany several times in recent years, produced by U.S. as well as French and Dutch soldiers, combining the complaints of soldiers and local youths.) The first distributors of the Fulda leaflet were arrested by U.S. and German Military Police but had to be released (no valid reason could be found for holding them). This failure to disrupt the committee made them heroes to their fellow soldiers and greatly increased their confidence. In early fall the Fulda activists learned about the EPOC union petition from members of the *FighT bAck* soldier committee in Heidelberg, who had come up to the border town (250 kilometers away), bringing copies of the petition. The idea of mobilizing for a union caught on quickly; within a month over 200 soldiers (approximately one-quarter of the unit's E-5s and below) had signed the petition.

When the Fulda soldiers began their union effort, they had serious questions about AFGE. They fully endorsed the idea of a union, but they knew little about the federation and were uncertain of its intentions. When they learned that AFGE did not strike and that it lacked a fighting tradition, their misgivings increased. After considerable discussion, though, most came to the conclusion that "a bad union is better than no union." Many would have preferred a more militant organization, but if AFGE was the only union willing to help, they would at least give it a try. AFGE was the only game in town. Moreover, as some soldiers noted, it was more important to get organized first and then deal with the union later. In any case they took the union's organizing plan seriously and went out on a limb to solicit signatures and openly advocate a soldiers' union.

Ironically, the soldiers' faith in AFGE was never reciprocated. As we have noted, the federation had a full-time office in Frankfurt, approximately 150 kilometers away. The union's representative, Chester Cole, could have gained over 200 potential new members in a single visit, enough to increase the union's total European membership by over 30 percent. In fact, however, Cole did nothing about the Fulda group and probably never even heard about it. Even if he had, one wonders how the Major would have related to this unruly crew of dope-smoking Pfcs.

Isolated from outside support, without the help of AFGE or sympathetic civilian lawyers, the soldiers fell easy prey to command repression. Two of the leading organizers were singled out as ringleaders and were "fired" through administrative discharge, in this case for alleged psychiatric disorders. The two Fulda "ringleaders" were abruptly summoned to appear at the 97th General Hospital in Frankfurt, ostensibly for a checkup. When the two arrived the next day, however, they were given sedatives (to calm them, they were told) and were immediately shunted off to psychiatric examinations.* The by-now heavily doped soldiers were labeled "drug-dependent" and were railroaded out of the military with medical discharges. Back at Fulda, meanwhile, organizing activity quickly faded. Bereft of its leading organizers and unable to link up with either soldiers or civilians, the committee ceased functioning by January 1977.

In many ways the Fulda story is typical of what occurred throughout the military in 1976 and 1977. The union's announcement sparked an initial upsurge of activity, which was quickly followed by repression, dispersion, and silence. During this period EPOC received petitions and letters from GIs all over the world, from Navy Seabees (construction crews) in faraway Diego Garcia in the Indian Ocean, from sailors aboard dozens of ships in the Pacific, and even from radar men at an obsolete antiballistic missile site in the wilds of Alaska. In almost every case, however, the initial contacts could

---

* It is important to note, when so much is written of the Soviet Union's pernicious use of psychiatry against dissidents, that similar methods are sometimes employed within the U.S. army. In a number of cases -- including those of Larry Johnson in Idar Oberstein, Babette Peyton from the 97th General Hospital in Frankfurt, and Sergeant Benjamin Simms at Hahn Air Force Base -- the army tried to use psychiatry as a method of eliminating dissent. Soldiers whose sanity was not in question a few months before are suddenly branded "insane" the moment they begin to show tendencies toward organized resistance.

not be sustained. The lack of local civilian support and the military's swift repression of such organizing soon draped a curtain of silence over most rank-and-file union efforts.

Ex-Sp/5 Tom Doran

One of the few cases where, because of personal contact, we were able to follow an organizing effort through to its premature, command-imposed demise was that of Sp/5 Tom Doran, who was fired from the 82d Airborne Division at Fort Bragg in December 1976. Doran, it will be recalled, had attended the 1974 International Soldiers' Congress in Amsterdam and had been one of those deeply impressed by the Dutch conscripts' union, the VVDM. In 1975 Doran reenlisted into the 82d Airborne at Fort Bragg and dedicated himself to a long-term effort of organizing among local soldiers, something few of his fellow GI resisters had been willing or able to do. A quiet and intense man, one of the few U.S. soldier organizers we know who was not into the drug scene, Doran had long recognized the importance of unionization, and even before his visit to the Netherlands had advocated a GI union at Fort Bragg. When the AFGE announcement came to his attention in 1975, Doran immediately recognized its significance and intensified his organizing efforts, founding the Fort Bragg-based Organizing Committee for an Enlisted Peoples Union. Doran worked closely with EPOC in Washington, D.C., on the pro-union petition and helped author EPOC's pamphlet on unionization.

Unlike most of his peers, Doran was able to contact the AFGE and work with the civilian union for an extended period of time. He not only introduced himself to the AFGE local at Fort Bragg (which was housed in a barracks building on post) but became quite close to several AFGE national leaders as well. Doran was the only active-duty soldier present at the union's Las Vegas convention. Although he did not speak before the full membership, he did address about 100 delegates at a meeting of Midwest districts called by national vice-presidents Kaplan and Miller. At one point Doran was even flown to Washington to consult with union officials at the national headquarters on how the military should be organized.

Given Doran's close relations with AFGE and the leadership's apparent confidence in him, one would expect that if any soldier were to receive union support against command repression, it would be him. In fact, however, when the crunch came, AFGE did exactly as much for Tom Doran as it did for the Fulda activists: nothing. While AFGE officials may have been ignorant of events at Fulda, this was not the case with Tom Doran. When Doran was notified on the morning of December 13 that he was to be discharged by that evening (despite a spotless record of over four years of service), he could see the railroad coming and immediately phoned for help from the union. When AFGE's general counsel and executive assistant to the president were notified of Doran's plight, they expressed concern and promised to "look into the matter"; nothing was done then or later. Left to face the command alone, Doran was rushed through out-processing in record time and by 6:00 P.M. that evening was an unemployed civilian. Neither the AFGE local nor the national union came to his aid. Even when he filed suit to get his job back, with help from the ACLU office in Atlanta, AFGE refused to get involved. The union simply deserted Doran, abandoning with him a strong base of support at Fort Bragg and nearby Pope Air Force Base.

Despite his firing, Doran continued valiantly to work for unionization and to support the burgeoning organizing committee that had grown up around his efforts. Along with active-duty organizers, he helped collect over 300 signatures from area servicemembers and continued to build the rudiments of a union local. When the union petition was presented to Congress and to the press in May 1977, Doran led the delegation. Doran maintained that since his discharge was illegal, he was actually still in the army. Appearing with the other active-duty soldiers, including the masked man, Doran forcefully argued for a rank-and-file union willing to fight for soldiers' rights.

The EPOC press conference, which occurred just as AFGE was beginning its membership referendum, was a last futile effort to press ahead with the faltering campaign to unionize the U.S. military. By the time Doran and his colleagues brought their appeal to Washington, the struggle for a soldiers union was already lost. The fact that the only mobilization of soldiers came from such tiny groups as the Fulda Soldiers' Committee and EPOC merely confirmed the hopelessness of the situation. AFGE not only failed to mobilize soldiers but left Doran and other GI organizers out on a limb, a limb that in almost every case the army command obligingly sawed off.

If . . .

Could it have been otherwise? Could the U.S. military have been organized? Certainly yes, given the widespread support for unionization that appeared in the ranks in 1977, and which no doubt still exists today. U.S. soldiers have shown a ready willingness to join a union organization. This attitude exists in nearly all highly capitalized countries and is part of the soldier's continuing struggle for greater say over the terms and conditions of service.

While the troops seem ready for organization, the established trade unions are not. Stodgy unions such as AFGE are incapable of the commitment required for organizing the military. The problem is not confined to U.S. labor, for, as we shall see in Chapters 11 and 9, the same tendency has occurred among French and German trade unions. Only a labor movement on the offensive, such as the upsurge that built the CIO in the 1930s, could possibly undertake this weighty challenge to both military and civilian establishments.

The sweetheart or company union deals that labor bosses have in mind simply will not work. Command repression will greet any union effort, no matter how timid. The military command structure is threatened by all forms of independent mass action, even the most innocuous. In this respect military commanders and their right-wing allies saw the significance of military unionism far more clearly than the unions. AFGE officials held on to the myth that organizing would not challenge command authority. But Strom Thurmond and his colleagues knew perfectly well that unionism could have profoundly disruptive consequences. It might alter relations between soldiers and officers, and thus weaken the command's ability to control "their" troops. This simply cannot be allowed, especially if GIs are to be sent off on unpopular missions abroad.

4

The Professional Military Unions
of Europe

When the American Federation of Government Employees announced its interest in unionizing the army, U.S. commanders shrieked in horror: "You can't run an army with unions." Imagine the disappointment of these generals when it was revealed that military unions have existed for decades in Europe, and that such unions are common in the armies of several of our loyal NATO allies in Northern and Central Europe.

To learn more about these unions, AFGE sent one of the authors on a research and fact-finding tour in 1976. What we found was an elaborate and highly developed network of organizations throughout the armed forces of Europe.[1]

Unions Everywhere

In the six countries studied--Sweden, Norway, Denmark, Belgium, Germany, and Holland--we identified more than sixty separate soldier associations. Sweden had three officially recognized unions, Norway seventeen, Denmark over twenty-five, Belgium three, Germany two, and Holland twelve. These groups range in size from the huge Armed Forces Association (Bundeswehr Verband) of Germany, with over 180,000 members, to a tiny Norwegian union of draft board officers with just fifteen members.

These professional military unions are vastly different from the conscript and soldier committees examined elsewhere in this book. Professional unions and soldier committees are two entirely separate phenomena, the former fitting comfortably with the military establishment, the latter often directly challenging command authority. Our elegant lunches in posh hotels with the professionals contrasted sharply with the spare coffee and cigarettes offered in the disheveled offices of the conscripts. The only conscript organizations with official union status are the Dutch VVDM and AVNM (see Chapter 7). Otherwise, the ad hoc committees that have been formed by low-ranking soldiers in nearly every European country are very much "unofficial" and bear no resemblance to the world of professional military unionism.

The professional organizations are composed almost entirely of career officers and noncommissioned officers. As one would expect in organizations of military careerists, the political outlook tends to be conservative. The associations are organized on a craft basis, according to branch of service, rank, occupation, and professional interest. In Holland, the organizations are even divided according to religious denomination (Catholic, Christian, and nonreligious). Ironically, officers tend to be the most highly organized, with a rate of union membership in the Scandinavian armies of over 95 percent.

These officer unionists often find themselves the subject of conscript barbs, and they naturally view soldier committees with misgiving, not to say trepidation. In Norway, an official of BFO (the Joint Organization for Officers and Sergeants) proudly proclaimed that his union had defeated Labor Party proposals in parliament to expand democratic rights for low-ranking soldiers. When we asked an official of the Regimental Officers' Union in Sweden about the Draftee Working Group in his country (a union-type committee that we shall examine in Chapter 8), he frowned sourly and dismissed such efforts as "communist subversion." By geography, the Swedish Officers' Union and the Draftee Working Group are very close, with Stockholm offices less than a mile apart; in political orientation, however, they are continents apart.

Part of the Labor Movement

Although these organizations are often more like associations than unions, the professional military unions share some important characteristics of civilian labor, especially unions in the public sector. Most of the military associations are affiliated with public employee unions within their country, which are in turn affiliated with giant labor federations (equivalents of the AFL-CIO). The resulting pattern of organization and affiliation is bewilderingly complex--a "jungle of organizations," as one Danish union official described it to us.

The pattern is fairly simple in Sweden, and we describe it here by way of illustration.[2] Three "official" military unions exist. The Swedish Officers' Union (SOF) consists of regimental or senior officers and has approximately 5,400 members, nearly all such officers in the armed forces. The

Company Officers' Union (KOF) is made up of lower-level officers and has about 5,000 members. The Platoon Officers' Union (POF) has about 9,300 members, consisting mainly of warrant and noncommissioned officers. KOF and POF, the two "lower" associations, are affiliated with the Central Organization of Salaried Employees (TCO-S), a large and powerful white-collar union federation. SOF is affiliated with a smaller public employee federation, SR-SACO, which is composed primarily of academically trained professionals.

The military associations gain important benefits from their affiliation with civilian labor. The large union federations that speak on behalf of the military organizations can mobilize considerable resources to back up their soldier and officer demands. In Belgium, the military union, SYNDIC, is affiliated with the Liberal Trade Union Federation, which engages in collective bargaining on behalf of its military affiliate. All of the Scandinavian military unions and several of the Dutch associations are also affiliated with one or another civilian labor federation.

These affiliations have given the professional military unions impressive powers. In Sweden they enjoy full collective bargaining rights. Swedish officers even have the right to strike, at least on paper, a point we shall discuss below. In Holland, Germany, and Belgium, the military unions lack formal bargaining powers, but they possess extensive consultative powers. All of these organizations, even the most limited, have obtained formal government recognition and have acquired a major voice in the determination of personnel policy, especially compensation, promotions, and work conditions. The governments are required by law to negotiate or consult with these organizations, and no change in service conditions can be made in these armies without the participation of the military unions. Ironically, the powers of these military organizations in Europe are in some cases greater than that of civilian unions in the United States such as the AFGE.

Interestingly, although the military unions are often but tiny parts of large civilian labor federations, they tend to wield considerable influence within them. They have come to play the role of brokers between competing unions within the larger labor conglomerates. In Norway, for example, the president of the 100,000-member state employee federation, Kartelet, is the former president of Norges Befalslag, a small military union with only 3,000 members.[3] Similarly, in Denmark, the chair of the "B" Officers' Union, with 1,700 members, is cochair of the 45,000-member public employees' union, COII.

The Dialectics of Military Unions

The history of professional military unionism can be divided into three separate phases. Initially the associations were organized for moral or social purposes. Some date back to the nineteenth century and were formed to honor "God, King and Country." Perhaps the earliest of these organizations was the "Society for Producing Useful Military Information," formed by British military engineers in 1810.[4] Such groups were created for purely professional or social ends and did not concern themselves with the material conditions of service.

Over time, especially in the 1930s and after World War II, these associations began to act and think more like unions. Questions about pay and compensation began to be raised. Military service became more of an occupation, less of a calling. The officer was less a father to his men, more a professional wanting decent wages and conditions. It was during this time, mostly in the years after the war, that the associations formally affiliated with larger labor federations. In Denmark, the "B" Officers' Union joined the COII labor federation in 1948. In Norway the union of "B" Officers joined the LO labor federation in 1961. Thus began what we consider Phase Two of professional military unionism.

In their earliest phase these organizations posed no threat to the military establishment. Indeed they were part of that establishment. Even in Phase Two, when the groups became more like unions and raised demands for more pay, there was no conflict with the command. The shop steward and the commander seemed to be getting along fine.

Phase Three, which is just beginning now, may change all of this. A new type of military union organization is emerging, based primarily on lower-ranking enlisted volunteers, noncommissioned officers (NCOs), and junior officers. These unions tend to be more militant, more willing to cooperate with the draftee and soldier committees, more unpredictable from the viewpoint of the command. The growth of these new NCO unions is still a new and relatively uncertain development but may have enormous potential significance for the future of resistance in the military. We shall examine this trend in more detail below.

A Record of Success

The professional military unions have focused nearly all of their energies on improving compensation and the conditions of service. In the process they have scored some major victories. Pay raises have been the paramount goal, and in most of these countries the unions have succeeded. The Scandinavian unions in particular have won substantial wage gains and have been able to maintain pay levels equivalent to those of civilian public servants. In Belgium and Holland military wages have also been raised. Generally speaking, the unionized armies of Northern Europe have much higher pay scales than the nonorganized forces of Southern Europe.

Wages are not the only compensation concern of the military unionists. As incredible as it may seem in the United States, several of these unions have also won the right to a forty-hour work week, with compensation for overtime. The unions have been able to negotiate limits on the amount of extra work-time permitted within a given year. Moreover, each hour spent on special maneuvers or weekend duty must be compensated with time off or additional pay. In Belgium, Norway, Holland, and Denmark, these rights have already been won, although in reality they are not always fully enforced. The unions must constantly fight to ensure that work hours are limited and that full compensation is provided.

In keeping with their professional orientation, the military unions of Europe have also won the right to participate in officer and NCO promotion boards. In Norway, union representatives have been sitting on promotion boards since 1966, with three of the eight members of the central board selected by the unions.[5] In Denmark, union influence is even greater, with two out of the three members on the central board selected by the unions.[6]

The European military unions are also raising potentially troublesome questions about occupational health and safety. It might seem peculiar that demands for job safety would appear within an institution predicated on the possibility of death and destruction, but the military unionists of Europe are very serious about these matters. They view military service as a profession and they want the same occupational safety standards enjoyed by other workers. Thus in Germany, Sweden, and elsewhere, unions have sought a greater role in monitoring on-the-job safety conditions and have even demanded the right to halt training operations or other forms of hazardous duty when they pose an unnecessary safety threat.

The military unions of Europe have a solid record of accomplishment. They have achieved large financial gains and have reduced the arbitrariness and inequity of military life. In many respects these efforts are completely acceptable to the command and have even helped to oil the military machine. Through their representation on promotion boards and in wage negotiations, for example, the unions serve as partners in personnel management. On the other hand, some of these union efforts inevitably create difficulties, despite innocuous intentions. The unions have imposed extra financial burdens on the military establishment and have placed certain limits on command prerogative. Their attempts to regulate work time and reduce hazardous duties pose particularly difficult questions. As we shall observe below, the constant striving of these unions to achieve civilian wages and working conditions create serious contradictions for the military.

Strikes in the Foxholes

When military unions were first proposed in the United States, opponents blasted the idea by raising the specter of military strikes. Images were conjured up of picket lines in the infantry, of troops striking in the midst of battle. A steady drumbeat of ridicule was aimed at union proponents: "You can't have strikes in combat." As a result many supporters backed away from the idea. These criticisms turned out to be much ado about nothing, for no military union in the world, not even the Dutch VVDM, has the unfettered right to withhold labor.

There is one group, however, that does have a limited right to strike, and it is, ironically, a group of officers. The Swedish officers' unions theoretically have the right to strike. They enjoy this privilege as members of the country's public employee federations. In reality, though, this power is severely encumbered by bureaucratic restrictions (a government labor board can rule against such actions by claiming it would have national security implications). A confrontation over the right to strike in Sweden occurred in 1971, when negotiations with the government over a new wage contract broke down. When the government refused to meet their wage demands, the officer unions reacted by announcing plans for a limited walkout by selected middle-level officers. The government responded not by arresting the would-be strikers, but by ordering a lockout of about 3,000 regimental officers, thereby threatening the military with temporary paralysis. Parliament reacted swiftly to the escalating confrontation and passed an extension of the old wage agreement. It is ironic, in light of all the alarmist cries about soldier strikes from military traditionalists, that the only attempted application of this right resulted in a reaction by the command that nearly crippled the army.[7]

Elsewhere in Europe military unions do not have even the theoretical right to strike. They must rely instead on more indirect means to enforce their demands. The most frequently used or threatened means of applying pressure is the "sympathy strike" by civilian public employees. Since negotiations for military wages are usually conducted as part of the larger bargaining process for all public employees, it is natural for the military and civilian members of the labor federations to work together. The Scandinavians are particularly fond of what they call "point strikes," in which a single, strategically located occupational group can strike on behalf of all the members of the union. For example, the Norwegian public employee federation, Kartelet, can threaten a strike by its small air-traffic controller division and thereby apply strong pressure on the government without having to call out its full membership. Such "point strikes" are threatened often, although used seldom, and are an effective means of backing union demands.

After the strike weapon, the most common means of trying to win support for union demands is the informal process of lobbying and insider persuasion. Before they resort to threats of strikes or other labor action, the public employee federations and military unions try to win support for their demands by meeting with the appropriate political officials within the government. This process is especially important in Scandinavia, with its tradition of consensus and social harmony. This insider lobbying is also aided by the frequent presence of Social Democratic governments in these countries. The major labor federations with which the military unions are affiliated tend to be major bulwarks of the Social Democratic governments, and their attempts at persuasion are thus likely to be effective.

The NCO Unions: Changing Dialectics

To date, the professional officer unions have not used their considerable powers to disrupt the military establishment. The bargaining and consultation sessions have been fairly tame. Militant tactics have not been used. This is not surprising, given the class and social composition of these groups.

For certain other organizations, however, particularly those of sergeants and junior or warrant officers, a different pattern of behavior is emerging. A transition toward more militant and authentic forms of trade unionism seems to be underway in several of these groups. The most prominent examples of this new type of union are the Central Organization for Contract Personnel of Denmark, SYNDIC of Belgium, and the Association of St. Martinus in Holland.

The Danish union, the Centralorganization Stampersonnel (CS), has approximately 14,000 members, all of them enlistees.[8] Of these, approximately 9,000 are volunteers or contract soldiers. These privates are not draftees, but rather enlistees who serve varying terms (or contracts) of several years' length. The Danish contract enlistment system is similar to that of the British volunteer force, although the terms of service are shorter. This new type of enlisted volunteer is becoming more prevalent in the Danish military, reflecting a general tendency in Denmark and elsewhere to deemphasize the role of conscripts and increase the proportion and importance of enlisted volunteers (see the next chapter). In the small Danish army, for example, the number of contract volunteers increased from approximately 3,000 in the early 1970s to nearly 10,000 a decade later. The number of draftees during the same period has declined by several thousand.[9] Most of these new contract volunteers now entering the army have also joined CS.

SYNDIC and the Association of St. Martinus are similar to CS in social composition and union orientation. The Dutch St. Martinus group is open to servicemembers "under the rank of second lieutenant" and is affiliated with Holland's civilian Catholic labor federation, the NKV. SYNDIC in Belgium is also based primarily among sergeants and enlisted NCOs, although approximately one-third of its members are junior or warrant officers. It is likewise affiliated with civilian labor, in this case the Liberal Trade Union Federation.

These unions represent social groupings within the military (especially contract volunteers) that did not exist in large numbers in previous years. The technicians, skilled volunteers, and middle-level supervisors who make up these unions represent a kind of "new class" in the army. They are also the potential source of a military resistance phenomenon. The union efforts of these organizations seek to elevate the status of what had previously been insignificant or lower-level social groupings within the army. Unlike the situation with the higher-officer associations, the members of these unions are not part of the command, and they have less of a vested interest in the military profession. They tend to view the military as just another job or as a way of learning a trade. They are not concerned about preserving the status quo within the ranks. On the contrary, their interest is in shifting the balance of power and privilege downward toward the middle ranks.

In keeping with these different interests, the NCO unions tend to employ more militant tactics and are more confrontationist in style. The Belgian union, SYNDIC, for example, has sponsored street demonstrations in which several hundred uniformed sergeants and junior officers have demanded better pay and conditions. These actions are similar to the demonstrations and rallies of conscripts and are a far cry from the gentlemanly manner of the higher-officer unions.

The efforts of these NCO unions also overlap with those of the soldier and conscript committees. Unlike the officials of the higher-officer unions, the leaders of CS and the Association of St. Martinus have friendly and cordial relations with their colleagues in the junior ranks. The Association of St. Martinus cooperates often with the Dutch conscripts' union, VVDM. In Denmark CS has helped Danish conscripts participate in and attend meetings of the European Conference of Conscript Organizations (see Chapter 8). The members of these NCO unions have no doubt been influenced by their younger colleagues. It is unimaginable, for example, that the Association of St. Martinus could watch the draftees gain a tenfold wage increase through militant tactics and still continue in the old polite manner. If the draftees can go out in the streets and win big gains, the sergeants cannot be far behind. (This same pattern occurred with the movement of NCOs in Italy; see Chapter 12.)

It is very difficult to characterize these NCO unions politically or in relation to soldier resistance. Although they have cooperative ties with the conscripts and occasionally employ similar tactics, the NCO unions do not fit the mold of soldier resistance. The members of these unions tend to remain in the army for relatively long periods of service (*lifers* the draftees call them) and are less antimilitary or hostile toward command authority. Moreover, these unions tend to be distrustful of political parties on the left, while soldier committees tend to cooperate with such groups. For example, CS voted against affiliation with the Danish labor federation LO a few years ago.[10] This was partly a rejection of the Danish Social Democratic Party with which LO is affiliated. The contract soldiers and sergeants voted against LO, according to the official we interviewed, because the Social Democrats in parliament tend to vote against military budget increases. The leaders of CS want more money for the military, so that pay and conditions can be improved, and they are suspicious of politicians on the left who vote otherwise.

These new NCO unions thus present the apparent paradox of more vigorous trade unionism coexisting with conservative politics. The meaning and implications of this development remain unclear. One thing is certain, though. As the role of volunteers increases in modern armies, the importance of unions such as CS will grow.

Normalization

As noted earlier, professional military unionism can sometimes place restrictions on military flexibility and prerogative. Even when the unions remain cooperative and polite toward the military establishment, their actions can have unintended, often radical effects. The quest for regulated work time is a case in point. As we have observed, the Scandinavian unions have won the right to a forty-hour work week. This is a very normal and logical development for civilian trade unionism, but it is highly unusual, not to say shocking, for the armed forces. Inevitably it means that commanders have less control over their troops and less time to carry out their missions. In the case of special military functions, such as sea operations, or combat exercises, it also means less capability.

As trade union activities advance within the armed forces, the command's previously absolute control inevitably becomes diluted. The hours of the day when a soldier is under military authority are reduced, and civilian standards are introduced into many features of military duty. These tendencies are especially important in the NCO unions. The changes are subtle but nonetheless significant, especially when viewed in an historic context. The concept of military service for today's unionized volunteer is far different from that of the doughboy draftee of earlier decades.

The Danish CS union is quite explicit about its purposes. They describe their goal as "normalization," the process of narrowing the gap between the military and civilian society. They want military service to be stripped of its feudal vestiges and integrated more closely with civilian life. This position is similar to that of the VVDM in Holland, which seeks to break down the difference between soldiers and civilians and to "make the army more like the society."[11] The Danish volunteers urge the elimination of punitive discipline and a more democratic form of leadership and decision making. They demand that soldiers be treated as citizens and be accorded the dignity and rights of full members in society. Again, this is a far cry from the tradition of rigid and unquestioning discipline.

This process of "normalization" faces inevitable limits, though. The army is, after all, a "special body of armed men." It exists as an instrument of destruction and repression and is the means by which the state and ruling classes defend themselves from external and internal adversaries. At a certain point the process of union-led democratization must reach limits beyond which it cannot go. Otherwise the distinctiveness of the military institution would be blurred altogether. It is significant that this "normalization" of the army is most advanced in Scandinavia, where class conflict and social discord are muted and armies are seldom used for unpopular purposes. In a sense the ruling elites of Scandinavia can "afford" to dilute the nature of military authority as other mechanisms of social control become more dominant. In the advanced welfare state, the democratization of the armed forces can reach its farthest limits.

5

The Volunteer Army:
Its Origins and Consequences

Introduction

In several of the highly capitalized nations of the West, a gradual but significant trend is developing toward professionalization of the army. The United States, Great Britain, Canada, and Australia have abandoned conscription and now rely totally on volunteer recruitment. In Denmark the proportion of conscripts has declined while the number of "contract" volunteers has correspondingly increased. In Holland, Denmark, Italy, Spain, and Belgium, the role of conscripts and their importance within the military has diminished. Even in the Soviet Union there is now talk of a volunteer force. In nearly every country there is an unmistakable trend toward downgrading the role of conscripts and relying more on volunteers and specialized professionals.

It might be expected that conscripts would be grateful for this easing of their military burden. But the soldier activists of Europe uniformly oppose the trend. At the 1979 international conscripts' conference in Malmö, Sweden (see Chapter 8), the assembled soldiers were unanimous in their opposition to the volunteer army and their support for conscription. Like many civilians on the continent, especially those on the left, European soldier activists view conscription as a safeguard of democracy. The conscripts see professionalization as a threat to their movement, as an attempt by the military establishment to isolate the army from democratic influences. They fear that professional soldiers will be less likely to challenge unpopular or repressive military policies. They know that soldier movements have virtually disappeared in the U.S. volunteer army, and that Britain's volunteer forces have seen no organized dissent at all.

The weakness of soldier movements in all-volunteer armies constitutes an important exception to our general rule about the armed forces of highly capitalized society. In this chapter we examine the volunteer army, its evolution and current consequences, and explain its relation to the general trend toward resistance.

Why the Volunteer Army?

In the United States, the decision to end conscription was overtly political. In 1968 presidential candidate Richard Nixon seized on the volunteer army idea as a means of countering the revolt among youth and defusing the powerful antiwar, antidraft movements then shaking the foundations of the U.S. system. Immediately upon taking office, Nixon appointed the Gates Commission to examine how the draft could be ended. The commission strongly endorsed the volunteer force concept, and its recommendations were adopted soon afterwards. In explaining its case for ending the draft, the commission warned that "efforts to escape conscription" were imposing severe costs on society and the armed forces. The commission was very explicit about the relation between military resistance and the volunteer force:

The draft creates ... morale and disciplinary problems which otherwise would not arise ... Dissent within the military presents particularly ticklish problems within the armed forces of a free nation. Problems raised by the forced military service of those who are unwilling or unable to adjust to military life will largely be overcome by voluntary recruiting."[1]

In Australia the decision to end conscription in late 1972 was similarly motivated. A strong antiwar and draft-resistance movement had emerged in opposition to Australia's participation in the Vietnam War. As in the United States, the unpopularity of the war and growing hostility to military service led the government to abandon conscription and return to purely voluntary recruitment.

In Britain the decision to end the draft also came in the aftermath of an unpopular military intervention, in this case the Suez campaign of 1956. Although the short-lived Suez fight did not generate the kind of mass military resistance that emerged in the United States during the long Vietnam War, the political and military controversy resulting from the unsuccessful campaign raised serious doubts about Britain's military policies.* The Suez debacle fueled demands for a major reduction in Britain's

---

* None of the unpopular colonial wars of the late 1940s and the 1950s generated the kind of mass soldier resistance that emerged a decade later, not only in the U.S. military during Vietnam but in other armies as well. The Dutch intervention in Indonesia, the French attempt to reconquer Indochina, the British police actions in

vast military establishment. (During this period the military budget in Britain absorbed approximately 10 percent of the country's gross national product, compared to less than 6 percent in the 1980s.)

As pressures for reducing the military burden grew, steps were taken to end conscription and trim the military budget. In 1957, then-Defense Minister Duncan Sandys issued a government White Paper calling for a radical revision of military policy: Britain's armed forces would henceforth become smaller and more mobile, conscription would be ended, and the military budget would decline relative to other government expenditures.[2]

Academicians have coined an apt phrase to describe this trend: "the decline of the mass army." According to the eminent Dutch military sociologist Jacques Van Doorn, the declining importance of conscription reflects broad social and political developments within the military and society at large.[3] Changing values and social conditions have resulted in declining legitimacy for the armed forces. American sociologists Morris Janowitz and Charles Moskos likewise trace professionalization to changes in the the structure and values of Western industrial society.[4] As the values and conditions of society have evolved, the importance of military service as an obligation and duty of citizenship has declined.

"Unilateral Disarmament?"

The decision to rely on volunteer recruitment in Great Britain was part of a larger, more fundamental decision to reduce the size of the armed forces and radically limit the missions and responsibilities of the military establishment. Accordingly, in the years following the issuance of Duncan Sandys' White Paper, manpower levels in the British military steadily declined. Total force strength went from 690,000 in the mid-1950s to 420,000 in the mid-1960s and 340,000 in the mid-1970s. Along with this drop in force strength came a withdrawal of British troops from many of their traditional colonial outposts, especially east of Suez. Except for the British army of the Rhine, overseas force commitments were drastically curtailed.

The volunteer forces of Canada and the United States have experienced similar declines in troop strength. Beginning in 1964, the Canadian government steadily reduced its troop strength, from 120,000 in 1964 to approximately 80,000 in the late 1970s. Similarly, while the draft was being phased out in the United States during the early 1970s, manpower levels dropped sharply. Total U.S. troop strength dropped from over 3.5 million at the peak

---

Malaysia and elsewhere, Washington's "UN" war in Korea, the eight-year French war in Algeria, the Franco-British intervention at Suez--none generated mass GI resistance. As we note in Chapter 1, soldier behavior changed only after time "T" in the 1960s.

of the Indochina war to just over 2 million in the 1970s. A large part of this decline was due to the withdrawal from Vietnam, but it should be noted that the leveling-off point of 2.1 million troops maintained into the 1980s is considerably below the pre-Vietnam strength of 2.6 million.

In Britain and Canada these reductions were motivated by a desire to reduce the cost of the military relative to other national priorities. Growing social expenditures required a reallocation of financial resources. In the United States, manpower reductions were based on a similar concern about the high cost of the military (especially after the large pay raises passed at the outset of the volunteer army). The reduced U.S. manpower levels were the best that could be achieved at the time and reflected the inevitable decline in troop strength that seems to accompany the all-volunteer force.

Although military budgets in the United States and Britain climbed again during the 1980s, the extra money did not lead to major increases in troop strength. Personnel costs have risen prohibitively. The military has been obliged, somewhat reluctantly, to increase the standard of living of its volunteers. Each soldier now costs the army far more than his or her predecessor did a few dozen years ago. Per-unit labor costs have risen both directly (pay) and indirectly (conditions) as the military competes in the labor market and must now spend more on such things as increased wages, improved benefits, and new barracks.* The large payroll and recruitment expenditures required to maintain a volunteer force serve as an impediment to easy expansion of the military.

General William Westmoreland argued against the all-volunteer force in 1973 on precisely this basis: "The cost of manpower expansion would be tremendous," he warned, and "such realization could serve as a deterrent" to military planning.[5] The Defense Appropriations Subcommittee of the U.S. House of Representatives made the same point when draft calls were ending: "The cost of recruiting additional personnel . . . might be prohibitive." The committee added: "The all-volunteer force appears to be a *purely peacetime concept,* in that even a relatively small increase in personnel strength would place a nearly impossible strain upon the recruiting capabilities" (emphasis added).[6]

The all-volunteer force seems to set limits on war-making capabilities. Military force levels are determined not by army generals but by what the recruitment "market" will bear. Without the easy option of increasing draft calls and thereby expanding forces at will, military planners lose a crucial element of flexibility. They must respond to any challenges with forces

---

* The greater part of military budget increases of the 1980s have gone for expensive new hardware, to increase the capital equipment per soldier. Karl Marx would have seen here confirmation of a basic law, the rise of the "organic composition of capital." The ratio, c/v, of hardware costs (constant capital, c) to labor costs (variable capital, v) continues to grow, even when v, the cost of labor, increases.

already in place or seek legislative approval for renewed conscription. Depending on the circumstances, it may be possible for armies to fulfill their missions within these constraints, but large-scale and lengthy military interventions certainly will become more difficult. Morris Janowitz described this transition in striking terms to the Defense Manpower Commission in 1975: "Manpower has come to operate and will in the future continue to operate as a crucial limitation and restraint on U.S. foreign policy." Janowitz went on: "The shift from conscription to the all-volunteer force is a form of unilateral disarmament."[7]

Recruitment and Unemployment

The challenge of recruiting a large military establishment on a purely volunteer basis is a formidable one. As we shall see, the U.S., British, and Canadian armies have all experienced periodic crises in attempting to meet this challenge, in the 1960s and 70s with the British, in the 1970s for the Canadians, and in the late 1970s for the United States. Military recruiters have been forced to adopt unaccustomed and sometimes troubling methods to reach their quotas, including the recruitment of "boys" in the case of Britain, and accepting large numbers of women and minorities in the case of the United States. Despite extraordinary public relations and advertising efforts, recruiters have found a frequently inhospitable and disinterested reception among the youth of today's highly capitalized societies. The only population sectors attracted to military service are those that benefit least from social modernization: rural youth and the marginalized, often nonwhite population of the old urban centers. Indeed, the volunteer armies would have long since entered into a permanent state of collapse were it not for the army's savior: high youth unemployment.

Defense officials do not like to admit that the volunteer recruitment depends on high unemployment. They prefer to believe that the recent successes of recruitment are due to their own wise management, or that young people are finally shedding their indifference to the military. The evidence is strong, though, that unemployment is a prime reason for the rise in the fortunes of volunteer recruitment.

In the 1960s former U.S. Defense Manpower chief Harold Wool wrote: "Studies of enlistment trends have shown . . . that enlistment rates have been positively correlated with fluctuations of youth unemployment."[8] A 1972 study by the University of Michigan's Survey Research Center also found a strong correlation between high unemployment and enlistment.[9] In 1978, the authors of the Pentagon's own comprehensive study of the volunteer army, *America's Volunteers*, reported that econometric figures confirm the linkage between military recruitment and high unemployment.[10]

A close examination of U.S. recruitment figures illustrates these trends. After a shaky beginning of recruitment shortages, the volunteer army experienced a brief respite during the 1975 recession. Recruitment then entered another period of declining results during the late 1970s, reaching bottom in 1979, only to be rescued again by the joblessness of the 1980s. It is particularly striking that the recruiting decline of the late 1970s occurred while annual enlistment quotas were dropping. The armed forces fell well below their goals in 1979, even though the enlistment quota for that year was lower than what it had been four years earlier. In 1975 the military signed up 456,000 recruits; in 1979 it recruited only 338,000.

The army is interested not only in numbers but in the types of recruits it finds. Commanders need what they call "quality" soldiers, those who have or can learn technical skills and can adapt to the rigors of military life. Thus, "qualitative" statistics are kept of the educational level and mental aptitude scores of those who enlist. Actually, the word *quality* here is a misnomer, since these statistics have little or nothing to do with the work skills, moral character, or personality of the individual being tested. In the case of Blacks and Hispanics, these figures are often discriminatory and fail to reflect the recruit's abilities. Educational and aptitude statistics tell us less about the soldier than about his or her social background. A decline in "quality" figures represents a lowering of the army's socioeconomic representativeness.

The evidence is clear that the educational levels of army recruits have dropped considerably since the end of conscription. According to Morris Janowitz and Charles Moskos, "the overall educational levels . . . of male enlistees is [sic] lower than either the equivalent civilian population or the army entrants of 1964, the last year before the war in Vietnam."[11] During the first eight years of the volunteer army, 45 percent of all male recruits were high school dropouts. The percentage of high school dropouts among army recruits in 1980 was higher than in 1960, even though the overall rate of high school completion for males aged eighteen to nineteen rose from 65 percent in 1964 to 80 percent in 1978. State Moskos and Janowitz: "While the national trend has been toward a higher percentage of high school graduates, army accessions are moving in the opposite direction."[12] The percentage of army recruits with some college has also dropped precipitously. In 1964 one in eight enlistees and one in six draftees had some college experience. In the current volunteer army, only one in twenty recruits has had college experience.[13]

The decline in the educational levels and mental aptitude scores of army recruits in the late 1970s led Congress to impose restrictions on recruiting standards. The fiscal year 1981 Defense Authorization Bill required the armed services to accept no more than 25 percent of Category IV recruits (those scoring lowest on aptitude tests) and restricted the army to no more than 35 percent high school dropouts. These restrictions have been maintained in the years since. When the standards were first imposed, many doubted that the army could meet them. But these efforts coincided with the advent of higher unemployment and underemployment. Since the rise of joblessness and the resulting improvement in the recruitment climate, the armed services have witnessed a marked improvement in educational level and aptitude scores and have had no difficulty meeting Congress's quality standards. The compulsion of economic necessity has forced many to join who previously would not have considered military service. Both quantitatively and qualitatively, recessionary conditions have helped military recruitment.

Blacks in the Volunteer Army

It was to be expected, and was predicted by many, that a military force founded on economic conscription would disproportionately attract those most afflicted by joblessness, particularly minorities. Statistics in Figure 5.1 confirm that black representation in the military rose in the early years of the volunteer force and has stayed at levels considerably above the black percentage in the overall population.

Figure 5.1
Blacks in the Military, Percent of Total Force
1977--1985

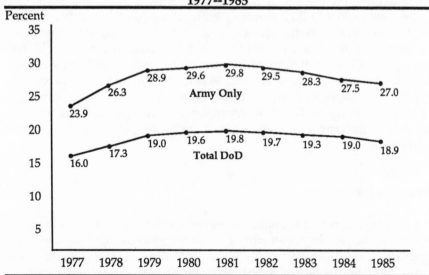

Source: Defense Manpower Data Center

While overrepresented in the enlisted ranks, they are underrepresented in the officer corps. In 1983, Blacks constituted only 9 percent of officers in the army.[14] They are even less represented among officers in the air force and navy.

The proportion of Hispanics, the fastest growing minority population in the United States, is far below that of Blacks. In 1983 Hispanics constituted just 3.8 percent of the army and 3.6 percent of the armed forces as a whole. (As with Blacks, though, discrimination is prevalent. In 1983 Hispanics made up 4 percent of the enlisted ranks but only 1.4 percent of officers.)[15]

After the early 1980s, the percentage of Blacks among new recruits leveled off and declined slightly. In part this was due to the general rise of joblessness among youth in the early 1980s (which increased the pressure to enlist on whites who otherwise might not have considered military service). Another factor, though, may have been a conscious policy by the military to hold down the percentage of minorities. The principal means of achieving this objective has been a systematic campaign by recruiters to shift their offices and other enlistment activities from urban centers to the suburbs. Throughout the United States in recent years, new recruitment offices have opened in shopping centers and other suburban locations, while previous stations downtown have been closed. The stated purpose is to recruit a broader cross-section of the population, not to exclude Blacks, but the end result is the same.

Concerning black enlistment and the so-called "quality issue," it should be noted that the black soldiers who have enlisted in the volunteer force have a considerably higher rate of high school graduation than whites. Although Blacks in civilian society trail whites in educational level, in the all-volunteer force Blacks have the edge. Since the advent of the volunteer army, according to Charles Moskos, the proportion of black army recruits with high school diplomas has been 64 percent, compared to 53 percent for whites.[16] As Moskos points out, black soldiers seem to be representative of their community in terms of education and background, while white recruits in the army tend to come from the least-educated sectors of their community.

Recruiting Women

In the armies of the United States and Canada, as well as in Belgium, France, and other European armies, women are increasingly faced with the question: Does liberation mean getting into the infantry? Of course the army could hardly be said to be promoting feminism. Far from it; military training is inherently sexist (with a heavy dose of aggressive machismo), and the military establishment has traditionally resisted opening the ranks to women. Faced with the recruitment problems of the volunteer era, however, military leaders have discovered a new interest in women. Since the end of conscription, the percentage of women in the U.S. armed forces has jumped from 2.4 percent in 1973 to 7.4 percent in 1979 to 10.1 percent in 1986. In 1990 women constituted 11 percent of the U.S. military. The percentage of women in the military has also increased in other Western armies, although nowhere as sharply as in the United States. While the infantry remains closed, some 90 percent of all military jobs are now open to women.

The armed forces are particularly interested in "quality" women. They can compensate for some of their problems in the recruitment of men by going "up" the quality scale in the selection of women. During the first few years of the volunteer army, all women recruits had to be high school graduates. Even today, women in the military tend to have higher educational levels and higher aptitude scores than do men.

No matter how skilled, however, women recruits are still asked, "Can you type?" and are assigned predominantly to clerical and service positions. Many jobs may be open, but most female recruits still end up doing "women's work"--behind the typewriter, the supply-room counter, or the nurse's station. Increased female participation allows the military to move skilled male recruits from administrative and service positions to "more important" technical jobs.

There may be a contradiction for the army in relying too heavily on women. Women who join the military nowadays tend to be independent minded and more than capable of looking out for themselves. They are certainly not what the sergeant would consider "duds." They exhibit a healthy disdain for the traditional military concept of women as servants of men or mere sex objects. This is not to say that women recruits in the volunteer army are free from sexual abuse. Sexual harassment and rape have become widespread on a number of U.S. military bases. A female soldier interviewed by the authors at Fort Bragg, North Carolina, claimed that nearly half the women recruits she knew had experienced rape or sexual harassment. The *Army Times* and other military publications have featured major reports on the subject. But women are rising up to counter this violence in the military as elsewhere in society, and in the process are challenging army traditions that equate military prowess with sexual aggressiveness.

Bringing women into the armed forces, the bastion of male sexism, thus creates problems for the military. This is particularly so in an era of rising feminism, where women are demanding equality and dignity. It is not surprising, therefore, that military traditionalists oppose the use of women in combat and that any further increases in the percentage of women in the ranks may be slow in coming.

GI and Gay?

The armies of most nations are not only sexist but also homophobic. Homosexuality among male and female soldiers supposedly doesn't exist. When gays and lesbians are discovered, they are eliminated, sometimes after brutal harassment and punishment, often with less-than-fully-honorable discharges. Although the percentage of gays and lesbians in the army is as high, or perhaps higher than in civilian society, they have long remained in the closet. In pre-T times they rarely confronted the army's homophobia but preferred to remain silent.

In recent decades, however, as part of the rise of soldier resistance in the post-T highly capitalized nations, homosexuals have asserted the right to be gay and GI too. In the United States, Holland and other highly developed nations, gays and lesbians in the ranks have come out of the closet to demand legitimacy and recognition. Just as soldiers have asserted the right to control the length of their hair, or have published newspapers to create independent sources of information, so gay and lesbian troops have confronted the command over sexual preference. As in so many aspects of GI resistance, the first victories for gay rights occurred in the Dutch army. An association of openly homosexual servicepersons now exists in Holland, the SH&K, with a claimed membership of 2,000.

The struggle for gay and lesbian rights has often been a painful and difficult one. The heroes who led the way often suffered great personal hardship in the process. Perhaps the most famous case in the United States was that of air force sergeant Leonard Matlovich. When Matlovich wrote to the Secretary of the Air Force in 1975 announcing that he was gay, he did so with the intention of staying in the military and asserting the right of a serviceperson to be homosexual. His was a conscious political act, similar to that of soldiers who advocated a GI union, designed to call attention to the plight of gays and lesbians in the military and win recognition for their rights. Although Matlovich had considerable support inside and outside the ranks and received extensive press coverage (including a cover story in *Time* magazine), he was discharged in October 1975. As Matlovich ironically noted after his release, "they would give me a medal for killing a man, but kicked me out for loving one."

Matlovich kept up the fight for gay and lesbian rights after his discharge, as did hundreds of other veterans and active duty soldiers. Many additional cases of individual confrontation with the military command took place all through the 1970s and 1980s. Matlovich himself died of AIDS in 1989, but the struggle he and others initiated began to bear fruit in 1990 when the U.S. Supreme Court ruled for the first time in history that a homosexual soldier, army sergeant Perry Watkins, had the legal right to re-enlist in the military. Slowly the bastion of military homophobia was beginning to give way before the repeated challenges of gay and lesbian soldiers.

The "Manning" Crisis of Canada

Canada has had an all-volunteer force since the end of World War II and thus has the longest experience with volunteer recruitment of any NATO country. For the first twenty-five years the relatively small, highly profes-sionalized armed forces of Canada achieved their recruitment objectives without strain or difficulty. The army faced no resistance or recruitment problems. Beginning in the 1970s, however, the Canadian volunteer system began to show cracks; the generals began to face many of the same problems that have plagued their U.S. and British counterparts.

The development of spot shortages and "quality" problems in the Canadian force was unexpected and, on the face of it, highly improbable. The army entered the 1970s with a very favorable recruitment outlook. Force levels were declining (following a decision to cut manpower in the 1960s), while the military-age population was increasing. The armed forces were very small in relation to the population (80,000 out of a total civilian population of 23 million, or only 1 soldier per 300 civilians). Only 12,000 new recruits were needed annually, which meant that just 1 out of 100 young male Canadians would have to be recruited. Nonetheless, beginning around 1973, the Canadian forces experienced what one study has termed a manning crisis, a steady deterioration in recruitment and reenlistment.[17] For the first time recruiters had difficulty meeting their quotas, and, more importantly, shortages began to appear in key job positions. The problems became particularly acute in the Combat Arms and Sea Operations special-ties, where recruiting difficulties and unusually high rates of attrition created turmoil and shortages.

Why did these troubles arise? Canadian researchers have traced them to "an apparent intolerance among high-quality--notably more educated--recruits for the conditions of service."[18] The Canadians have faced the same paradox evident in other volunteer forces. The highly educated and skilled youth who are most desired by recruiters tend to be the least interested in military life. Most do not join the military, and those who do tend to leave early. Studies of shortages for enlisted technicians or combat soldiers trace them to discontent over military discipline and the conditions of service. The skilled volunteer leaves the military not only for financial reasons but because of military restrictions and harassment. Even in the relatively relaxed and reformed Canadian military, the quality of life is better on the outside.

The Boys of Britain

The British army has found a truly unique but also unsettling solution to the problem of volunteer recruitment. The British have filled the ranks of their armed forces by enlisting boys aged fifteen to seventeen--what they euphemistically term "pre-adults," or "junior leaders." Recruiters have always believed in "getting them young", but the British have gone to extreme lengths. In this way they have managed to maintain the much-reduced manpower levels of their volunteer force.

Soon after the British military draft was ended, the familiar problems with recruitment began to appear. Military officials responded by lowering the enlistment age and expanding the percentage of "boy" recruits, first gradually, and then in increasing proportions. The British army and navy had always had a tradition of boy drummers, buglers, and tailors. When the recruitment squeeze of the volunteer force began to appear, though, this so-called junior entry program was overhauled and enlarged. As a result the percentage of boys among recruits climbed steadily. Between 1956 and 1966 the number of "junior soldier" training units in the army more than doubled, even while the overall size of the armed forces was declining.[19]

As in other countries, those who enlist in the British volunteer force tend to come from disadvantaged socioeconomic backgrounds. Many are "school leavers," the same as high school dropouts in the United States. In Great Britain unemployment and economic hardship tend to be geographically concentrated, particularly in the declining industrial regions of the North and in small, rural towns. It should not be surprising that military recruitment is also concentrated in the same regions. A disproportionately large percentage of recruits come from the aging industrial centers of Liverpool and Manchester and from the rural regions of Northern England and Scotland. By contrast, in the more prosperous London area, the rate of recruitment is abnormally low. Thus the same pattern emerges as elsewhere. The volunteer force disproportionately attracts the disadvantaged, while society's more educated and privileged sectors avoid military service.[20]

Quiet in the Ranks

The British army is the exception in Europe: It has experienced no organizing or resistance movements. In Britain as in Canada, Japan, Australia and New Zealand--all with volunteer armies--soldier newspapers and committees do not exist. The absence of resistance in the British army is especially curious in light of its grimy, often bloody intervention in Northern Ireland. Researchers report that the war in Ireland is apparently bad for recruitment, but it has not sparked any organized protest in the ranks.

The absence of a soldiers' movement in contemporary Britain is all the more striking in light of that country's long history of enlisted revolt. From 1647 to 1649 the soldiers of the New Model Army, led by elected "Leveller" agitators, swung the course of the English revolution far to the left. In 1797, during the anti-Jacobin war against revolutionary France, both major British fleets, at Spithead and Nore, passed for weeks into the hands of antiauthoritarian sailors. In more recent times, several major mutinies and rebellions erupted in the British armed forces near the end of World War I and during the Allied intervention in Russia--in Etaples, Murmansk and elsewhere.[21] In the 1920s, Britain experienced a remarkable "lower decks movement" in which soldier newspapers and union-type committees spread throughout the enlisted ranks. As late as 1931 there was a major strike in the home fleet at Invergordon.[22]

Why is there no soldiers' movement in the British armed forces today? One factor is the relatively small size of the military. The British army is truly a professional force and is relatively isolated from society. The population per soldier ratio is nearly 160, compared to approximately 100 in the United States. The British army can thus be more selective in its recruitment. It is more insulated from what sociologists term the "mass army effect." As noted above, the more modern and affluent regions of Great Britain are underrepresented in the military, while the more economically backward areas are overrepresented.

But the ranks of the British army have not been completely quiescent. Although official statistics are hard to obtain, rates of unauthorized absence and desertion increased slightly in the 1970s. A small number of soldiers have deserted from Northern Ireland. One soldier interviewed by *The Guardian* in 1975 claimed that sixteen soldiers stationed at the Long Kesh internment camp deserted with him to protest British policies there.[23] Notwithstanding such isolated incidents, the British armed forces have seen no recent organized soldiers' movement similar to those in other Western nations.

Unionization in Britain?

The present calm in the British armed forces could be shattered by a familiar development: soldier unionism. In recent decades, two major civilian unions in Britain have proposed organizing soldiers. At least one independent group has also formed to begin preparing for a union. As in the United States and other industrialized nations, pressures are mounting for unionization of the army.

The first call for unionization in the British military came in 1969 from the giant Transport and General Workers Union, one of the largest and most powerful in the country. Union leader John Cousins wrote to the Labour government of that time to ask if his union would be permitted to sign up servicemembers. The government replied coolly, stating that while no law prohibited membership in a union, "a serviceman who withdrew his labour could be charged with failure to obey a lawful command." As controversy and opposition to the proposal mounted, the Transport and General Workers' Union backed away from the plan and subsequently dropped it altogether.[24]

A more recent attempt at military unionization was undertaken in 1978 by the Association of Scientific, Technical, and Managerial Staffs (ASTMS). ASTMS is a relatively new, largely white-collar union composed of middle-level technicians and managers. In a press announcement of April 1978, ASTMS General Secretary Clyde Jenkins announced the union's desire to organize the military and claimed that a number of junior officers had already joined the association. In keeping with the character of its civilian membership, ASTMS expressed primary interest in organizing officers and middle-level technicians. ASTMS said the principal focus of its military union work would be improving pay and compensation, but the union also expressed opposition to the repressive and undemocratic nature of military discipline.[25]

As with the Transport and General Workers' Union, though, ASTMS has been blocked in its plan to organize the military. The controversy and criticisms have been intense, and the association has thus taken no steps to realize its plan. Individual sergeants and officers continue to work with ASTMS quietly and informally, but an official organizing drive has been postponed. The creation of an actual soldiers' union in the British army thus remains for the future.

While these halting efforts were emanating from civilian labor, an impassioned plea for unionization emerged from within the ranks, articulated in the remarkable pamphlet, *The Soldiers' Charter*. Written in the early 1970s by soldiers and civilians in response to the Transport and General Workers' Union proposal, the charter argued strongly for military unionism:

John Cousins declared that "unionization of the service would make the possibility of a military coup d'etat more remote." And he was right . . . the only guarantee for the labour movement against the sort of "blind obedience" of soldiers which leads to coups and dictatorships is a powerful trade union movement in the army. With soldiers' committees and the right to organize, the army ranks will be in a position to think for themselves. They could refuse to be used against our movement in, for example, a general strike . . . in this context, the question of trade union rights for soldiers can be seen as more than simply a matter of Labour's duty to a long-neglected section of the working class. It is also a matter of elementary self-interest in securing the future of our movement.[26]

Although developed independently in Britain, *The Soldiers' Charter* was remarkably similar to soldier declarations in other countries, such as the "Appeal of the 100" in France or the program of the American Serviceman's Union. The charter demanded "the absolute right for all servicemen to form soldier committees and to join a soldiers' union," as well as more liberal leave policies, and a sweeping reform of the military justice system. The charter also called for a revision of haircut regulations, abolition of the mess system, a guarantee of privacy, and the abolition of that peculiar British custom, the "batman" or servant.

The charter movement may have had a very bold and articulate program, but it lacked any mass following. Only a few copies of the charter were circulated, and it is doubtful that even a tiny proportion of the army's volunteers ever heard of it, much less read it. In part this was due to command repression. The charter was labeled "subversive literature" the moment it appeared and notices were posted that copies were to be turned over to the command. But such repression is normal. Commanders have attempted to quash soldier newspapers and pamphlets in every army. What is significant in the British army is that it worked.

Australia: The Dog that Didn't Bark?

It is easy to understand why the all-volunteer Japanese, Canadian, and post-Suez British armies have seen no organized resistance. But the apparent absence of a GI movement in Australia seems less explainable and puts considerable strain on our thesis that the youth of highly capitalized societies no longer blindly accept military discipline. The Australian case becomes all the more puzzling when we note that:

- Australia is certainly above the GNP/Capita threshold (see Chapter 1, table 1.1);

- Australian troops fought in Vietnam alongside U.S. servicemen for more than ten years (from July 1962 to December 1972);

- Conscription ("National Service") was reintroduced by the Conservative government in 1965 to supply troops for the Vietnam intervention; and

- A strong draft-resistance and antiwar movement developed in civilian society in the late 1960s, and in 1972 this movement played an important role in ending twenty-three years of conservative government.

Meanwhile some 500 Australian soldiers died in Vietnam, apparently without a murmur of protest from the ranks.

At first sight it seems as if our hypotheses of antiauthoritarian tendencies among the soldiers of highly capitalized countries cannot be applied to this island-continent.* Do Australian soldiers differ completely from those of the United States, or those of economically similar European countries? Does this case invalidate our general theory?

We discussed this enigma with many Australians, including some leading activists of the anti-Vietnam War movement. All seemed surprised to learn that GI resistance, let alone organized GI movements, existed anywhere. None of the left-wingers had been in the army themselves and they had never considered possible contacts with soldiers. They doubted that any troops would have questioned the war effort.

After a detailed study of disparate sources, however, we learned that many soldiers did indeed question the war. Although there was no organized GI movement in Australia, there were various forms of resistance, growing in strength towards the end of the Vietnam war. From a warrant officer, for example, we learned that as the Australian Labor Party leader Whitlam announced his victory over the pro-war Conservative government in December 1972, numerous National Servicemen (draftees) watching the returns on television spontaneously yelled: "That's it!" and walked out of their barracks. In a number of different army camps the conscripts simply went home. As the warrant officer noted: "There was nothing the army or government could do about it." The new prime minister, Whitlam was forced to "follow the movement"; he discharged all draftees and, as promised, abolished conscription.[27]

A 1972 survey of National Servicemen's attitudes found that of 34,065 soldiers who had completed their service between 1965 and 1969 only 384 (1.1 percent!) were willing, despite considerable inducements, to transfer to the regular army. Among a control group that was questioned, 17 percent said they "hated" the military, and another 26.5 percent said they "didn't like" the military.[28]

Why were these feelings so unknown to the left, to Australian antimilitarists? The Australian peace movement seemed unable to conceive of soldier resistance. Although initially this was also the case in the United States, by the late 1960s U.S. GI resisters had established many links with the civilian antiwar movement. Antiwar GIs (including one of the authors)

---

* At least one GI paper, *Sydney FTA*, was published in Australia, but it was edited by U.S. civilians and distributed among U.S. servicemen on R & R in Sydney. The New South Wales branch of the Builders Laborers Federation gave union "tickets" to U.S. deserters, to enable them to remain and work in Australia, but no such aid was given to Australian soldiers.

marched in the front ranks of peace demonstrations from San Francisco to New York. Why did dissidents in the Australian ranks remain so isolated from their potential civilian allies? Why did the Australian draftees of the Vietnam era not become, as they often did in the United States, a bridge between the military resistance and antiwar civilians?

We believe that this development was blocked by a simple question of inadequate numbers:

Table 5.1
Comparative Population to Soldier Ratios
Vietnam Era: 1964-1973

	Australia	USA
Maximum troop strength	85,000	3,500,000
Population	14 million	220 million
Civilians per soldier	165	63
Max. draftee strength	8,000	700,000
Civilians per draftee	1,750	314
Maximum draftee per soldier ratio	9%	20%

At its peak strength during the Vietnam years, the U.S. military had 1 soldier to 63 civilians; the Australian, 1 to 165, nearly three times less. When we consider only draftee soldiers, the difference becomes even greater: The U.S. military had about 314 civilians per conscript, the Australian 1,750, almost six times less. Even at the height of the Vietnam War, the Australian military remained far more isolated from society as a whole than did the U.S. Furthermore, within the military, the draftees made up less than 10 percent of the Australian forces, only half as much as in the United States. Both the U.S. and the Australian armies contained an explosive mixture of reluctant draftees and economically underprivileged volunteers, but the ratio was quite different, with a considerably greater proportion of draftees in the United States than in Australia.

Another factor that played a role in the low level of Australian GI resistance was the pervasiveness and ease of draft avoidance and the resulting lack of draft-induced volunteering. This is brought out by a study of Australian draft statistics:

Table 5.2
National Service in Australia

Total Registered: 1965-1972[29]	804,286	100%
Actually Called Up:	63,790	8%

We see that although antiwar Australians complained loudly about the draft, in fact during eight years of conscription, only 63,790, less than 8 percent of those registered, were actually called up. These figures show that in practice it was far easier for Australians to avoid the draft than it was for Americans; draft-induced volunteering played no important role in Australia, and many such potential resisters remained outside the army.

In the latter stages of the Vietnam War, when the civilian peace movement reached its peak, the draft calls became even smaller. Australian draft resisters went into hiding and, in a few cases, to jail, but they did not go into the military. After 1973 any chance for an alliance between left-wing activists and soldiers evaporated when the Labor government abandoned the draft and switched to a smaller all-volunteer army.

Nonetheless, the behavior of Australian volunteers does seem to conform to that of rank-and-filers in other "post-T" volunteer armies: In 1974 and again in the 1980s Aussie soldiers attempted to unionize their army. In 1974 this effort was actively opposed by Robert Hawke, then head of the ACTU (Australian Council of Trade Unions) and later prime minister of the (conservative) Labor government. Hawke and his colleagues reportedly saw no role for a soldiers' union inside the labor movement. In the 1980s an independent "Armed Forces Federation" was formed, which in 1986 claimed 10,000 members (out of a total armed forces of 75,000). However, many AFF activists have left the Australian forces, which, as the Canadian military, are having trouble retaining "quality" troops. It is still uncertain how the Armed Forces Federation will fare, but it is clear that the Australian soldier of today is far closer in behavior and attitudes to his contemporary in the United States or Europe than to his ancestor at Gallipoli.

Conclusion

The concern that a volunteer army might spell the end of the soldiers' movement is in part well founded. Rank-and-file newspapers, independent petition drives, soldier committees, these and other phenomena so evident in other highly capitalized nations hardly exist in the volunteer armies. Even the proposals for unionization that have emerged in Britain and the United States have come from civilian labor unions outside the ranks.

The lack of an organized soldiers' movement does not mean that resistance is entirely absent, however. The very social isolation of the volunteer army, which helps to prevent internal dissent, is in itself a reflection of widespread antipathy toward the military. Most young people in highly capitalized countries shun the armed forces and want nothing to do with military service. Those who have viable social and employment options on the outside simply do not enlist. This avoidance of the military takes place despite the fact that entry-level wages in the volunteer army are often higher than for civilians in the same age group and despite the massive huckstering and public-relations efforts of military recruiters.

This indifference to volunteer recruitment can perhaps be considered a form of antimilitarism. It is highly class-specific, however. The situation is somewhat analogous to that which exists within the conscript army of West Germany. In the Federal Republic many middle-class youth avoid the military through conscientious objector procedures. Tens of thousands of young people annually elude service through an ethics paper chase, while working-class youth are consigned to the draft. In Britain and the United States, the middle classes exempt themselves altogether by simply turning their back on recruitment lures.

The class character of the volunteer army helps explain the different nature of soldier resistance in these forces. As we observed in Chapter 2, middle-class soldiers tend toward organized "dissent," while more economically disadvantaged recruits are prone to "disobedience." The middle-class, college-educated soldiers who publish newspapers and form committees no longer serve in the volunteer armies. The younger, less-educated and less-affluent recruits who do serve are more likely to go AWOL than to form a soldier committee. They vote with their feet or their fists, not with a newspaper or petition.

The soldiers' movement may be absent in the volunteer armies, but the general phenomenon of resistance to the military remains. Increased rates of "wastage" in the British army, record discharge and attrition levels in the U.S. military and the "manning crisis" of the Canadian and Australian armed forces all suggest that resistance to the military continues. The changing social values and behavior of youth in highly capitalized society have had an impact even on the volunteer army.

6

The Debate on Military Unions

When the American Federation of Government Employees announced its intention to unionize soldiers in 1975, the reaction was one of universal condemnation. From all sides of the political spectrum came howls of opposition. Right, center, left, everyone was opposed. Strom Thurmond and his military colleagues shrieked in horror, while Pentagon managers shuddered in disbelief. Liberals and social democrats spoke out against "politicizing" the army. Even pacifists and leftists rejected unions as "helping the military."

Why does military unionism arouse such condemnation? What are the arguments used against unionization and what do they reveal about political attitudes toward the role of soldiers in society?

Military Absolutism

We begin with the most vocal criticism of soldier organizing, that of the military establishment. According to the U.S. Defense Department, the collective bargaining process cannot be applied to the military because command authority would be eroded, which in turn could lead to a decline in national defense capability. Strom Thurmond, Senator John Stennis, and other longtime patriarchs of the U.S. Senate Armed Services Committee would agree. Unionization is wholly incompatible with the military chain of command, would undermine the authority and position of the commander, and might make it impossible for the military to carry out its mission. Nearly every military and veterans' organization in the United States has expressed similar sentiments. The same attitudes prevail in Europe. French General Marcel Bigeard once labeled soldier unionism an "enterprise of demoralization."

This position holds that soldiers will not fight unless subjected to rigid and unyielding discipline. Absolute and unquestioning obedience is required at all times. Any dilution of command authority will weaken military effectiveness and lead to chaos.

Although assiduously propagated and widely held, this absolutist position is fundamentally flawed. In the first place it fails to recognize that excessive discipline can actually hinder morale and combat effectiveness. More importantly, this view misunderstands the nature of combat motivation. Numerous surveys have shown that soldiers fight not because of discipline or fear of punishment, but for other reasons: to protect their buddies, for self-preservation, to return home safely, or out of a deep-seated belief in the cause. A multivolume study of motivation during World War II, *The American Soldier*, authored by Samuel Stouffer and a team of sociologists, found that "leadership and discipline" were the least important factors in motivating men to fight.[1] Similar studies during the Korean and Vietnam Wars showed that buddy relations, self-preservation, and a sense of purpose and self-esteem are more likely to produce combat effectiveness than harsh discipline and punishment. Genuine discipline comes from within, not without.

In Vietnam it was well known to U.S. GIs and officers alike that the Vietcong were tenacious warriors, or as it was said in soldier slang, "their gooks fight better than ours." The GIs were not told, however, that their highly motivated adversaries in the NVA (North Vietnam Army) and NLF (National Liberation Front) were allowed to question and criticize their officers. Despite (or because of) such democratic practices, the communist troops fought heroically.

The authors once asked a Vietnamese infantry captain how his NVA unit could mount concentrated attacks in the face of devastating B-52 bombardments. (The B-52s' bombs were guided by seismic sensors that could detect the vibrations caused by any large walking group.) Captain Ho Nam described it this way:

The entire company, every soldier, studied a model of our objective for days. Then we dispersed and split up into 50 or 60 groups of three men each. Each group took a different route, walking the long way around--two or three days. Then, at the planned hour, close to the target, we met, attacked and immediately dispersed again. The B-52s got perhaps one or two of these three-man groups."

Captain Ho was reminded that in the U.S. army at the time most such small groups, necessarily without officer leadership, would have "got lost" under way and avoided combat. The captain responded: "But we knew what we were fighting for."

The soul of the army, as traditionalists say, is the ordinary soldier. If GIs (and the society from which they are drawn) support the mission of the military, the armed forces will perform effectively, and soldiers will battle courageously. Under these circumstances, where the cause is just, an improvement in conditions and transfer of power to the ranks through unionization could actually improve morale, increase readiness and enhance performance. Unions or any form of democratization need not hinder an army's ability to fight as long as a common sense of purpose prevails.

Civilian Control, Or "No Politics in the Military"

That right-wing military traditionalists oppose GI unions is hardly surprising. Less expected is the opposition of liberals and social democrats, people who normally accept and favor unionization in civilian life. This center-left position is based primarily on the classical view of civilian supremacy over the military, on the concept that there should be "no politics" within the army. The armed forces should be strictly subordinate to civilian control. Generals must obey their civilian masters, and inside the ranks no challenge from below can be permitted. Authority relations must remain absolutely vertical, with the whole institution theoretically subservient to civilian political leadership. Power is supposed to flow from civilian leaders on top down through the ranks, with no one, general or private, allowed to buck the chain of command.

Thus, when General John Singlaub challenged the intention of the Carter Administration to begin troop withdrawals from South Korea in 1977, the administration had him reprimanded and fired (although the force reductions were in fact halted). Likewise, German Air Force generals Frank and Krupinski were dismissed by the Social Democratic Government in 1976 when they red-baited a leading Social Democratic Party member of Parliament, Herbert Wehner.

Just as the liberal believers in civilian control reject a political role for the officers, so they also oppose a greater voice for the ordinary soldier. Soldiers cannot be trusted any more than generals. Just as they oppose free speech for General Singlaub, so they also oppose it for Sp/5 Doran, or Pfc. Johnson. The enlisted soldier should stay in the barracks and quietly follow orders.

Of course the liberals do not oppose all rights for soldiers. They point out that eighteen-year-old GIs now have the right to vote. As with all citizens in a democratic society, privates can choose between potential commanders-in-chief--for example, between a presidential candidate like Barry Goldwater, who favored war, and someone like Lyndon Johnson, who promised that American boys would stay home. But once the commander-in-chief has been elected, soldiers must obey orders, and go to

'Nam.

The problem with the civilian control argument is that the armed forces are already highly politicized. The assumption that democratically elected civilian governments exercise absolute control over an obedient and neutral military apparatus is totally unreal. The flow of power is not unidirectional. The secretary of defense may issue policy directives, but the parameters within which he can act are powerfully shaped by the Joint Chiefs of Staff, their allies, the arms industrialists, and dozens of military associations and lobby groups.

The leading general officers in the armed forces today wield enormous political influence. Since World War II, as C. Wright Mills has shown in *The Power Elite*, the military chiefs have become a central element of the political establishment. As heads of the largest institutions in society, they inevitably exert vast sway over the direction of national affairs. Through their political and public relations networks and their highly evolved system of dispensing weapons contracts according to political criteria, the Pentagon chiefs have established themselves as a formidable center of political power. Their fortunes with the top civilian leadership may ebb and flow (rising with Reagan, perhaps sliding a bit with Carter), but their institutional presence at the heart of political power in the United States remains constant.

The question is not whether the armed forces should be politicized--they already are--but whether they should be steered in elite or democratic directions. Should the military serve the narrow interests of generals and arms industrialists, or the wider interests of civil society? Unless one assumes an identity of interest between generals and privates, an illusion shared by few GIs, the emergence of soldier organizations can help to counteract the excessive power of top military officials. Through democratic organizing within the lower ranks, the power of generals to use the army against popular wishes can be lessened.

As is so often the case, the ordinary soldier often understands these issues quite clearly. Many of the soldiers with whom we have talked support unionization precisely because they feel it will depoliticize the military. They feel that one of the biggest problems with the army is its excessively political character. They point not only to the sweetheart deals in Congress and elsewhere that rob them of their benefits, but to what they interpret as the overly political nature of the Vietnam War. "If war is hell for privates, it is good for generals." They feel that the generals and politicians got into the Vietnam War to advance their careers and their own interests, with little thought for the costs of the war to soldiers and society. For these soldiers, union organization offers the possibility of ensuring a more accountable military policy.

Unionization of the army would not introduce politics into the military.

It would only begin to counterbalance the traditional right-wing military politics that already exist.

The Communists: Trust the Generals

It may come as a surprise to many Americans, conditioned to think of communists as firebrand radicals, but the major communist parties of Western Europe, particularly the French and Italian, oppose unionization of the military. The primary objection of the Eurocommunists is that unionization would upset the general officer corps and provoke a rightist counter-reaction. The parties believe that nothing should be done to provoke the generals, and since nothing is more threatening to commanders than organized soldiers, GI resistance is considered "adventurist" and must be opposed. Soldiers should be kept quiet in the barracks. The communist and liberal positions are in some ways quite similar. Both are based on the fear that organizing soldiers will disturb the generals. They also assume, or rather hope, that undisturbed generals will then stay out of politics.

The Eurocommunist fear of military intervention is quite rational, especially when one remembers the established tradition of overt military interference in politics in France, Italy, and Spain. Although French governments seldom mention their origins, the present regime, the Fifth Republic, was founded in a military coup by Charles De Gaulle in May 1958. Three years later the general himself had to face an abortive right-wing countercoup, led by four "felon" generals in Algeria. In Italy, rumors and worries of a military putsch are frequent. And every communist of Carillo's generation in Spain remembered how the Republic of the 1930s brutally succumbed to a forty-year military dictatorship. A Jimmy Carter or Helmut Schmidt would hardly expect his generals to march up and shoot him, but Marchais, Berlinguer, and Carillo could not be so sure.

The Eurocommunists have been deeply influenced by events in Chile, specifically the 1973 military overthrow of Salvador Allende, and by what they feel are the coup's lessons. During an interview at Italian Communist Party headquarters in Rome, a spokeswoman for the party told the authors that the greatest mistake of the Popular Unity government was its failure to gain support among officers and the middle class. According to the Italian Party, adventurist elements provoked the generals into breaking Chile's tradition of democracy and crushing Popular Unity.[2]

The facts show otherwise. The Allende government tried very hard to please and reassure the military chiefs. Army pay was increased forty percent, and new privileges were offered to officers. Meanwhile, leftist supporters of the government within the ranks were left to fend for themselves. The few meager efforts to support soldier organizing by the

MIR (left revolutionary movement) were deemed "ultraleftist." No aid was offered, for example, to the leftist petty officers in the Chilean Navy who on August 8, 1973, took over their ships in Valparaiso to preempt the right-wing putsch attempt by their officer superiors (see Chapter 15).

Even as the tanks were beginning to roll in Santiago on September 11, 1973, communist members of the Allende government continued to believe that the generals could be trusted. In the end, only five or six of the army's two dozen top officers remained loyal.

To expect that generals of any country will look more favorably upon a communist government (or communist participation in a left government) if the party opposes organizing in the barracks seems highly naive. No matter how "responsibly" the party tries to behave, the military chiefs will still oppose communism. Even when the armed forces are led, as in Chile, by exceptional democrats such as generals Rene Schneider and Carlos Prats, the majority of the general staff can sweep them aside and quickly establish predominance (especially, as is often the case, when actively abetted by the CIA). The class allegiance of higher-ranking officers is usually linked to the upper classes, to the major capitalists and large landowners. To attempt to win favor among these sectors while abandoning the party's natural constituency within the lower ranks seems a curious and self-defeating policy for a left-wing organization. In effect, the communist position denies the significance of class conflict within the ranks. Class analysis may apply to the factory and to society in general, but not to the army.

A 1977 book by British party theoretician Jack Woddis, *Armies and Politics*, makes this point explicitly: "A concept of 'rank and file soldiers vs. officers' could produce unwanted divisions and tensions in the army."[3] Woddis magnanimously admits that "differentiations" do exist in the military, but he insists that the conflicts between officers and soldiers are "secondary" to the larger contradiction between monopoly capital and labor. This may be true in the abstract, but it affords little comfort to the soldier struggling for justice within the barracks. The party's analysis cuts it off from its natural constituency, the enlisted majority within the ranks, and weakens its ties with working-class youth who serve as soldiers.

Underlying the political objections of the communist party, we believe, is a profound psychological discomfort with the spontaneous, often uncontrollable nature of soldier resistance. A deep gap separates the antiauthoritarian GI resister and the disciplined communist party functionary. The communist penchant for controlled and orderly activity ("working-class discipline") finds little comfort in the world of soldier organizing. The bureaucratic mindset of communist party officials simply cannot cope with the spontaneity of soldier resistance. It should be remembered that the Communist Party of France played a key role in restraining and limiting the Paris uprising of May 1968. In the same way the party has reacted negatively to the "wild" actions of the soldier committees. The fear of an uncontrollable mass seems to frighten communist leaders almost as much as it does military officers.

The Pacifists: No Army, Not A Better Army

The other left-wing objection to unionization is that of the pacifists. They fear that unionization will improve the army and make it more efficient, that contented soldiers will be better killers. Pacifists feel that organizing aimed at improving day-to-day conditions in the barracks is at best unimportant or at worst counterproductive.

This sentiment is well illustrated in the 1976 experience of the Friends' Peace Committee in Philadelphia, a longtime Quaker-supported organization active in southern New Jersey. For several years the Peace Committee had sponsored the Friends Military Counseling group at Fort Dix. As the reader will recall from Chapter 3, in December 1976 news of organizing among Fort Dix and McGuire Air Force Base troops created a front-page sensation and scared AFGE into suspending its preparations for unionization. Ironically, the newspaper stories that frightened AFGE equally repelled the pacifist overseers of the Friends' Peace Committee in Philadelphia. They were shocked to learn that the counseling office they were funding was working with GIs who wanted to unionize the military. Just as AFGE called a halt to any further efforts, so the radical pacifists reigned in their feisty project and put a stop to union advocacy. The Quaker leaders wanted no part of anything that might "make the army better."

"Efficiency" and "Effectiveness"

Not only pacifists but many radicals fear that a more efficient army will also be more effective, that it will be a better instrument of repression. The GIs themselves, for all their visceral antimilitarism, know better.

Some definitions are in order. The Random House dictionary defines efficiency as "competency in performance," the ability to carry out day-to-day operations smoothly, with a minimum expenditure of time and effort. Effectiveness, on the other hand, implies the accomplishment of a desired purpose, the achievement of an "intended or expected result." The question for the army becomes: What is the "purpose?" An efficient army is not necessarily effective for all purposes. It depends on whether the soldiers agree with the intended result. In an army where soldiers have power and can question the mission, even the most efficient organization cannot guarantee success. Whether the efficient army will be effective depends on the "purpose."

It is a well-known, though embarrassing fact, among NATO officials that the long-haired, unionized Dutch conscripts move their tanks faster and more efficiently across the countryside than do their short-haired, "disciplined" NATO colleagues. Unionization has improved efficiency. As we shall see in the next chapter, however, the effectiveness of the Dutch army varies enormously with the mission. It is nil for such tasks as strike breaking or foreign intervention. No Dutch government today would dream of sending conscripts to reconquer Indonesia (as they did in 1946-1949). Effectiveness is only fair when Dutch troops are sent as part of U.N. forces to Lebanon, where some conscripts object to the anti-Arab bias of the "peace-keeping" force. But effectiveness is very high when they are combatting Moluccan terrorists at home and rescuing Dutch hostages, a task they consider necessary and important. Unionized, efficient soldiers will be effective only when they believe in their mission.

Beware the Labor Bureaucracy

On the far left are a variety of often sectarian Marxist-Leninist groups that, while supporting the right of soldiers to organize, vehemently oppose unionization. Their opposition is particularly aimed at cooperation with such established unions as AFGE in the United States or OeTV in Germany (see Chapter 9). These left-wing groups argue that a military union of this sort would replicate business unionism within the ranks. They fear that a bureaucratic union, to prove its "respectability," would bend over backwards to assist the command in maintaining workforce discipline. A conservative AFGE or OeTV-type union would break up existing soldier groups and throw out the radicals. These suspicions are strengthened when labor bureaucrats of AFGE or OeTV openly state their preference for organizing careerists rather than low-ranking soldiers. It is feared that the union steward, far from calling strikes in the foxholes, might become an assistant to the command.

This left-wing objection to bureaucratic unionism is an important one. It is often heard from the GI activists themselves. The problem is similar for workers in civilian industries: The battle against the union bureaucracy is often as fierce as that against the boss.

It is a common and disappointing experience for workers to realize that their unions (supposedly vehicles for class struggle) often become as conservative and hierarchical as the company. Nearly all unions, regardless of the particular industry or political system, tend to become isolated from and sometimes even hostile toward their members. The worker on the shop floor and the highly paid union official are worlds apart. The fundamental problem is not merely that some labor bosses are "sell-outs" but rather that a permanent union bureaucracy inherently tends toward ossification and separation from the rank-and-file. One of the few U.S. unions that has tried to avoid these problems is the United Electrical Workers (UE), whose constitution prohibits any official from making more money than the highest paid shop floor worker. It is perhaps not entirely accidental that UE was the largest union expelled from the CIO in 1949, for "communism."

Another union that has tried to avoid the pitfalls of bureaucratization is VVDM of Holland. The conscript union's democratic decision-making process, its lack of a large permanent bureaucracy, and the constant rotation of its leadership, all described in the next chapter, make it one of the most uniquely democratic union organizations in the world. Even here, however, union officials are occasionally criticized as distant and insensitive to soldier needs. The problem seems unavoidable. The moment a soldier moves from the tank to the typewriter, he begins to lose touch with the membership; in particular, he is no longer subject to the daily trials and harassment of barracks life.

But problems tend to produce their own solutions. The bureaucratization of unions in the United States and elsewhere has led to the development of movement-style organizations, such as the Shop Stewards' Committees in Great Britain and groups like PROD* and Steelworkers Fight Back in the United States, which operate within the unions but maintain a separate identity.

Similarly, the growth of soldier unionism in Holland was accompanied by the emergence of an independent caucus, the BVD, the League for Conscripts. This caucus worked actively within the mass union, VVDM, but also maintained a separate organization. BVD supporters were good union members but they were also strong advocates of greater mobilization and radicalism. In 1979, for example, when Dutch troops were sent as part of the U.N. force to Lebanon, VVDM took no position beyond defending the individual soldiers who did not want to go. BVD, on the other hand, strongly opposed the entire operation as biased against the interests of Palestinians.

The history of labor shows that the major gains of the working class have come from mass movements. The basic function of the union is to guarantee gains won through prior struggle. The movement at the base is more important than the trade union bureaucracy. The same applies to the military. Resistance in the barracks is a precondition for authentic soldier unionism. Indeed it is precisely the prior existence of such resistance that makes military unionization so potentially important. Without constant

---

* Professional Road Drivers, a dissident group within the 2-million-member Teamsters Union.

mobilization from below, a union will weaken, lose its original meaning, and ossify. The best answer is an approach that is both "in and out"-- working from within to protect the union and preserve earlier victories, while pressing against the hierarchy for greater democracy and activism. Unions need both skeleton and muscle: a structure to guarantee previous gains and the constant flexing of grass-roots activism. Soldiers need both a union and a movement: an institution which can protect the rights they have won and a movement to constantly extend those rights.

Military Unionism and Democracy

It is obvious that the authors strongly support unionization. We do so because union organizing would make the military more democratic and would reduce the prospects of using the army against popular wishes.

At a minimum, military unionism would extend the civil liberties of enlisted people. Any union operating in the military would be forced to fight for free speech and basic organizational rights. As the German OeTV has demonstrated, even a conservative union must first assert the right to distribute literature, solicit members, and organize on base. In effect, a union must fight for the rights that enlisted people have sought for years. In defending its members and organizers, a union must argue for greater democratic freedoms. It is interesting to note that AFGE's 1976 investigation into the legalities of military unionism focused on the major court cases of the GI movement, including *Spock v. David*, 421 U.S. 908, 1975; *Dash v. Commanding General*, 401 U.S. 981, 1971; *Stolte v. Laird*, 353 F. Supp. 1392, 1972; and *Cortright v. Resor*, 325 F. Supp. 797, 1971. The right to organize would be a central battleground in any attempt to unionize the military.

Beyond the extension of civil liberties, military unionism would forge closer links between labor and the armed forces. Especially in volunteer forces such as those of Great Britain and the United States, unionization could mitigate the inherent tendency for the military to become isolated from society, to become a state within a state. The importance of closer ties between soldiers and workers is obvious from even a cursory glance at the history of labor. In U.S. history the battles of Homestead and Ludlow are but two of the more blatant examples of antilabor action by the military. While such bloody assaults are infrequent today, postal workers and truckers still face military intervention. In France and Spain the army has been used frequently to break strikes. Any development that weakens the military's ability to break strikes, as unionization would certainly do, strengthens the hand of the working class.

Most importantly, military unionism would alter the political orientation of the armed forces and facilitate enlisted opposition to unpopular policies. Some object, as noted above, that military unions might hinder enlisted resistance, but it would be a mistake to exaggerate the possibilities of such bureaucratic unionism. If soldiers no longer fear their officers, why should they listen to union bosses? In any case, a union trying to discipline the troops would not get very far in today's military. Company unionism simply will not work. Soldiers will not stick their necks out for a union that refuses to fight for their rights.

A far more likely result of unionization is an increase in GI resistance. The existence of an organizational forum where soldier grievances could be aired independently would be of enormous value. It would separate soldiers from the chain of command, at least for brief periods, and would allow for autonomous action. Horizontal relations would grow at the expense of vertical authority. The possibilities for collective action against the command would greatly increase. Particularly during times of crisis, such as a potential Vietnam-type intervention or a domestic strike-breaking operation, the prior existence of organized locals could greatly facilitate the growth of enlisted opposition. As one retired military officer told us, "If we had had a soldiers union earlier, maybe we might have avoided the tragedy of Vietnam."

Military unionism would have a profoundly democratic influence on the functioning of the armed forces. The struggle to alter the terms of service, even if originally concerned with "peripheral" issues such as pay and benefits, fundamentally alters the nature of military authority. When the soldier has won the ability to determine the conditions of service, when he has fought for and gained the right to say, "Sir, I object," the absolutist underpinnings of military authority begin to crumble. The opinions and attitudes of the low ranking soldier can no longer be ignored. The functioning of the military increasingly depends on his willing support.

On the previous occasions in history when armies have been used against the interests of the people, soldiers were powerless and without influence. Today this is changing. The struggle for improved conditions is altering power relations within the ranks and raising the ordinary soldier to a new status and influence. Democratic society can only benefit as a result.

The "Hair Force" of Holland

A short distance from the gleaming shopping center and central rail station in Utrecht is the tiny, nineteenth century army base, Hojel Kazerne. This ancient brick structure is a relic from the past, complete with high ceilings from the age of cavalry. But Hojel Kazerne also has a modern look. The soldier greeting us at the gate has hair down to his shoulders. As we enter, he escorts us down a long hallway to the offices of the Vereniging Van Dienstplichtige Militairen (VVDM), the Dutch Conscripts' Union.

Inside are five or six soldiers "on duty," garbed in bluejeans and sweatshirts, performing their military duty as officials of the union. The long-haired youths are busily pecking away behind typewriters, talking on the phone and peering over documents and reports. The walls are lavishly postered with protest banners. The corners of the office are piled high with stacks of newspapers and files. Half-filled coffee cups lie about everywhere, and the air is heavily laden with cigarette smoke. The ambiance is decidedly unmilitary and disheveled, more like a movement office than an army barracks.

From these modest quarters has emerged one of the most remarkable soldier organizations in the world. Since its founding in 1966, the VVDM has created a uniquely activist form of soldier unionism and compiled an extraordinary record of achievement. Dutch soldiers have dramatically transformed the nature of the army, civilizing military service and changing traditional authority relations. Nowhere else have the radical implications of military unionism been so starkly outlined.[1]

The Roots

Small and relatively peaceful, the Netherlands has traditionally had little significance in military affairs. It seems an almost forgotten denizen of NATO. Yet Holland has a substantial armed forces for its size (with a relatively high soldier-to-population ratio) and is the homebase for over 100 U.S.-operated nuclear weapons, as well as the designated recipient of a new, highly controversial force of 48 ground-launched cruise missiles, later negotiated away under the INF Treaty. The Dutch population of 14 million supports an armed forces of approximately 100,000, including 46,000 conscripts, most of whom serve twelve months.

Although the induction system is supposed to be universal, less than 40 percent of the draft-age population actually serves. Nonetheless, the Dutch army is very much a "mass army," and it is subjected to the same social and cultural forces that affect civilian society.

Holland is one of the world's most affluent, highly industrialized nations. As such it has been a crucible of the political and cultural transformations associated with highly capitalized society. The youth rebellion and social upheavals of the 1960s surfaced early in Holland and created lasting effects.

The most dramatic and colorful expression of this social upheaval was the Provo movement. Combining utopianism and derision, anarchism and political theater, the Provos first emerged in Amsterdam in the 1960s. Although a strictly local phenomenon, the Provos had an influence far beyond Amsterdam. Described by one observer as political "dadaists," the Provos expressed a total refutation of society.[2] Through outrageous behavior the Provos provoked repression from police forces unable to react in a liberal manner to their unconventional ways. By poking fun at traditional values, the Provos exposed the authoritarian underpinnings of liberal society. Challenging what they called "monolithic mass society," they urged a more playful, nonhierarchical order free of monotony and routine. Related to the Provos were the freewheeling Kabouters (literally, the Gnomes), who gained national attention in the late 1960s by winning several city council seats in Amsterdam on a radical environmentalist program.

These antiauthoritarian movements had an enormous impact on other young people, and they inevitably seeped into the armed forces. Everywhere in Dutch society students and young workers were showing new assertiveness. Traditional academic associations, youth groups, the established political parties, the Catholic Church, all experienced movements toward greater democracy and progressivism.

At the same time new theories of "human relations" began to take hold among government and corporate administrators. As hierarchy and rigid authority were being challenged from below, new concepts of cooperative management were being developed at the top. The trend toward greater tolerance among managers even took root within the military. The old model of discipline and punishment began to give way to a more rationalist approach based on cooperation and responsible leadership.

In such a setting it was almost inevitable that the armed forces would face the same kind of democratic leavening sweeping the rest of Dutch society. The anachronisms of military life became increasingly untenable to conscripts intent on greater creativity and self-expression. With democratic movements appearing in every realm of national life, the armed forces could not long remain insulated. Also, as we have noted in Chapter 4, the Dutch military had already long accepted unions (so-called interest organizations) for officers and career NCOs. Thus, when the attempt was made to form a union of conscripts, there was little of the shock and outrage that later greeted such developments in other countries.

Innocuous Beginnings

VVDM was founded at Elias Beeckman barracks in Ede in summer 1966 in an unassuming, almost whimsical manner. As the first chair, Huub Oosterbeek, later recalled:

Three of us were walking from the station to the barracks Sunday evening, July 20. There was social unrest in the country—strikes and Provos. Then someone suddenly said, "Why not have a trade union for soldiers? Everyone else has one." The next day our company commander asked what we wanted to talk about . . . somebody called out, "about the union." I was shoved up front and that was the first time anyone talked seriously about it.[3]

The officers at Ede actually helped the union. A number of progressive commanders happened to be stationed there, and they thought that a union could help channel conscript grievances into controllable outlets. They also hoped that a conscripts' union could be a partner in their own efforts to improve and modernize the military. When conscripts thus broached the idea, they faced not the repression that greeted their French counterparts eight years later but shrewd receptivity.

From the outset the Dutch conscripts' union had a dual character: an authentic democratic impulse from below and a management initiative from above. Much of the early history of VVDM revolves around the interaction of these two tendencies.

On August 4, 1966, VVDM formally came into being with Oosterbeek chairing the first meeting. Within days the battalion commander gave permission to organize, and within a few weeks 250 soldiers at Ede were unionized. In early September a VVDM pamphlet found its way into the hands of a major newspaper, and the story of a fledgling conscripts' union burst onto national headlines. As Oosterbeek described it, "the whole press was on the line."[4] The media generally were quite sympathetic to VVDM (they seemed allured by its Provo-like unconventionality), and they maintained a friendly relationship with the union for several years. The widespread press coverage was a valuable windfall, accelerating the union's growth and attracting a flood of membership requests from barracks throughout the country. Even the minister of defense gave his support, declaring that the union seemed like a good idea and should be allowed to continue.

As VVDM grew in the early years, it was aided by a range of privileges and rights granted by the Ministry of Defense. The union was given free office space at Hojel Kazerne. It was given virtually free reign to recruit members throughout the military. In 1968 the union was given the important benefit of dues checkoff, so that union dues were automatically deducted from military paychecks and paid directly from the ministry to the union. This was an important step that placed the union on firm financial footing. Another significant development for the union came in 1968 when the ministry exempted the elected members of the board from military duty and allowed them to fulfill their service obligation by working full-time for the union.

Many of the rights that civilian trade unions struggle for years to obtain were simply handed to VVDM on a silver platter. The command's assistance was such that Oosterbeeck later remarked: "We almost got more support from the army leadership than from the conscripts themselves."[5]

Not only did the government recognize and support VVDM, it also began to implement some of the reforms demanded by the union. Anachronisms such as brass polishing and military trains were abolished. The number of personal inspections was reduced, and soldiers were allowed to wear civilian clothes off-duty. Pay was also increased, the first in a series of wage boosts that would soon make Dutch conscripts the highest paid in Europe.

One of the most important reforms of these early years was the creation of a direct link between the union and the Ministry of Defense. Beginning in 1968 the union entered into an arrangement known as "organized consultation." Under this system, problems on the military base could be brought directly to the ministry in Den Haag without going through the chain of command. This was, and still is, a significant change in the nature of military authority and gave conscripts an independent channel for raising grievances and concerns. They could go around their local commanders directly to the Ministry of Defense.

As the union gained legitimacy and won improvements in conscript life, membership grew rapidly. By early 1968, just a year and a half after its founding, VVDM had nearly 5,000 members (about 10 percent of all conscripts). Although the union remained tame and nonconfrontational during these first two years, it had already made a major difference in conscript life. The young VVDM played a crucial role in reducing the arbitrariness of military life and laid the groundwork for the emergence of a militant soldiers' movement.

The Awakening

As VVDM developed, so did soldier resistance. Independent activism and protest movements unconnected to the union began to emerge within the ranks. The leaders of the union soon found themselves in a difficult quandary. On the one side military commanders pressed them to contain radical stirrings within the ranks. On the other side union members demanded greater militance and activism. For a time the union's leaders tried to straddle the fence, but before long the pressures from below pushed VVDM to the left and transformed it into an activist, fighting union.

By 1969 independent demonstrations and protests began to occur, usually focused on local conditions and grievances. The central board of VVDM was seldom involved in these protests, some of which took on a decidedly radical, antimilitary tone. One such action was a demonstration by thirty-two soldiers in the town of Middelburg. The conscripts were protesting the custom of military parades. Their reason: They did not want to be involved in anything that made the army look good.

At about the same time an influential article appeared in the union newspaper *Twintig* (Twenty, named for the age at which most conscripts served). A soldier named Van Schuur wrote a piece entitled "The VVDM has to fly," arguing for militant tactics and greater confrontation with the brass. The VVDM needs wings, argued Van Schuur, particularly a left wing.

In keeping with the new spirit of militance percolating through VVDM at the time, a letter was sent to the Defense Ministry, signed by 143 soldiers of the 103d Medical Battalion in Ermelo. The letter was inspired by the U.S. war in Vietnam. The soldiers stated that they could not guarantee their loyalty if issued orders with which they disagreed. This was too much for even the enlightened Dutch officers. They could not tolerate soldiers extending their newly-won democratic rights to a questioning of orders. The military intelligence services launched an investigation, but the case was later dropped to avoid adverse publicity.

As activist pressures grew, the number of union locals increased, and the internal workings of VVDM became more democratic. In the first two years the main power of VVDM had been with the central board, a group of seven soldiers elected by their fellow union members to serve as national officers. As the number of locals and the membership grew, however, power began to shift more toward the grass roots. The main decision-making body became the General Assembly, a kind of soldiers' town meeting open to all union members, although attended mostly by leaders of the locals. Held twice a year, the assembly took increasing control over union policy and began to chart a more left-wing course.

Another sign of the increasing vigor of the grass-roots movement was the emergence of GI newspapers. A growing number of the union locals began to publish their own papers, publications that in style and content closely resembled the underground newspapers then emerging within the U.S. military. The development of these local newspapers, written and published independently of the national union, marked an important turning point for the soldiers' movement. As in other highly capitalized nations, the emergence of a lively soldier press symbolized new relationships of knowledge within the ranks and marked a new level of soldier organization.

Although Holland is a small and highly cosmopolitan nation, the Dutch soldiers' movement initially had almost no contact with the American GIs moving through the country. Amsterdam was a key station on the Underground Railroad of deserters leaving the U.S. Army in Germany. (See Max Watts, *U.S. Army Europe: Von der Desertion zum Widerstand in der Kaserne, oder wie die U-Bahn zur RITA fuhr.*) In the 1966-1969 period, U.S. soldiers knew nothing of the burgeoning Dutch conscripts' union. Even those joining the American Servicemen's Union were unaware that a legal soldiers' union had been formed and was flourishing in the army of their NATO ally, Holland. Many of the Dutch soldiers building the VVDM were strongly opposed to the Vietnam War, but they did not yet consider that their union had any role to play in the growing American resistance. For the Dutch GIs, beginning to transform their army through unionization, desertion was a marginal phenomenon. For most young Americans, feeling utterly powerless inside the "green machine," even the concept of military unionism seemed far distant.

After 1969 this separation began to break down. In the U.S. army desertion became a relatively minor aspect of the movement. Even though the absolute number of AWOLs/desertions remained high and continued to grow, on-base organizing and the formation of soldier committees spread rapidly. The Dutch VVDM, meanwhile, evolved from a relatively tame company union into an activist organization questioning all aspects of military life. Soon the paths of the two movements would cross.

The BVD: The Union's Gadfly

During this time, as the Dutch soldiers' movement was taking off, an important new force arrived on the scene, a small but potent organization known as Bond Voor Dienstplichtigen (BVD), the League for Conscripts.

BVD played a key role as a kind of union within a union, a pressure group of activists providing support for the larger union but constantly pressing from the grass roots for more action. The growth and achievement of VVDM owed much to the support and prodding of BVD.

The BVD first appeared in 1967 as a group of conscientious objectors. It grew out of the climate of protest associated with the Provos and reflected the growing antimilitarist leanings of Dutch youth. The early members were mostly conscientious objectors doing alternative service in hospitals and the like. At first the goal of BVD was to get rid of the army. But as time went on and political understanding changed, the goal became to change the character of the army, to make it more democratic by organizing from within. Their message changed from "Don't serve" to "Join up and work for the union." With this approach BVD emerged as a strong and important presence within VVDM and the soldiers' movement. Over half the members of BVD were civilians, recent vets, and women activists who assisted the active-duty members and provided key support to their efforts. In May 1970 the group began publishing its own monthly newspaper, *De Soldat-enkrant*, described as "the voice of resistance in the army."

For nearly fifteen years BVD served as the conscience of VVDM, constantly calling for mass action at the barracks level to advance union demands. Their slogan was "out of the negotiating room and into the barracks." They also provided a sharp political focus for the soldiers' movement, from challenging the Dutch role in NATO to resisting deployment of nuclear cruise missiles. During its fifteen-year history, BVD served as a model for how to build and support the soldiers' movement.

The Salute

As Dutch soldiers gained increasing rights and became more active, they began to take exception to certain military customs and traditions that they considered obsolete in a democratic army. The conscripts were no longer willing to play the role of mere pawns, and they objected to previously accepted rituals that reinforced rank privilege. Saluting in particular came to be seen as a demeaning vestige of the old system, and an important movement developed within the ranks to do away with it.

The pioneer in the saluting campaign was Henk Van der Horst, who was a VVDM activist in the base at Oirschot. In 1970 Van der Horst shocked his colleagues and local military commanders by declaring that henceforth he would no longer salute anyone. Van der Horst's public announcement excited many of his fellow conscripts, but it outraged his commanding officers. They responded swiftly and harshly (by normally tolerant Dutch standards) and sentenced him to eight months' imprisonment, equal to his remaining time of service.

Far from quieting the situation, the army's stiff sentence against Van der Horst proved counterproductive and sparked widespread indignation within the ranks. Many soldiers agreed with Van der Horst that saluting was ridiculous and anachronistic, and they were concerned about the harsh sentence meted out to their fellow unionist. VVDM responded to these concerns and came to the aid of Van der Horst by organizing a defense campaign.

Soon the VVDM leadership went beyond merely defending Van der Horst. The union decided to take up his cause and launched a campaign to put an end to mandatory saluting. Their choice of tactics was both unusual and inventive, and was strongly influenced by the example of the free-wheeling Provos and Kabouters: they decided to use the weapon of ridicule. The union called for a "national saluting day," urging soldiers on that day to salute anyone and everyone, regardless of rank, civilians included. The first saluting day was held on July 1, 1970, and proved to be a rollicking success. Once again the press helped the conscripts by providing wide-spread news coverage. Soldiers saluted everyone--garbagemen, other conscripts, policemen--thoroughly lampooning the saluting regulations.

The union kept up the fight for two more years, demanding that saluting regulations be changed. In summer 1971 a second national saluting day was held, with soldiers sending postcards to the government objecting to mandatory saluting. Several thousand cards were actually sent to the Ministry of Defense under the heading "Greetings from the barracks." In Havelte there was a demonstration of around 600 soldiers to protest saluting and other military restrictions. In 1972 there was a third national saluting day. This time soldiers were urged to act "normally," that is, to refuse to salute. Many soldiers participated in the action, and a number of demonstrations were held, including an action at one base where 150 soldiers clapped, waved, and cheered as their officers came through the gates after lunch.

In 1973, after three years of struggle, the saluting campaign finally achieved victory. Elections that year produced a new, Social Democratic government coalition in Holland. The new officials, especially Defense Minister Henk Vredeling, brought with them a more progressive and democratic view of the military. Vredeling was much more sympathetic to the views of the conscripts than were his predecessors. In fact, he was once quoted as saying, "My whole life I have been against discipline . . . I am in fact absolutely allergic to uniforms."[6] Under Vredeling's leadership the Ministry of Defense finally responded to the union's demands. New regulations were issued making saluting optional. According to the new rules, the salute would no longer be automatic but would have to be earned by officers through respect and enlightened leadership.

Hair Comes Down

Perhaps the most dramatic campaign in VVDM's history, a struggle that gained the union recognition throughout the world, was the fight for free hair-length. As we have already seen with soldiers in the U.S. army, the issue of hair length can become an important symbol in the GI's struggle for greater freedom and independence of mind. So it was for the Dutch soldiers in 1971, as a major campaign developed in opposition to mandatory haircuts.

As in the case of the saluting campaign, the impetus for the haircut struggle came from an individual act of resistance. In May 1971 conscript Rinus Wehrmann announced on his first day of service that he would refuse to get a haircut. Once again the commanders overreacted and court-martialed Wehrmann, sentencing him to two years' imprisonment. This draconian sentence against Wehrmann caused shock and outrage among conscripts (and among many civilians as well) and sparked a major campaign of protest. Petition campaigns and demonstrations occurred throughout the country. In Amersfoort, 300 soldiers held a demonstration on base, one of the first such actions held on a military installation. A civilian demonstration was held at Den Haag.

The Wehrmann case and the question of hair length quickly became major controversies. In the face of mounting protests, both in the army and in civilian society, the government beat a hasty retreat. In July the government announced that haircuts would henceforth be optional, and Wehrmann was released from detention. The union had won a sudden but complete victory. The "hippie army" (or, as the Dutch prefer to call it, the "hair force") was born.

Repression Begins

In the wake of the haircut victory the VVDM leadership faced competing pressures. On the one hand membership was growing rapidly and soldiers in the barracks were pressing for additional actions and struggle. On the other hand the Ministry of Defense was growing impatient at the soldiers' continued demands and urged the union to restrain its members. The ministry itself was under pressure from local commanders and officers who were uncomfortable with the growing challenges the conscripts' movement posed to their traditional authority. Initially VVDM called for a cooling-off period, but this was quickly shattered by increased government repression and censorship of local soldier newspapers. In one incident the government hauled in the conscript editors of a paper entitled *Left Face* (the same title used by soldier activists in the United States, Germany, and elsewhere) and accused them of "demoralizing the army." The most famous case of repression, though, came in fall 1971 when two editors of the paper *Alarm* (one of them a member of BVD) were sentenced to several months' detention. These arrests touched off another round of protests and demonstrations, including a demonstration in Amersfoort that drew nearly 600 conscripts.

As the battle over censorship of soldier papers mounted, the Dutch conscripts once again employed the tactics of comic derision and ridicule. When local commanders attempted to censor the newspaper *Stomp*, the soldiers claimed that the paper had more than 150 editors (the entire membership of the union local). When military police came to question the editorial staff, a large group of soldiers appeared, and the security forces needed a fleet of trucks to haul them away. In the face of such tactics the dour bureaucrats of the military appeared silly and helpless.

After several more years of confrontation that included considerable pressure from progressive members of parliament, the government finally agreed to a compromise. The most important change was that local commanders could no longer hand out punishments in matters concerning freedom of expression. This did not end all restrictions on the soldier press, but it did mark another victory for VVDM and the soldiers' movement.

Whenever soldiers were repressed or the government threatened to withdraw newly won rights, BVD and other groups formed action committees to defend soldier rights. One such effort in 1972 was known as the "hairy walnut" ("hard as a walnut but not as bald"). In response to rumors that hair would be restricted again, soldiers solemnly pledged never to have a haircut. Civilians also came to their aid. In one public statement entitled "This is too much," 350 prominent citizens signed an appeal to the government to ease its pressures. Among the signers were eight future government ministers. With such wide support, and especially with its mass following in the barracks, VVDM easily withstood these early trials and firmly established itself as a force to be reckoned with in Dutch military affairs.

1971 was the peak year for VVDM's membership. Victory in the haircut struggle, the ongoing saluting campaign, the union's highly visible protests and demonstrations, all contributed to a flood of membership and support. By the end of the year union membership totaled an incredible 30,000, 70 percent of all conscripts. A public opinion poll taken that same year revealed that 86 percent of all soldiers thought VVDM was doing a good job at representing their interests. Although government repression against the union continued to flare (in one incident the ministry briefly detained all seven members of the VVDM central board), the union enjoyed a wide following in the army and in civilian society.

The Campaign for Compensation

While the most visible campaigns of VVDM focused on saluting and other issues of personal freedom, the union also maintained from the outset traditional trade union demands for improved pay and compensation. It was the latter issue, the call for greater compensation, that came to dominate the union's agenda throughout the 1970s, and that remains an active concern to this day. The central controversy of this struggle has been the conscripts' demand to be compensated for overtime duty. The soldiers have insisted that all extra duty, including weekend assignment and field maneuvers, be compensated with an equal amount of free time. The soldiers emphasize that their primary demand is free time, not extra pay. They want to reduce the amount of time they are on duty and thereby limit military control over their lives.

The struggle over compensation raises fundamental questions about the process of "normalization" (as noted in Chapter 4). The conscripts feel that differences between civilians and soldiers should be reduced. They do not want commanders to have control over their free time and personal lives. They want to be treated more like civil servants, with the terms of service determined in negotiation and bargaining rather than by command fiat. Military officers understandably resist this demand and have tried to cling to their power and privileges. When they are forced to concede on the compensation issue, for example, commanders prefer to give extra money rather than time off. The struggle over these differing concepts of military duty has been an important theme in the Dutch soldiers' movement.

Although demands for compensation have been part of the union's program since its inception, the first major actions on the issue did not come until 1973, when VVDM sponsored a "national compensation week." Hundreds of soldiers gathered at demonstrations in the towns of Zwolle, Ede, Eindhoven and Den Bosch. At De Wittenberg a demonstration occurred on base. Petitions circulated in barracks throughout the country and were signed by thousands of conscripts. A second action week followed in December of that year, with additional demonstrations in Amsterdam, Havelte and t'Harde. Dutch soldiers stationed in Germany also took up the call for compensation and participated in actions in their bases there and at Breda in Holland.

The climax of the initial compensation campaign came in February 1974, when VVDM sponsored an enormous mass demonstration in Utrecht. On February 14 some 8,000 soldiers gathered for one of the largest soldier demonstrations in recent history. The union hired buses to transport soldiers from bases all over the country. After work the buses pulled away from dozens of barracks, and by early evening a huge throng had gathered in Utrecht. Nearly one out of every five Dutch conscripts was present. The 8,000 soldiers marched in uniform through the streets of Utrecht and then assembled at a rally to hear speakers demand full compensation for overtime.

The Ministry of Defense responded to the union's show of strength with an offer for limited compensation reforms. The leaders of VVDM rejected the offer, however, and in a move that caused some internal dissent and controversy, decided to call for another round of mobilization, this time employing more militant tactics. VVDM called for a "national action day" of protests and rallies on base on May 8, not accidentally the anniversary of the 1945 victory over Nazi Germany. The actions were set for noontime, with the explicit intention that they would extend past the lunch hour into duty time, thus becoming a kind of de facto strike. As the date for the action approached, the government warned that any strikes or work delays would be illegal. The union went ahead regardless, although the actions were less successful than hoped. Approximately 1,000 soldiers participated in May 8 actions on six bases, in some cases remaining off-duty for several hours.

In response, the government not only refused demands for compensation but also delayed a promised pay increase that would have brought Dutch conscripts up to the civilian minimum-wage level. The union reacted by sponsoring another mobilization campaign in June 1975. This time regional demonstrations were held in major cities. The demands of the actions were threefold: compensation for overtime, higher wages, and payments for food and lodging (the conscripts wanted the current deduction for room and board paid to them directly in cash). Approximately 4,000 soldiers participated in the demonstrations in five separate locations.

In July 1975 the Dutch soldiers finally gained a victory in the fight for compensation and higher wages. The Ministry of Defense granted some of the union's demands and raised conscript wages to what was at the time nearly the top level in Europe, indeed the world. The union could feel justly proud of its accomplishment. After a lengthy campaign involving tens of thousands of soldiers throughout the country the union had achieved another in its impressive string of victories.

f-15, Not F-16

During the campaign for compensation and higher wages in 1975, VVDM sponsored a modestly sized rally at the beginning of May that well illustrated the contradictions posed for military authorities by a unionized army. Approximately 400 soldiers gathered in the town of Leiden to demonstrate at an appearance by then-Prime Minister Joop Den Uyl. The important aspect of this rally was not its size or venue but the nature of the demands. As the soldiers chanted and demonstrated across the street from the prime minister's appearance, their slogan was, "f-15, not F-16." By that they meant that the government should give soldiers an f-15 pay raise (fifteen guilders, or about six dollars) rather than purchase the F-16 aircraft from the United States. (A multibillion dollar aircraft sale was then being arranged between Holland and the United States.) The soldiers were demanding a different set of priorities for military dollars. They were insisting that improved conditions for rank-and-file soldiers would be wiser and more beneficial than the purchase of new combat aircraft from the United States.

The incident was a minor one, but it clearly reflected the challenges that unionized soldiers can pose for the military command: How to balance the soldiers' demands for more pay with the defense establishment's perceived need for technological hardware. Soldier unionism can create pressures for diverting resources away from weapons procurement toward higher wages and benefits.

Solidarity with Unions

As VVDM focused more attention on compensation issues, the union began to develop closer relations with the civilian labor movement. VVDM always had had good relations with labor youth groups, which provided support for many of the soldiers' early campaigns. During the 1970s, as economic recession and austerity measures put downward pressure on wages, the soldiers found greater common ground with the unions. This closer relation became particularly crucial after the government raised the soldiers' pay and linked it to the civilian youth minimum wage. Wage trends for civilian workers thus began to have a direct effect on soldiers.

Given this common economic interest, it is not surprising that VVDM and the civilian unions began to work together. In 1977, when civilian unions staged a solidarity action in support of a walkout at the Rotterdam docks, soldiers came to their aid. VVDM organized support actions at several bases. Thousands of soldiers signed petitions supporting the strikers. VVDM representatives spoke in uniform at a number of labor demonstrations. Another example of this joint action occurred in 1980, when the civilian unions sponsored a mass protest campaign against reductions in worker wages. During an October 1980 demonstration at Utrecht around 1,500 soldiers joined in a demonstration of 5,000 workers to call for higher pay.

Although VVDM has worked closely with the labor movement in the last decade, the union remains officially independent of the established labor federations.* VVDM has participated in joint projects with the FNV federation, particularly in providing employment training and assistance for conscripts returning to civilian life, but they have shunned formal ties. Discussions have taken place from time to time between the soldiers and the civilian unionists about possible affiliation or merger, but the soldiers have backed away. They fear that they might be swallowed up by the giant labor federation and that the more conservative style of the civilian unions might limit their freedom of action. (In 1990 VVDM finally decided to join FNV.)

While many Dutch soldier activists support efforts toward labor solidarity, they are generally distrustful of an affiliation with the civilian unions. As one BVD leader phrased it, "we want cooperation at the base, not at the top." They are all for closer ties with labor, but they do not want to weaken VVDM's fighting spirit. As soldiers have found in Germany, the United States, and elsewhere, GI activism does not fit well with established trade unionism.

Reaching Out

Holland has a long tradition of internationalism, of outward vision and interest in the rest of the world. Thus it was quite normal for the Dutch soldier groups, in particular the highly politicized BVD, to take an active interest in what soldiers elsewhere were doing. In the early 1970s the Dutch began to reach out toward soldiers in other armies, especially to those of the U.S. Seventh Army in neighboring Germany. To the delight of American GIs and the fury of their superiors, long-haired Dutch soldiers in uniform turned up at U.S. barracks in Mannheim, attempting to testify in court-martial proceedings against soldiers charged with "long hair." Dutch soldiers in the thousands also signed petitions in support of English-based U.S. airman Dan Pruitt in his court case against military haircut regulations (see Chapter 2).

The Dutch also made contact with soldier activists from other countries. By the early 1970s they were meeting with German, French, and Italian organizers, in addition to the Americans. Everywhere the Dutch were spreading the idea not only of "In union there is strength", but also

---

*Traditionally Holland had three major labor federations: the CNV, Protestant and conservative, with some 240,000 members; the NKV, Catholic and fairly progressive, with approximately 400,000 members; and the NVV, mildly socialist and affiliated with the Labor Party, with over 600,000 members. In the 1970s the latter two federations merged into a single giant labor coalition, the FNV.

"Soldiers of all countries unite." Thus it was quite logical that the Dutch would organize what history will record as the first International Soldiers' Congress in Holland in November 1974 (see Chapter 1). The Amsterdam Congress concluded with a mass meeting in Utrecht where soldiers from ten nations joined together to sing the *Internationale*. The congress was considered a great success by its participants, but it did not lay the groundwork for a permanent international organization. Although France, Portugal, Italy, and other countries saw unprecedented soldier movements in the following years, and the U.S. army soon faced the beginnings of a unionization drive, the contacts established in Holland in 1974 slowly lapsed. Most of the soldiers who had come to Amsterdam lost contact with their colleagues both at home and abroad. Only the Dutch-organized groups maintained consistent work over the years.

BVD and VVDM had very practical reasons, apart from their philosophical interest, for maintaining international contacts with other armies. Their exceptional conditions of service, the high pay and more humanitarian forms of discipline won through union struggle, were constantly under pressure from Holland's NATO allies, who did not want to pay such (relatively) high wages in their armies. It made obvious sense for the unionized Dutch soldiers to help GIs in other countries improve their conditions, so that the disparity could not be used to lower wages or benefits in Holland.

An important part of the Dutch army is stationed abroad, mostly in the northern part of West Germany. The Dutch soldiers there have long been disadvantaged by their relative isolation and by poor conditions. A major complaint has been that while their mates in Holland have weekends off (100 free days per year), the soldiers in Germany have but 77 days free. In the mid-1970s the VVDM mounted a major campaign for "100 days." The drive culminated in a mass march of some 1,000 Dutch soldiers, mostly in uniform, through the northern German city of Hamburg on April 30, 1977. To increase the effect of their protest the Dutch had explained their slogan of "100 days now" to the somewhat bemused German soldier committees in the nearby barracks. A small group of German soldiers understood the point and stuck their necks out to march behind the Dutch demonstrators. The German draftees, unprotected by a recognized union, took considerable risk when they expressed such solidarity, but in this instance their command played it cool. There were no repressive measures, and in fact no publicity whatsoever. It was a sign of the changed times that 1,000 protesting soldiers could march in uniform through West Germany's largest city and be utterly ignored by the media.

The International Soldiers' Organization first envisioned in Amsterdam in 1974 remained a dream until, quite unexpectedly, the Scandinavian soldier groups, ignored by other GIs or dismissed as "company unions," converted it into reality. It was not the Dutch but the Danes and Swedes who called a conference in Malmö in February 1979 that succeeded in establishing the first permanent, still-functioning European Conference of Conscripts' Organizations, ECCO. VVDM served as the secretariat for this organization, though, and the Dutch have been active participants at every conference (see chapters 8 and 18).

Consolidation and Competition

As the Dutch soldiers' movement grew rapidly and matured in the 1970s, VVDM found itself confronted with an ironic fate: The very successes that had brought it so much strength were beginning to dissipate the union's energy. Beginning in the early 1970s, union activists began to feel a sense of malaise, as the movement first leveled off and then began to decline. The halcyon days of growth and favorable publicity were over. Having achieved a sweeping transformation of military service, VVDM began to find its victories harder to come by. In addition, a rival, more conservative conscripts' union was founded, an organization that would eventually grow to surpass the VVDM. Government repression and animosity also increased. In nearly every respect the conditions that led to the historic development of VVDM were changing.

One of the most important aspects of this change in circumstances was the souring of relations with the government. As the union became more aggressive in its demands and action programs, the previously cozy relationship between VVDM and the military leadership became adversarial. As we have seen, early conflicts emerged in 1972 over the soldiers' saluting actions and the command's censorship of local papers. Conflicts continued in 1973 and afterwards, despite a new government coalition, when even the new social democratic Defense Minister Vredeling grew impatient with the soldiers' militant tactics and tightened pressures on VVDM.

In the latter part of 1975 military commanders began to attack VVDM at a highly vulnerable point: its ability to recruit new members in the barracks. The union's very life blood was challenged. Previously VVDM had enjoyed easy access to the barracks every two months, as approximately 6,000 conscripts are inducted and processed into the army. VVDM would use these recruitment periods to talk with and sign up as many members as possible. Beginning in 1975, however, commanders began to stretch the rules, claiming that the new conscripts must be kept on duty for extended periods and that they could not be available to the union recruiters.

Faced with these restrictions on their ability to gain new members, the leaders of VVDM were forced to take drastic action. The union ignored command restrictions and decided to enter the barracks as usual. As a result, union organizers quickly fell victim to punishment. More than twenty leading VVDM activists, including all the members of the national board, were harassed and briefly detained.

Further troubles developed for VVDM from an incident in February 1976 at the 44th Armored Infantry Battalion in Zuidlaren. Some 200 men refused to muster for duty to protest poor conditions in subfreezing weather. Although the VVDM leaders did not initiate this action, which came to be known as the "incident of the cold feet" (so dubbed by an increasingly unfriendly civilian press), the union came under renewed attack for allegedly condoning the refusal of orders.

Hampered in its recruiting efforts and under increasing attack inside and outside the army, VVDM saw its fortunes and membership steadily decline. By 1977 VVDM membership had declined from its peak of 30,000 to less than 20,000.

One of the developments that seriously stung VVDM was the founding of an alternative, more conservative conscripts' union, the AVNM, the General Association of Dutch Servicemen (Algemene Vereniging Nederlandse Militairen). AVNM was founded at the end of 1972 by conservative soldiers associated with the VVD, Holland's largest right-wing party. AVNM declared that it was in favor of improving conditions for soldiers but that it opposed the militant tactics of VVDM. The new union rejected calls for mass action and instead placed greater emphasis on negotiation. Drawing its support primarily from country youth and conservative students, AVNM gradually developed a considerable following in the ranks. By the late 1970s membership reached 5,000. By the mid-1980s, as VVDM continued to decline, AVNM membership grew to 10,000, surpassing that of VVDM.

If there is any consolation for the activists of VVDM in this situation it is that the rival union has steadily moved toward activist politics. As AVNM has acquired more members, it has had to become more active to gain and keep conscript support. The two unions have supported the same demands for higher wages and have worked together on a number of campaigns. There have even been talks about a possible merger. Discussions to this effect were conducted for a while but were broken off in 1984.

The "Dilemma of Success"

The irony for VVDM is that its very successes have led to its difficulties--what former activists have termed the "dilemma of success." Because of the sweeping democratization that the union has fostered, soldiers have fewer rights left to demand. The initial goals of the union have been met.

The union won in its fight for improved conditions and for elementary rights of expression and freedom. Conscripts who enter the army now take these hard-won freedoms for granted. It is harder to motivate soldiers to take risks and join protests when so many gains have already been won.

Consider the record of accomplishment of VVDM during its first ten years:

- a 1,200 percent pay raise, with salaries now pegged to the civilian minimum wage
- free hair length
- optional saluting
- almost-free publication and distribution of independent GI newspapers
- a major increase in the amount of free time and number of holidays
- limited forms of compensation for overtime (as of the early 1980s compensation terms were eight hours off for every 24 hours on extra duty, plus extra pay of ten guilders, about four dollars)
- an easing of military regulations and disciplinary procedures
- abolition of military trains
- a reduction of spit and polish
- improved living conditions and eased restrictions within the barracks

VVDM has succeeded in democratizing the Dutch army and introducing trade union relations into the ranks. The arbitrariness of military service has been reduced. There have been great improvements for the average conscript. But this very achievement has dampened the impulses that led to the creation of the movement.

The decline of VVDM in the 1980s has been part of a general reduction in political activity among youth in most highly industrialized nations. In Holland as in the United States and other countries, the student and youth movements that were so prominent ten or twenty years earlier have faded. There has been an unmistakable diminution of political activism among youth and a corresponding lack of experience among those entering the ranks of the army.

A special factor contributing to the decline of the Dutch soldiers' movement was a decision by the government, made in 1979, to lower the entry age. Where conscripts once entered at age twenty ("twintig"), now most were eighteen, and some were even seventeen. Where students once could fulfill their military obligation after college, now most served before their studies. For VVDM this was a severe blow, since the union had always received its greatest support and drawn its leaders from older conscripts, most of whom were students who had completed school and were finally fulfilling their military service obligation, sometimes at age twenty-five or older. Fewer conscripts are now in this older age group, and this has further contributed to the decline of activism.

Another factor was the army's decision to reduce the time of service for army conscripts to twelve months. Furthermore, as in many other countries, the establishment has made it increasingly easy for "antimilitarist" youth to avoid the draft. From the government's point of view it is better to have potential "troublemakers" emptying bedpans as conscientious objectors in hospitals or even "home free" studying than stirring up resistance inside the army (see, in particular, Chapter 9).

By 1984 the VVDM had shrunken to a membership of just over 7,000. The union had declined to one-quarter of its previous size, and it now had to compete with a rival, more conservative organization, AVNM. But while VVDM has faced lean times quantitatively, it has made major advances qualitatively. The political focus of VVDM and the Dutch soldiers' movement has sharpened in recent years. The union is now placing greater emphasis on fundamental questions relating to the purpose and mission of the armed forces.

Soldiers Join the Peace Movement

Beginning in the late 1970s, as a new cold war set in between the United States and the Soviet Union and nuclear tensions mounted, peace issues became more important for people throughout the world. This was especially true in Europe and the United States, where large movements emerged to speak out against the worsening nuclear arms race. This antinuclear movement rose with particular fervor in the Netherlands, and it was perhaps inevitable that the citizen soldiers of the Dutch army would also be drawn in.

For VVDM this involvement began in the late 1970s, when NATO officials endorsed the deployment of the neutron bomb as a tactical nuclear weapon in Europe. Like many in Europe and North America, the Dutch conscripts were outraged by the idea of a weapon that kills people but preserves property. They also knew that neutron weapons are designed to be used on the battlefield and thus make the risk of nuclear war greater. Within the VVDM General Assembly the issue was hotly debated, and a resolution was adopted strongly opposing the neutron bomb.

The nuclear issue quickly became even more heated in 1980 following the decision by NATO ministers in December 1979 to deploy 572 cruise and Pershing II nuclear missiles in Western Europe. Forty-eight of these ground-launched cruise missiles were to be based in Holland, and the Dutch people thus found themselves at the center of a major new escalation of the arms race. Almost overnight a vast new peace movement emerged.

The Dutch soldiers played an active part right from the beginning. In 1980, VVDM launched a major educational campaign on nuclear policy. A soldiers' conference on nuclear arms was held in January 1981, followed by local educational sessions in barracks throughout the country.

Meanwhile, individual soldiers began to take the issue into their own hands by refusing guard duty at nuclear weapons sites. The first such incident occurred in August 1980 when a conscript refused a direct order to perform guard duty at a nuclear weapons depot. Such incidents began to spread to other barracks, and before long some eighty Dutch conscripts had refused orders to guard nuclear weapons sites. In every case the resisters were brought before courts-martial and sentenced to varying degrees of punishment.

When the first refusals occurred in 1980 and 1981, a major debate ensued at the VVDM General Assembly. Although VVDM did not initiate or encourage such acts, the union felt it had to come to the aid of the individuals involved. Defense campaigns were organized for the accused soldiers, and the union provided legal assistance. Petitions of support were circulated urging that the accused be freed. In some instances these petitions were signed by up to 5,000 soldiers. Due in part to these defense efforts, the soldiers who refused orders generally received light sentences, usually just two or three weeks detention.

As a result of these cases and the wide debate within the union, VVDM was forced to take an official position on the issue of nuclear weapons in Holland. The position adopted by the union was fairly moderate by Dutch standards, but it clearly reflected a rejection of official NATO policy. VVDM stated that they were opposed to any new nuclear weapons, particularly the ground-launched cruise missiles, and they favored the eventual withdrawal of all nuclear weapons from Dutch soil.

AVNM also became involved in the nuclear weapons debate. The rival union took no position on nuclear weapons per se, but it defended the right of individual soldiers to refuse orders. In effect, AVNM was forced to adopt the same stance as VVDM, providing defense and support for individual resisters who refuse to guard nuclear weapons. Like VVDM, AVNM provided attorneys to defend soldiers court-martialed for refusing nuclear duty.

As the peace movement spread within the Dutch army, a new independent soldiers group emerged, Soldiers Against Nukes. This group was formed in the early 1980s (the initiative came from members of the BVD) to work exclusively on nuclear arms issues and the defense of individual resisters. Most of the members of this group were also VVDM members.

In the early period of the antinuclear peace movement, in 1980 and 1981, the conscripts were joined in their protests by a small group of officers and professional soldiers. An organization known as the "Peace and Security Council of the Armed Forces" was formed with a membership of approximately 50 officers, mostly lieutenants and captains, including some chaplains. One of the founders of the groups was Air Force Captain Meindert Stelling. This council cooperated with VVDM in the soldiers' peace conference of early 1981 and other public education efforts. After this initial period, though, the officers' group became less active. The members faced heavy criticisms from their officer colleagues, and most of the original founders soon left the military. As we have noted elsewhere in the book, especially in our discussion of Portugal, movements among low-ranking officers have had an impact in some nations below the capital accumulation threshold, but such movements have not been able to sustain themselves in any of the most highly capitalized nations, including Holland.

The conscripts, on the other hand, remained active and became an integral part of the peace movement. Dutch soldiers were a regular fixture at the large political rallies against nuclear weapons. During the massive November 1981 demonstration in Amsterdam, for example, 500 soldiers marched in uniform in a crowd of nearly 400,000. During the even larger antinuclear demonstration in Den Haag in fall 1983, another 500 conscripts marched in uniform.

The union's participation in the peace movement was not without its strains. The soldier activists found themselves facing a problem similar to that encountered by U.S. GI organizers during the Vietnam peace movement: animosities between peace protesters and soldiers. The problem arose at a "peace camp" established in Holland near a major nuclear weapons base, where civilian protesters frequently held demonstrations. Occasionally the civilians vented their anger and frustration at individual conscripts, screaming epithets and occasionally hurling objects at them. The conscripts on the base naturally demanded that the union do something to correct the problem. VVDM was thus caught in the middle. It tried to educate the peace movement that individual conscripts are not the problem, but it could not control everyone who came to a demonstration; meanwhile, union members on base were angered by abuse from a peace movement to which VVDM belonged. As was the case in the United States during the Vietnam War, the union found that a great deal of education was needed within the civilian peace movement so that it could see soldiers as allies rather than enemies. The lesson was an important one. If soldiers and civilians could work together in a common campaign for peace, the chances of preventing nuclear war and reversing the arms race would be greatly enhanced.

The Dutch conscripts have set an example for soldiers everywhere. In more than two decades of political struggle they have pushed through a sweeping democratization of the army and have fundamentally altered the terms and conditions of military service. They have shown that ordinary soldiers can make history, and that it is possible to create a more democratic military and perhaps even bring about a more peaceful world.

8

"Bad Company": Company Unions and the Soldiers' Movement of Scandinavia

By the late 1960s the Social Democratic governments of Norway, Sweden, and Denmark knew that soldiers were becoming restless. They had seen the news from Holland and faced burgeoning civilian youth movements at home. To protect themselves from soldier resistance, the Scandinavian governments opted for a preemptive strike. They introduced company unionism--a novel and quite remarkable approach to taming the troops. Their slogan became: "If you can't beat 'em, join 'em."

In all three countries the governments established representation systems for draftees.[1] First the conscripts were permitted to elect spokesmen (known as "tillitsmann") who would represent soldier interests at the company level. After some years these spokesmen were then allowed to elect regional and national representatives, and a permanent office and central committee were established. These national conscript committees were allowed to consult with the command, publish newspapers, represent soldier grievances, hold national conferences, and draw up demands for improving soldier conditions. The soldiers were given all the forms of unionism, but none of the substance.

The Scandinavian governments were careful to avoid even the hint of real trade union power. The conscripts could discuss their grievances with the command, but they were given no contractual or bargaining rights. They could draw up a program, but they had no formal means of enforcing it. The systems were designed by the command to be management tools, a "firebreak" against the spreading flame of soldier resistance.

The company unions of Scandinavia are a means of taking the heat off the command by providing carefully controlled outlets for soldier activism. The conscripts can elect representatives, set up an organization, present demands, and consult with the command. But all of this is conducted within carefully circumscribed limits. Elections are supervised by the command, all funding comes from the government, meetings are held within government offices, the agenda of discussible issues is limited to so-called "welfare" problems, and, at least in the case of Norway, commanders and military officials can participate in and vote on conscript decisions. These systems conform to the traditional Scandinavian approach of co-option and accommodation rather than repression and punishment.

The fact that the governments of the region had a long and harmonious relationship with various officer and NCO unions no doubt made it easier for commanders to accept company unionism. Social Democratic officials could rightly point to the military's cordial (one could even say cozy) relationship with these professional unions as proof that the armed forces would survive representation for conscripts. This would be considered "horrifying" in such Western countries as France and the United States, but in Northern Europe the traditions of social democracy permit a unique form of top-down conscript unionism.

These representation systems were introduced in response to changing social conditions and growing youth pressures both inside and outside the military. In all three countries the systems began innocuously, with spokesmen elected at the unit level but no national coordination. As youth activism and political pressures mounted in the 1960s, however, the representation systems grew more extensive. By the early 1970s each country had a national organization and central office. This change--from a system of isolated local representatives to a nationally coordinated network--was a crucial watershed (time "T") and marked the emergence of an independent soldiers' movement.

Just as the national conscript organizations were being established in the 1970s, leftist youth groups in each country tried to establish independent soldier committees outside the company union structure. Some of these leftists, including various Maoist groups, consciously ignored the tillitsmann system. They seemed to operate, using an analogy from U.S. labor history, like the Industrial Workers of the World (IWW), outside the established labor system, completely freewheeling and wild. As far as we have been able to determine, however, none of these original organizing efforts survived. Some independent soldier groups were formed for a time, but the company union structure remained the focus of soldier attention.

In Scandinavia, soldier resistance has emerged inside the company union structure. Despite elaborate command efforts to prevent organizational independence, the soldiers have progressively fought for greater autonomy and genuine trade union rights. The top-down company unions are being transformed by bottom-up soldier activism.

Two contradictory social processes exist within one institutional setting: command-imposed co-option versus draftee-initiated independence. Starting slowly from humble origins, an autonomous trade union movement has begun to emerge among Scandinavian conscripts. To the greatest extent in Sweden, to a lesser degree in Denmark, and hardly at all in Norway, an independent union movement has surfaced within the established representation system. What began as a top-down controlling mechanism has metamorphosed into a bottom-up movement for democracy.

Norway

The trek to the Huseby, Norway's Pentagon, takes one beyond central Oslo to the rugged hills of the city's outskirts. Norway's military headquarters are housed in an unpretentious modern office building, surrounded by a small army camp.

As we ambled along the base's main roadway, we watched a team of conscripts on work detail. They were a motley crew, busily defending their country in the age-old tradition of low-ranking soldiers everywhere: raking leaves, picking up cigarette butts, and manicuring the lawn of what appeared to be an officers club. Their languor and blank stares of boredom made us feel very much at home, and helped deflate the sense of intimidation public relations officials had tried to instill in us. After several inquiries at the front desk, we discovered the tillitsmann central office down several long corridors deep inside the Huseby. We opened the door to a small, unassuming office occupied by three young draftees in civilian clothes. This tiny, mildly disheveled alcove was the headquarters for Norway's conscripts, the central office for the army's tillitsmann or "representative" system.

The soldier representatives were initially skeptical toward us ("You're not from the CIA, are you?"), but after we explained our involvement in the U.S. GI movement and the then-burgeoning drive for a soldiers' union in the United States, they opened up to us and launched into a lengthy description of their system.

In each company or small unit in the Norwegian armed forces, soldiers are permitted to vote for one of their colleagues as the unit representative, or tillitsmann. There were 96 such representatives when we visited Norway. These are elected by the conscripts, with a voter turnout rate over 90 percent. These elections are organized and supervised by the local commander. The elected representatives then serve on a unit "welfare board" that determines barracks social life, including sports events and movie schedules. The company commander is the chair of this welfare board and controls and limits its proceedings.

The locally elected representatives also participate in national affairs. The ninety-six tillitsmann elected at the local level periodically meet to elect eleven members for a national draftee committee (three of these eleven are assigned as staff to the central office--our hosts today). This central committee also includes two members from the Ministry of Defense, two senior officers from the military leadership, and two base commanders. The central committee meets five times a year, but, like the local welfare board, its official powers are narrowly circumscribed. The conscripts are not allowed to bargain over conditions of pay, and they have no means of ensuring compliance with their demands.

Once a year all of the elected conscript representatives gather for a national conference where policy guidelines are discussed. Here again, however, the military command is very much in control. The conference is entirely arranged and organized by the Ministry of Defense. One-quarter of the delegates are from the Ministry of Defense and the military command. In 1976, for example, 36 of the 132 voting delegates to the conference were military officers and Ministry of Defense representatives.

Our conscript hosts at the Huseby valiantly tried to defend their national conference and noted that the last meeting had adopted a strong program for improving soldier life. Their demands had included:

- a doubling of conscript pay,
- the payment of an adequate separation bonus,
- an increase in the number of free trips home (from four to eight),
- equalization of working hours for soldiers and officers (which would mean a considerable shortening of the soldiers' work day), and
- unlimited overnight passes off base.

When we asked what power the conscripts have to enforce these demands, they conceded that the system is stacked against them. They have no formal bargaining rights and no real power. They can press their demands during consultation, but military officials are entirely free to ignore them. The draftees cannot push too hard; they must constantly look beyond the negotiating table to the possible harassment and repression they may face on the parade ground. The soldier representatives never entirely escape the private-general relationship and have thus far remained fundamentally dependent and powerless.

When we asked the three conscripts if they could visit local tillitsmann representatives and investigate grievances, they looked at each other nervously and admitted they could not. They cannot even visit a military base or talk with a local tillitsmann without the permission of the base commander. A company union indeed.

The embarrassed soldiers heatedly explained that they are not content with this dependent position and are eager to gain greater autonomy. They reported that many soldiers are now discussing the need for an alternative organization that would more closely resemble a real union. They enthusi-astically pointed to the experience of Swedish soldiers and said they hoped to follow this model in building a "free union" (we shall examine this Swedish model next). They noted that the demand for autonomy had come up even within the national conference (over the objections of the officers) and that debate on the question was intensifying.

As our interview stretched into its second hour, the atmosphere became more relaxed and discursive. The conscripts opened up about their experi-ences and wanted to know more about soldier organizing in other countries.

Suddenly the door banged open, and a sternly countenanced official from the Ministry of Defense strode into the office loudly demanding why foreign civilians had been allowed to visit the draftees without his permis-sion. "You must have the approval of the ministry." The arrival of the official had an immediate intimidating effect. The three draftees who a minute before had been agreeably chatting quickly ducked behind their typewriters and buried themselves in paperwork. The rap session was abruptly halted, and we were unceremoniously ushered out of the office and out of the building. It was a sad but fitting end to our glimpse of the Norwegian tillitsmann system.

As we departed the Huseby and walked back through the base, the troops we had noticed on our arrival were still "at work" with broom and rake, a glint of impertinence breaking through their torpor.

Sweden

The contrast between the offices of the draftees working group in Sweden and the tillitsmann headquarters in Norway is instructive. The Norwegian draftees are housed deep within the central military headquar-ters, tightly controlled by the military establishment. We found the offices of the Varnpliktiga Arbetsgruppen (VAG), Draftees Working Group, in downtown Stockholm in a commercial district, far from the eye of the General Staff and close to many political and trade union offices. The cluttered rooms had a distinct "movement" atmosphere: a mimeo machine, stacks of old newspapers, political posters on the walls. Two of the VAG representatives (one an active-duty conscript, the other a recent vet) gra-ciously took time to speak with us when we visited in 1976 and explained the workings of their system. They told of the growing strengths and independence of the Swedish soldiers' movement.

The basic organizational structure is the same as in Norway. Approxi-mately 200 soldier representatives are elected in company-sized units all over the country. These local representatives in turn elect a nine-member national committee, of whom two are selected as staff for the central secretariat. As in Norway and Denmark, these elections and organizational arrangements are completely controlled and financed by the government. The local representatives (called "foertroendevalda", literally, "one chosen in confidence") have only limited advisory power. The national draftee board consults with the government but has no formal bargaining rights.

Unofficially, however, the system works quite differently. Whatever the government's intent, the soldiers have used the representation system as a vehicle for building a feisty and independent soldiers' movement. They have sponsored widespread soldier protests and demonstrations. The largest actions, including sick-call strikes and petition campaigns, have involved as many as 30,000 troops (sixty percent of the entire army). Nearly sixty independent GI newspapers have been established at local bases, and an autonomous national newspaper called *Kanonen* (Cannons) has been founded (as a counter to the government-sponsored draftee paper, *Varnplikts Nytt*). Separate committees, considered the first locals of an independent union, were established beginning in the early 1970s at several bases (twenty such groups existed in 1979). Perhaps most importantly, an independent fund has been established through soldier contributions to finance union activity and build toward the creation of a completely autonomous structure. The soldiers have used the government's top-down apparatus to build a bottom-up soldiers' movement. As a VAG staff person expressed it, "We're building our own trade union inside their system."

Like the representation arrangements of Norway and Denmark, the VAG system evolved in stages. It began in the 1960's with the election of "foertroendevalda" in local barracks. By 1970, however, it had developed into a coordinated national organization with a central committee and permanent office. Pressure for these initial changes came not just from soldiers but from activists in the youth section of the ruling Social Democratic Party. The young Socialists demanded a voice for citizen soldiers. Senior Social Democratic officials accepted this demand in the hope that this would improve management and channel conscript complaints into controllable outlets.

The soldiers had different ideas, though. From the very beginning they sought greater independence and pressed for radical change. The idea of an autonomous union, for example, was raised at the first national conference in 1970 and has been continuously pursued ever since. These pressures have come mostly from soldiers in the barracks (often over the objections of or with only reluctant support from the VAG national committee).

Rank-and-file activism among Swedish soldiers first emerged in 1971. It coincided with the appearance of the first independent local newspapers. The first large-scale protest action took place in 1972 when approximately 1,000 soldiers at several bases engaged in a "sick-out," simultaneously going on sick call to press demands for free evening passes to leave the barracks at night. The action was initially organized outside the VAG national committee, but when the government reacted harshly (for Sweden) and brought legal charges against seven of the soldiers involved, the VAG became involved. A large defense effort was mounted on behalf of the soldiers (strongly aided by major civilian youth organizations). As a result the seven conscript-activists were acquitted. The sick call action and subsequent trial were important developments for the soldiers' movement, demonstrating the potential of mass action and leading to a new, more assertive VAG leadership.

One of the largest mobilization of the Swedish soldiers' movement came in 1973, when the VAG launched a campaign to increase the separation bonus paid to each departing soldier from 250 kroner (approximately $50 at the time) to 1,000 kroner. The call for 1,000 kroner became a rallying cry for soldiers throughout the country, and a massive petition drive was started. A series of demonstrations and small-scale strikes also swept the army. In spring 1974 the government responded to this growing movement with compromise, increasing the bonus from 250 to 400 kroner. The soldiers refused to accept the offer and remained adamant in their demand for a full 1,000 kroner bonus. Protests continued, and the petitions drive was pressed. By the end of 1974 the VAG call for 1,000 kroner had been signed by an amazing 30,000 soldiers.

In 1975 the weight of these mobilization efforts finally produced results. The Ministry of Defense conceded to the soldiers' demands and instituted a full 1,000 kroner separation payment. They also granted, a few months earlier, overnight passes and additional time off. These benefits marked the first major victory of the soldiers' movement and confirmed the importance of rank-and-file mobilization.

Buoyed by the success of their 1,000-kroner campaign, VAG activists met a few months later and took steps to begin building an independent union. For the first time they convened a national conference that was financed and organized independently of the government. The VAG activists also founded their own newspaper, *Kanonen,* and established a separate fund to finance these activities. The first independent trade union locals were also formed during this time. By 1976 Swedish conscripts were on their way to independent unionism.

The conscripts received valuable help in their efforts from professional military unionists and the civilian labor movement. During the height of the campaign for 1,000 kroner, VAG called together Sweden's three professional military unions to explore the possibility of mutual cooperation. Although no formal assistance was offered, some limited support for the VAG campaign was expressed by the union of platoon officers (the equivalent of NCOs in the United States). Several platoon officers subsequently worked with the conscripts and signed their petition. More significant aid came from several civilian unions. VAG asked for and received statements of support from the miners', paperworkers' and metalworkers' unions. (These unions may have been attracted by VAG's stand against the use of soldiers as strikebreakers.) VAG activists place great importance on these connections with labor and see them as a means of ensuring a more democratically accountable armed forces.

The Swedish soldiers' movement has been built on a trade union program for improving the economic and social conditions of military life. VAG's main demands are:

- free travel on trains and buses,
- forty-hour work week, with compensation for overtime,
- higher pay and benefits,
- safer working conditions,
- improved medical care, and
- reform of the military justice system.

Denmark

We first met the Danish national conscript committee on a trip through Copenhagen in 1976.* At the time its members seemed complacent and docile--a stark contrast to their feisty brothers in Sweden. The soldiers we interviewed said they preferred "negotiation, not confrontation" and did not want a union.

When we visited just three years later, however, the climate had changed. The national conscript committee had just resigned in protest over the government's censorship of their newspaper. Danish soldiers were holding demonstrations, and the beginnings of a movement for independent unionism were emerging. Cooperation was giving way to conflict.

We found the militancy of Danish soldiers particularly striking in light of the generous wages and privileges they enjoy. The organization's

---

* The Danish "spokesmen" system (Forretningsudvaldet Vaernepligtige Menige Talsmaend) is very similar to that of Sweden and Norway. Local "spokesmen" are elected in every small unit or company, and these in turn choose a national committee that serves as a full-time secretariat. The local "spokesmen" represent conscripts in meetings with the command, but, as elsewhere, their opinions are merely advisory. The national representatives can consult with the Ministry of Defense and top commanders, but they have no bargaining rights.

This Danish system was first established by a Social Democratic government in 1968. It began on a local level only, with no national coordination or central office. Under pressure from the party's youth section, however, the national committee and headquarters were established in 1973.

previous path of accommodation had apparently paid off handsomely. Danish conscripts are the best paid in the world, better paid even than the unionized troops of Holland. (As of late 1979 their take-home pay was approximately $1,000 per month.) These high wages were theirs without a single demonstration or strike. While their Swedish colleagues had mounted a major campaign to get an adequate separation bonus, the Danes were simply awarded the relatively generous standard of 2,400 crowns (nearly $500). They had also been granted the right to free public transportation. The rights and privileges that soldiers battled for in other lands were theirs for the asking.

But the Danes were not content with good pay. They also wanted better conditions in the workplace and the barracks and greater freedom to speak their minds. They began to make demands and to use more militant tactics. They were influenced in this by the example of the Danish National Committee for Conscientious Objectors (those who perform alternative civilian service have their own separate representation system.) The soldier "spokesmen" and the conscientious objector representatives have often cooperated and worked closely together. The methods of political activism employed by the conscientious objectors, especially their use of demonstrations and strikes to improve conditions, gradually had an effect on the conscripts.

As the soldiers wrote increasingly critical articles in their newspapers and as they began to report on politics and on soldier unions in other countries, conflict between the spokesmen committee and the government inevitably followed. The differences broke into the open in 1979 in a confrontation over government censorship. The immediate occasion for the dispute was a proposal by the Danish conscripts to host an international soldiers' conference in Denmark. The Danes had met with the Spanish organization, UDS (Union of Democratic Soldiers, see Chapter 13), and had been impressed by their accounts of soldier struggles in their own country and elsewhere. They also agreed with the Spanish proposal to hold a conference of soldiers from all over Europe. When the Danish conscripts announced their intent to convene such a meeting in Denmark, the government reacted harshly. The Ministry of Defense said that such a meeting would "embarrass the Danish government." It forbade the use of state funds or facilities for such a purpose and demanded that the conscripts have nothing to do with it.

As the dispute over the proposed international soldiers' conference intensified, so did the confrontation between soldiers and the command over control of the national newspaper. The specific issue was editorial direction of the paper, *Soldaten*. Although financed by the government, this official journal of the spokesmen committee had until then been written and edited by the conscripts themselves. In February 1979, however, after complaining for months of articles that it considered "antimilitarist," the Ministry of Defense took control of the paper and imposed new editorial policies.

The ministry no doubt expected that its clampdown would end the growing feistiness within the ranks. As so often with the GI movement, however, increased repression only brought heightened activism. When the government took control of *Soldaten,* the entire conscript editorial board resigned. As they did they vowed to follow the example of their Swedish colleagues and found an independent newspaper. Within weeks a new soldier newspaper, *Kanonen,* appeared in the barracks. The Swedish disease had sprung up in Copenhagen. (The new paper, which first appeared in May 1979, was a great improvement aesthetically over *Soldaten.* In place of cheesecake nudity and pics of government officials, *Kanonen* offered tabloid coverage of working conditions and barracks life.)

When the rescheduled international conference was finally convened (across the sound from Copenhagen in the Swedish town of Malmö), the Danish conscripts were told by the government that they could not attend. Fed up with company unionism, the Danish delegates defied the command and left to join their fellow soldiers from other countries. They were on the road to Sweden.

ECCO Is Born

The 1979 conference that sparked such a row between Danish conscripts and their officers had a significant impact well beyond the borders of Scandinavia.[2] The March gathering in Malmö was the first international soldiers' conference in nearly five years (the last had been the anti-NATO congress organized by the Dutch BVD in November 1974). It brought together soldier representatives from Denmark, Sweden, Norway, Finland, Holland, West Germany, Belgium, France, and Spain. The Malmö meeting also paved the way for a larger soldiers' conference eight months later (at Putten in the Netherlands) and created the first international coordinating body for the soldiers' movement--the European Conference of Conscript Organizations, ECCO.

The surroundings in Malmö (arranged by the VAG of Sweden) were luxurious compared to those of the Amsterdam conference five years before. Musty auditoriums and sleeping-bag accommodations were replaced by a comfortable downtown hotel, the St. George. The character of the groups represented at the meeting was also different from previous gatherings. The four Scandinavian countries in attendance (including Finland) were represented by their officially recognized national conscript committees. The Dutch were represented by the officially recognized

15,000-member VVDM. Five out of nine of the national delegations could thus fairly claim to represent substantial percentages of their armies. Small ad hoc committees were present as well, but these took a back seat to the official national committees. The attendance at the Malmö meeting thus may have been small (about thirty people), but those present spoke with the voice of tens of thousands. From these modest beginnings came the historic transnational soldier organization, ECCO.

The Malmö meeting was followed a few months later by a larger, more formally structured conference at Putten, Holland. This gathering, arranged by the VVDM, took place at a civilian labor center thirty kilometers from Utrecht.[3] Ten countries were represented at Putten (Holland, Belgium, France, Spain, West Germany, Switzerland, Denmark, Sweden, Norway, and Finland). The total number of delegates was also larger (approximately 100), and the range of represented organizations wider.

At both conferences soldiers exchanged information on their mutual problems and concerns and pledged to work towards closer international cooperation. Despite their many differences of language and culture, the participants at Malmö and Putten found their mutual experience as soldiers a strong bond of common interest and outlook. The soldiers found themselves in agreement on many issues, particularly the political importance of maintaining conscription and fighting for the democratic rights of soldiers.

The final declarations at Malmö and Putten revolved around two fundamental and interrelated propositions:

1. Conscription is a "progressive conquest" (in the words of the Putten statement)that narrows the gap between armed forces and society; the participation of the whole society in national defense is essential to democracy; the trend toward professional armies *(mercenary* they were called) must be opposed;

2. If soldiers are to be "citizens in uniform," they must have the same rights as civilians; this includes the right to form unions; as the Putten conferees declared, "Only those military men who live through democracy and believe in it will feel obliged to defend it."[4]

Since the founding of ECCO in 1979, the participating organizations have maintained communications (with the Dutch VVDM providing secretarial coordination). Annual conferences have been held and the groups have continued to work for the principles enunciated at Malmö and Putten (see Chapter 18).

Finland

It was at the Malmö and Putten meetings that European soldier activists (and the authors) were first introduced to the unique soldiers' union of Finland, Varus Mies Liitto. This is one of the most unusual groups in the entire soldiers' movement. It might best be described as a communist-influenced company union. It is a conscript representation committee similar to that in other Scandinavian armies, except that in this case it is approved and strongly influenced by the official communist party. The organization's bylaws specifically refer to Finland's treaty of friendship and cooperation with the Soviet Union. Yet the union has some of the same quarrelsome attributes of its Scandinavian neighbors and has a program urging pay increases, a forty-hour work week, and abolition of military courts.

Varus Mies Liitto was founded in 1970, at a time of increasing political activity among youth. The structures of the system (and its co-optive intent) are the same as in the rest of Scandinavia, but there are some important differences. One is that the Finnish organization has formal membership, whereas the other Scandinavian unions are open to all conscripts but do not have a paid membership list per se. The Finnish group is a regular membership organization, more like the VVDM in Holland than the company union structures of the other Scandinavian countries. The Finnish union has approximately 12,000 members. Of these, however, only 3,500 are active-duty conscripts (out of an army of 36,000). Of the members, 8,500 are civilians, mostly recent veterans or youth representatives of the various political parties in Finland.

The Finnish conscripts also differ from their colleagues in pay and conditions of service. Compensation in the Finnish army is among the lowest in Europe. The 1980 conscript wage of approximately $42 per month put the Finns near the bottom of the list for European soldiers, down with the long-suffering French. Other forms of compensation were also meager. The separation bonus at the end of the conscripts' eight-month tour of duty was only $37. Free trips home were few and far between. In addition, Finnish soldiers were among the few remaining in Europe who did not enjoy free passes in and out of the barracks; soldiers could leave the base only one evening a week, and then only until midnight.

The Finnish soldiers union has been working hard to remedy these conditions. In this regard it closely resembles its Scandinavian counterparts. The union regularly holds meetings in local barracks, produces and distributes a national soldiers' newspaper and holds twice-a-year national congresses. The union relies heavily on consultations with government and defense ministry officials, but it also employs such techniques as hearings and mass petition drives. The union's strong ties to the official communist party and other forces within the ruling government coalition provide considerable leverage.

The Finnish soldiers' union has a strong peace program. It was the only organization at Malmoe and Putten that injected issues of disarmament into the discussion. They urged a resolution in support of the Helsinki agreements and world peace. The other soldiers at the conferences were a bit bemused by their Finnish colleagues. As one soldier put it, "We're all for peace, but we don't want to pass resolutions about it." Some soldiers considered the whole discussion a diversion and wanted to return to the real problems of fighting for better pay and conditions. Others perhaps suspected that they were being used to support Finnish (and Soviet) foreign policy and wanted no part of it.

In the end, the ECCO conference approved a communique on the issue of peace that even the Finns had to agree made the point well:

In previous history soldiers of different countries have met only on the battlefield. Today we meet peaceably to build democratic armies everywhere. We will fight in our armies so that they cannot act as aggressors or fight against their own population.[5]

9

Sons of the Wehrmacht: Pacifists and Unionists

In the wake of World War II, with the Nazi war machine smashed and society devastated, German political leaders of all persuasions proclaimed: "Never again." Never would the scourge of militarism be allowed to rise again. Germany would be kept permanently free of all armed forces. For several years, from 1945 to approximately 1950, the politicians kept their promise. Even Franz Josef Strauss, later chief of the right-wing Christian Social Union (CSU), exclaimed at the time, "May my arm be cut off if it ever again raises a rifle."[1] (In the early 1960s Strauss became minister of defense, without anatomical loss.) For a time the country maintained a strong aversion to all things military. The West German Constitution or "Basic Law," adopted in 1949, specifically authorized the right of conscientious objection even before a new army had been created.

As the Cold War intensified in the early 1950s, however, initial hopes for a pacified West Germany crumbled. With the German economic recovery well under way (amply aided by U.S. capital), the bitter memories of a few years earlier faded. Plans for rearmament began to appear, often at the behest of the United States. Within the Federal Republic itself, the initial revulsion to rearmament also began to diminish. By the mid-1950s, only the Social Democratic Party and a few others continued to oppose a German army.[2] The majority, represented in the governing coalition of the Christian Democratic Union, CDU, and the CSU, strongly advocated a new army and reintroduction of the draft. As the inevitability of rearmament became clear, the opposition launched a campaign known as "Ohne Mich": "Without Me," or "Count Me Out." Even this opposition soon faded. The new West German army, the Bundeswehr, was officially founded in 1956 without major incident.

While the Social Democrats ultimately acceded to rearmament, they exacted a series of reforms designed to make this new army more democratic. The concept of the "citizen in uniform" was proclaimed, to replace the traditional model of the fanatically obedient, unquestioning warrior. The previously self-contained German military was to be reformed. Conscientious objector procedures were established. The old military justice system was abolished. (The military command may only impose minor summary punishments, with a maximum of twenty-one days' detention. All major offenses, including such strictly military ones as desertion, must be tried in regular civilian courts.)

A system of elected soldier representatives was also introduced into the Bundeswehr.[3] In each company or small unit, conscripts were permitted to elect one of their own as vertrauensmann (literally translated, "one who can be trusted") to represent the interests of the conscripts in consultation with the command. (This institution was first employed during the Weimar Republic in the early 1920s, at a time of similar reaction to militarism and to right-wing coup attempts by early Reichswehr generals in 1919 and 1920. Significantly, this democratic innovation was abolished by Hitler in 1935.) The Social Democrats and other left-wing critics hoped that these democratic reforms would hold the armed forces accountable to society and prevent military despotism.

Given the earlier widespread opposition to rearmament and the draft, one might have expected that the new German Bundeswehr would soon experience considerable internal dissent. In fact, however, no such opposition appeared. What remained of the antimilitary movement focused on opposition to nuclear weapons, sponsoring huge annual "Easter marches." The civilian protesters devoted little attention to the constantly growing Bundeswehr. Where masses of citizens had a few years before shouted "Ohne Mich," young workers now quietly submitted to the draft and dutifully followed orders. Despite the easy availability of conscientious objection, the level of pacifist refusal remained at manageably low levels. The twelve-year period from 1956 to 1968 saw little resistance to the Bundeswehr, in or out of the ranks.

Youth Objects

In 1968 this situation began to change dramatically. Suddenly the level of pacifism and conscientious objection in Germany began to rise sharply. The nation of Hitler and Kaiser Wilhelm gave birth to the largest youth pacifist movement in the world. Within the ranks, German conscripts showed signs of a decisive break with the past. Soldier committees and newspapers began to emerge, and petitions and protest actions appeared. These changes occurred not in response to any shift in military conditions (the same military policies applied as before) but as part of a general rise in youth antimilitarism and political activism in West Germany. As in the other highly capitalized countries, a fundamental change occurred in the behavior of youth toward the military. Whereas in the United States this change initially took the form of desertion and draft resistance, and in Holland a conscript's union, in West Germany it first led to mass conscientious objection.

Beginning in 1968 the rate of conscientious objection skyrocketed, rising to 35,000 in the early 1970s, to 69,000 in 1977, and then to 77,000 in 1988. (See Table 9.1.) For a time this rising tide of conscientious objection threatened to engulf the army. In 1977 a new law, long promised by the Social Democratic government, further liberalized application procedures, leading to a brief pacifist stampede. This law allowed potential draftees to obtain alternative civilian service (eighteen months instead of the military's fifteen) "on simple demand." It eliminated the requirement to pass "conscience" examinations, which are easy for middle- and upper-class youths but often intimidating for the less educated. For a time conscientious objector applications soared and (together with medical deferments) began

Table 9.1
Conscientious Objection in the Bundeswehr

Year[4]	Total Number of Applications	Total Number of Recognitions
1967	5,963	4,739
1968	11,952	5,588
1969	14,420	7,500
1970	19,363	9,521
1971	27,657	11,033
1972	33,792	13,132
1973	35,129	16,649
1974	34,150	18,621
1975	32,565	18,496
1976	40,618	(unavailable)
1977	69,959	18,475
1978	39,720	17,525
1979	45,515	22,300
1980	54,315	30,250
1981	58,090	33,000
1982	59,776	32,574
1983	68,334	22,148
1984	43,875	23,929
1985	53,907	37,146
1986	58,964	43,390
1987	63,073	42,635
1988	77,044	57,793

to threaten the ability of draft boards to deliver the more than 200,000 conscripts required annually by the Bundeswehr. At this point the German Supreme Court, acting on a request of the opposition CDU party, first suspended and then overturned the "objection on demand" law as unconstitutional. Although conscientious objector procedures remained easier than before, the applicant could no longer receive automatic deferment.

For a time objector applications declined to more "normal" levels, but the steady rise in pacifism continued into the 1980s. In 1988 C.O. applications and acceptances reached an all-time high.

As a whole, conscientious objectors are far more numerous in West Germany than in any other country. Although many objectors are individualists who eschew organized resistance, others have helped create one of the largest antimilitarist groups in the world: Deutsche Friedens Gesellschaft-Verein der Kriegsdienstgegner (DFG-VK), the German Peace Society-Association of War Resisters, a fusion of several older antiwar organizations. With over 25,000 members, more than all of the early New Left groups in Germany combined, the DFG-VK has spread pacifism far beyond its usual university confines. In many small towns and villages, DFG-VK groups have channeled the diffuse antimilitarist sentiment of young Germans into organized activity. In some locations they have also aided not only German but foreign (U.S., French, and Belgian) soldiers stationed in nearby barracks.

The vast majority of West Germany's conscientious objectors operate "within the system," applying for C.O. status and accepting alternative service. However, there is a small group of "total objectors," young men who feel that any cooperation with the draft law is an unacceptable compromise, and some who simply refuse to participate in the bureaucratic paper-chase required to obtain legal C.O. status. These objectors are occasionally imprisoned "to make an example."

Tolstoy's Teaching

Near the end of his life the great Russian author and religious pacifist Leo Tolstoy penned his famous "Notes For Soldiers," urging young men to refuse military service:

If you indeed desire to act according to God's will you have only to ... throw off the shameful and ungodly calling of a soldier.

Tolstoy's exhortations have since become the rallying cry of pacifists the world over: If youths would simply refuse to serve, wars and militarism could end. Tolstoy might have been very pleased by the example of modern Germany, where pacifism is widely pursued as a means of preventing war.[5]

While one might sympathize with Tolstoy's sentiments, his ideal has never been realized in practice. Indeed, one could argue from the opposite viewpoint, that pacifist objection actually weakens military resistance and reinforces command control over the army. It is the opinion of some, for example, that conscientious objection in Germany has had a negative impact on soldier organizing, screening from military service precisely those draftees most likely to resist. The more educated and middle-class sectors of the youth population, the "intellectuals" most able to articulate opposition to war and violence, are channeled into alternative service, while the poorer and less-educated classes serve. Thus conscientious objection can be considered the least disruptive form of antimilitarism. It allows the individual objector, usually middle class, to keep his conscience (if not his hands) clean, while the system of violence against which he objects continues to function undisturbed. This was the view adopted by the draftee radicals of Holland in the late 1960s, especially those of the BVD. They decided to give up the pursuit of conscientious objection and chose instead to enter the army and organize within. Conscientious objection during a period of rising soldier resistance merely serves as a safety valve for the command, diverting from military service those people most likely to support democratic movements within the ranks.

It would be unfair to Count Tolstoy, however, not to mention some recent historical circumstances where his ideal came close to realization. One occasion, the most striking, occurred in the United States during the Vietnam War. Draft refusals and conscientious objector applications reached such mass proportions by the late 1960s that the Selective Service System had to be first changed and then abandoned. By 1972, for example, there were actually more conscientious objector applications than inductions.[6] This resistance clearly played a major role in the U.S. withdrawal from Vietnam. The other occasion of mass refusal was the previously noted flood of conscientious objectors in Germany in late 1977. Our two examples show that Tolstoy's ideal is theoretically possible but difficult to achieve in practice. In the U.S. situation, draft refusal did, in fact, help to cripple the war effort. In Germany, however, when mass legal objection began to reach menacing proportions, the state simply changed the rules of the game and slammed the flood gates shut.

The "Citizen in Uniform" Stirs

The traditional image of the German soldier is of the unquestioning storm trooper fighting tenaciously to the last. He may grumble over the hardships of military life, but his sense of discipline remains absolute. Even during the latter phases of World War II, with Nazism facing certain defeat, the vast majority of German soldiers continued to show unparalleled loyalty and devotion to duty. The plots against Hitler, the only organized opposition within the ranks, were all the work of high-level officers. The soldiers did not take independent action.

In recent years this has begun to change. Although German soldiers have not displayed the mass opposition evident in Holland or France, organized protest has emerged within the ranks. After 1968, at approximately the same time that conscientious objection began to rise, active-duty soldiers started to speak out and organize committees. From its inception the Bundeswehr had granted the soldier many theoretical rights, but it was not until the late 1960s that these rights were exercised.

As in other countries, the soldiers' movement in Germany has been characterized by ad hoc soldier committees and underground newspapers. Local groups come and go, but the total number of committees, approximately 25, has remained fairly constant since the early 1970s. Focusing on a wide range of issues, from poor conditions and low pay to criticism of NATO missile policy, the soldier newspapers circulating within the Bundeswehr are remarkably similar to soldier journals in other lands. This peacetime leftist soldiers' movement, small though it may be, is unprecedented in German history.

The first group to support soldier resistance was the official (pro-Soviet) German Communist Party, DKP (Deutsche Kommunistische Partei) not to be confused with the KPD or other so-called "K" groups, which were New Left and sometimes "Maoist." The DKP is one of the few "official" communist parties willing to endorse military organizing. In 1970, the youth movement of the DKP, Sozialistische Deutsche Arbeiter Jugend (SDAJ), Socialist German Workers' Youth, began to establish soldier committees known as ADS (Arbeitsgruppen Demokratischer Soldaten, or Working Groups of Democratic Soldiers). The SDAJ also published a national soldiers' newspaper, *Links Um*, "Left Face," produced every three months to coincide with each draft call.*

In their local work, the ADS committees have adopted a narrow trade union program, concentrating on improved canteen (or snack bar) services and better pay. (After receiving 165 marks per month for years--a mere $80--conscripts finally won a munificent raise in 1978 of one mark per day,

---

* The title of this newspaper was the same as that of many GI papers in other countries, but the cheesecake nudity plastered on the cover of each issue was very atypical. With one (Austrian) exception, none of the hundreds of issues of other independent GI papers we have seen employ this sexist device. Indeed, some Allied soldiers in West Germany have actually refused to distribute *Links Um* for this reason. As one American GI remarked, "It can't be worth much if they have to put that on it to get it read."

raising them to slightly below $100 per month. Their unionized Dutch colleagues at the time received over $350 per month.) ADS groups have also addressed more political issues such as the role of the Bundeswehr within NATO, but their primary emphasis has been on improving the conditions of service.

Although ADS groups have on occasion attracted hundreds of soldiers to May Day parades and other protest activities, their "straight" demeanor and the encumbrance of their political affiliation (anticommunism remains strong in West Germany) have limited their appeal. In recent years the DKP seems to have deemphasized its work in the army, and ADS groups have lost support in the barracks.

The decline of the ADS groups did not mean the end of the German soldiers' movement. By 1975 a new type of independent soldier organizing began to grow, concentrated in groups known as AMAK (Antimilitarist Working Groups) or Soldaten Kommittees. Often formed through the initiative of soldiers and recent veterans, these less sectarian committees usually attracted considerable support within the barracks, particularly in Southern Germany (where the ADS groups have always been weak). In fall 1976, these groups came together for the first time in a national soldiers' movement conference. Held in Stuttgart in November, the gathering attracted almost a hundred representatives from sixteen separate soldier committees. Also attending were American GIs stationed with the U.S. army in Germany, and representatives from soldier committees in the Netherlands, Italy, France, Switzerland, and Austria.

A Case Study

The West German AMAKs developed more spontaneously than the communist-inspired ADS groups. The impetus behind these committees and the dynamics of their operation can perhaps best be illustrated in the experiences of Berndt Plagemann, who was drafted into the Bundeswehr in 1974 and helped found a soldiers' committee in his unit in Southern Germany while serving as a panzergrenadiere.[7] Plagemann's political career began one day when he decided to object to the "voluntary" contribution for the maintenance of German war graves (the contribution is in fact made obligatory by command pressures: "Anyone who wants a weekend pass will volunteer"). For many years soldiers had grudgingly complied with this voluntary/obligatory payment for the upkeep of Nazi graves. Plagemann not only challenged the requirement publicly, while standing in formation, but also wanted to explain to his fellow soldiers why they should join him in refusing to pay for Nazi war graves. To the astonishment and shock of his commanders, Plagemann received very widespread support from the (until then) silently contributing GIs in his unit. (Plagemann's wide popularity and the broad support for his actions probably explain how he managed to stay out of jail.) Out of this rather elementary company-based action soon grew an active soldiers' committee that continued to flourish even after Plagemann completed his fifteen-month tour of duty in 1975.

By November 1974 the soldier committee in Plagemann's unit had grown to the point where it was in touch with soldier groups in other lands and heard about an international soldiers' conference being held in Amsterdam. The committee was interested in finding out about the soldiers' congress sponsored by the Dutch conscripts and decided to send Plagemann as a delegate. Plagemann attended semiclandestinely, claiming to his commanders that he was sick on leave, while in fact using the extra day for the journey to and from Amsterdam. Like his U.S. counterpart, Specialist Tom Doran (see Chapter 3), Plagemann was greatly impressed by the Amsterdam congress--by the strength of the Dutch soldiers' movement and the pervasiveness of soldier resistance throughout the armies of Europe. He returned to his unit and the local committee with a renewed sense of commitment and continued to organize in his last months of service and for several years afterward.

After his discharge, Plagemann maintained communication with his old unit and made contact with soldiers and recent veterans from other bases. For several years Plagemann functioned as a kind of informal coordinator for the AMAKs of southern Germany. Thanks in part to his work, a thin but effective network of soldiers' committees was established throughout the region.

In recent years leftist splinter groups have tried to take over the AMAK committees. While the AMAKs are clearly left in political orientation, they usually object to the leadership pretensions of these outside groups. Having come together to throw off the yoke of command authority, the soldier activists do not take kindly to new authorities, no matter now benevolent or "left." While the sectarian groups have been able to establish a few committees, their influence within the ranks has been rather limited. During the 1970s and 1980s the nonauthoritarian, self-initiated AMAK committees remained the most effective and dominant form of soldier organizing in the Federal Republic.

Imperial Storm Clouds

While the young people of Germany have thrown off the legacy of the past, some of their elders seem less clear. Strong historical forces seem to be casting Germany once again in an imperial role. German industry and finance now dominate much of Europe and play a vital role throughout the world. Within NATO, the Federal Republic took the lead in urging deployment of the controversial Cruise and Pershing II missiles.

West German interests have also grown beyond the Continent. In the name of combating terrorism, German security forces have struck within Africa (in Mogadiscu in 1977) and are stationed at airports in several countries. In Zaire, an area of over 100,000 square kilometers has been "leased" from the Mobutu government for "rocket experiments." Peaceful, of course. According to veteran journalist Tad Szulc, these experiments include the development of cruise missiles.[8] In South Africa, West German scientists worked closely with the state firm SASOL-II to develop advanced nuclear processing technology. In Iraq, German firms aided Saddam Hussein's development of chemical weapons.

Of course, even the slightest hint that the Federal Republic has militarist designs is vehemently rejected by German authorities. The official position remains that the Bundeswehr serves only defensive purposes and will not assume an external role. Nonetheless, the German armed forces have become very powerful. Prior to German unification active-duty force levels in the Bundeswehr stood at approximately 495,000--just below the legally authorized ceiling of half a million--and the entire "mobilization base" (including reservists who could be quickly mobilized in an emergency) was 1.2 million. In 1990, as part of the political arrangements for gaining approval of German unification, it was agreed that the size of the Bundeswehr would be reduced to below 400,000. Nonetheless, the German armed forces have the capability of playing a dominant role in European and international affairs.

The growing external role of the West German state has been accompanied by bouts of repression and political conformism at home. Again, this runs counter to the official image, so often extolled by the nation's leaders, of Germany as a bulwark of liberal democracy. It was the Social Democratic government of Willy Brandt, perhaps the most liberal in the post-war era, that first introduced the so-called "Radicals' Decree" and its major provision, the "Berufsverbot." Under this measure anyone considered a radical or political extremist is barred from federal, state, or local government employment. This is a very broad and sweeping dragnet, for it limits access to a huge category of employment, including all government service and public teaching positions as well as nationalized industries such as transportation. Governments are authorized to set up courts of inquisition, with authority to judge a citizen's views and rule on his or her employment prospects.

Although the Berufsverbot is supposedly designed to purge radicals of both left and right, it has been aimed primarily at communists and other leftists. Hundreds of thousands of German citizens, in particular recent university graduates, have been investigated under this system to determine if they have signed petitions or attended demonstrations sponsored by groups considered unfriendly to the state. In the 1980s the West German parliament, the Bundestag, considered and passed a sweeping measure under which any citizen attending a rally where violence occurred could be considered responsible for that violence, regardless of who started it.

History does not repeat itself in identical form. State authoritarianism in Germany today is not accompanied by brown shirts and the goose-step but by an atmosphere of moderation and legalism. It occurs in a period of affluent consumerism rather than mass austerity. Political controls are more subtle but not less efficient. Racism and crude anticommunism are replaced by an all-encompassing "antiterrorist" ideology. The modern state is thus more ambiguous than its predecessor: The machinery of repression is cloaked behind a veneer of tolerance and formal democracy. Novelist Heinrich Böll evoked the image of modern Germany aptly in the novel (later made into a film) *Katerina Blum*: An aggressive police apparatus hounds the citizen as pious officials intone paeans to the liberal democratic order.

Unionism in the Bundeswehr

So far we have examined two contradictory trends in German military affairs: the rise of pacifism and antimilitarism among youth, and the growth of state and military power. Into this complex web we now add a third factor, the prospect of soldier unionization.[9]

So far unionism in the Bundeswehr has been a relatively innocuous affair. Indeed genuine soldier unionism has so far failed to materialize. Two major organizations are now active in the Bundeswehr: the Armed Forces Association (the Bundeswehr Verband) and the Union of Public, Transport and Communications Workers (OeTV). The Bundeswehr Verband is the largest and most powerful military association in the world, with over 190,000 members. It is right-wing and promilitary in political outlook. The Verband organizes over 70 percent of the Bundeswehr's permanent officers ("Berufssoldaten"*) and contract soldiers ("Zeitsoldaten"†).

---

* Berufssoldaten are professional "soldiers," permanent officers and career cadre, who make up the leadership of the military. They are considered lifetime civil servants. Politically they fit within the mold of the traditional German officer corps--right wing.

† Zeitsoldaten are contract "soldiers" who serve volunteer enlistments ranging from a minimum of two to four years up to fifteen years. These contract soldiers, usually lower-level officers and non-commissioned officers, have grown in proportion to

The Verband also claims to have 20,000 conscript members, who serve only fifteen months and are drawn primarily from the working classes.

The OeTV is Germany's second largest union, with approximately 1 million members. Two thousand of these members are active-duty soldiers, mostly "Zeitsoldaten": sergeants and junior officers. Although OeTV has not yet done so, some officials within the union have suggested that it accept conscripts as members. This could have an important effect on the inner workings of the Bundeswehr, as we shall discuss below.

The Bundeswehr Verband: The Army's Partner

When we first visited the Verband headquarters in 1976, we were startled by the polished modern surroundings and precise business-like manner of its staff--vastly different from the relaxed environment of soldier committee offices.[10] Our official briefing featured a multimedia slide show presentation that reverberated with military music and bombast. We were shocked, for we had hardly expected to be regaled with marching music. The Verband's chair, Colonel Heinz Volland, greeted us in a clipped military fashion, answering our questions by the number. It reminded us of a command briefing. The ambience was warm and cordial, but the atmosphere was decidedly Prussian. We arrived in search of a soldiers' union and found instead an association of military careerists.

Bundeswehr Verband officials accurately refer to their organization as an association, not a union. It can best be compared to a giant-sized Association of the United States Army, the AUSA. The Verband was formed in July 1956, within weeks of the formal establishment of the Bundeswehr, and its development has closely paralleled that of the armed forces. It grew steadily during the 1960s, as the Bundeswehr itself expanded, and today stands as a powerful and massive organization with extensive services and benefits for its members and close ties with top military officials.

The Verband has no formal relations with the labor movement and has few of the union perspectives of the professional military organizations elsewhere in Europe. Nonetheless, it exerts considerable influence over military pay and conditions. The Verband has no collective bargaining authority, but it is accorded formal consultative status: no changes in the terms of military service can be instituted without the Verband's participation. Association officials meet regularly with high government and Defense Ministry officials and are generally able to ensure that their

the rest of the Bundeswehr in recent years. Ideologically they are more diverse, displaying loyalty to the armed forces as a profession but often viewing the military as merely an occupation and a stepping stone to later employment.

opinions are well represented in policy formulation. The Verband is in many ways a giant partner in the management of the armed forces.

While the Verband is not directly linked to other unions, it has maintained friendly relations with the 125,000-member police union, the Gewerkschaft der Polizei (GdP), and with the Deutsche Angestellten Gesellschaft (DAG), the German Employees Society, an independent conservative organization with approximately 500,000 members. In 1976-1977, some elements of the Bundeswehr Verband attempted to form a coalition with these groups, hoping to spearhead a drive to build a right-wing alternative to the established labor federation, the Deutscher Gewerkschafts Bund (DGB), the equivalent of the AFL-CIO. These projects received a setback in the spring of 1978, however, when the police union, GdP, abandoned its previous independent position and became the seventeenth affiliate of the DGB. The police union's affiliation with the DGB, rather than with a more conservative coalition, shows that the growing militancy of public service employees has spread even to that traditional bulwark of "law and order," the German police. The Verband's hopes for leadership in a national right-wing labor coalition were derailed, at least momentarily.

The Draftees' Sweetheart

While the Verband is seeking to widen its role horizontally within society, it is also trying to expand its influence vertically down into the draftee ranks of the military. Its claimed membership among conscripts has increased from 10,000 to 20,000, and the association seems quite serious about gaining others. As if to confirm these intentions, the Verband has designated one of its sixteen national board positions for a conscript, thus giving draftees formal representation within the organization.

The Verband's attempts to organize conscripts are fraught with contradictions, however. As we have emphasized in Chapter 3 and elsewhere, a sweetheart union among rank-and-file soldiers simply will not fly. In order to attract draftee support, the association will have to show militancy, but such activities are incompatible with its conservative nature. The duality runs deep: The organization has been predicated until now on a harmonious, almost unitary relationship with the military command, but organizing among conscripts will inevitably cause conflict with that command. This dilemma poses very serious obstacles for the association and is likely to complicate its attempts to gain a large conscript following.

For their part, most German conscripts dismiss the Verband as a tool of the command and ignore its appeals for membership. When we suggested to conscripts of a soldiers' committee in Mannheim that the Verband might unionize draftees, they scoffed at us. Their attitude was similar to that of

U.S. GIs when the possibility of using AUSA as a vehicle for presenting GI demands was discussed in the early 1970s: "No way!"

A conscripts' congress organized by the Verband in 1976 illustrates the association's almost comic attempts to control draftees.[11] The meeting was held in the headquarters of the CDU, the Konrad Adenauer House in Bonn (appropriately named for the prime minister who presided over West Germany's rearmament). The Congress was not the usual raucous gathering characteristic of soldier conferences elsewhere, nor did it resemble the regional conferences of German soldier committees we have attended. Rather, it was an orderly, disciplined affair, administered and controlled from above. This supposed conscripts' congress was entirely run by high-ranking officers and NCOs and led by none other than Colonel Volland. The conscript participants displayed little enthusiasm for the proceedings. Half of them came in uniform, not because they wanted to but because they had been ordered to do so by their commanders.

Interestingly, the Verband had invited representatives of the Dutch conscripts' union, VVDM, to attend as observers. Two of the world's largest military associations, one far to the right, the other left-wing, thus met face to face. The Dutch conscript leaders found the Verband's orderly meeting curious and unreal, a far cry from their own free-wheeling congresses. The main topic of discussion, according to the VVDM observers, was how to make the Bundeswehr more popular among German youth. The real problems and grievances of draftees were hardly mentioned. The VVDM participants noted that most of the German conscripts with whom they spoke considered the meeting a joke and thought the whole affair a waste of time. For their part, the VVDM observers brought a condensed history of their union, filled with description of militant mass action, which they distributed to the conscripts in attendance (no doubt to the chagrin of the officers in charge).

A comic postscript to the conference was the Verband's clumsy attempts to manipulate the Dutch conscripts as well. Before leaving the congress, the Dutch representatives had invited the principal German draftee spokesman, Gunther Fischbach, and his two assistants to attend the next VVDM assembly in Holland. When the Dutch invitation came to the attention of the Verband headquarters, Colonel Volland sent a letter saying that some of the conscripts might be able to attend, but that a high-ranking NCO from the Verband would also come along. Outraged at this interference in their communications with fellow soldiers, VVDM fired off a heated reply saying that they had not invited any officers and that this was not the way things were done in Holland. The Verband apologized for its gaffe, but in the end the three German conscripts found themselves on weekend duty at the time of the assembly and were unable to attend.

In fall 1977, the Dutch VVDM again was invited to attend the Verband's annual conscripts' conference, but, their sense of humor exhausted, the VVDM's leadership did not send any delegates. One of the authors attended, though, and found little changed from the previous year. When the outgoing ex-Private Fischbach ran over his thirty-minute time limit, he was sharply reprimanded by the senior NCO chairing the plenary sessions. All of the panel meetings were directed and chaired by high-ranking military officers.

The panel discussion concerning the liberalized conscientious objector law then in effect was particularly revealing. Interestingly, the conscript "delegates", who had been picked by local Verband leaders, NCOs, and officers, to "represent" other conscripts at the conference, were initially in favor of the "objector on demand" law. But the fregattenkapitaen chairing the panel, after politely listening to some opposing views, soon steered the discussion into more desired directions. As each soldier spoke, the officer interceded with counterinformation and, when the occasion demanded, with authoritative-sounding lies. (A draftee: "But, under the old law, some people were imprisoned for conscientious objection." The officer: "No, that is false, no one was jailed . . ." As a matter of fact, there were still unrecognized conscientious objectors in jail at the time of this discussion.) This technique prevented the few draftees who felt any real interest in the matter from pushing their arguments. In the end, a resolution opposing the "objector on demand" law as "unfair" to serving draftees was passed (by assent; no vote was taken) and forwarded to the plenary session.

OeTV: The Feeble Giant

While the Verband has enjoyed close relationships with the military hierarchy and has flourished over the decades, OeTV has encountered stiff opposition in its attempts to organize within the Bundeswehr. The military leadership has been openly hostile to this labor movement initiative, and they have placed numerous roadblocks in its path. The legacy of antagonism between the General Staff and social democracy is plainly evident in the persistent difficulties faced by OeTV's military organizing efforts.[12]

According to Article IX of Germany's Basic Law, the right to form labor organizations is absolute. No distinction is made between civilians and soldiers, or between careerists and draftees. When the new German army began to take shape in the early 1960s, OeTV decided to test this principle by proposing to organize soldiers. OeTV already represented nearly 60,000 civilian employees of the German army (plus 15,000 German civilians employed by the U.S. military), and the union saw itself as the natural vehicle for organizing soldiers. In 1964 the union began its long and arduous struggle to gain a foothold in the military. The union's first bid to organize ran into a stone wall, when then-Defense Minister Von Hassel barred OeTV from the barracks. The minister argued that servicemen were already adequately represented by the Verband (an interesting commentary on the association's cozy relationship with the government).

When the Social Democrats entered the government coalition in 1966, OeTV received its first legal recognition, but its organizing abilities were still severely restricted. After lengthy court battles and the resignation of several leading generals, OeTV finally won the right to operate within the Bundeswehr in 1971. The final agreement was arranged in November of that year by then-Defense Minister Helmut Schmidt. These arrangements supposedly placed OeTV on an equal footing with the Verband, but the actual experience of the two organizations leaves OeTV at a decided disadvantage. While the union must attempt to organize without any cooperation from the command, the Verband is allowed to meet on post. The Verband can also use the military postal system and regularly receives unit rosters from commanders.

Partly because of the restrictions it faces, OeTV's organizing efforts within the ranks have had a very paltry result. Incredibly, this towering force within the DGB, a union of more than 1 million members, has been able to garner only 2,000 military members after two decades of organizing. As noted, this weakness is largely due to the command's favoritism toward the Bundeswehr Verband. Another important factor, though, in our view, has been the union's unwillingness to organize among conscripts.

The OeTV leadership has adamantly refused to organize draftees, arguing that conscripts are not "employees" and are therefore outside the national wage system (which covers only the career soldiers, Berufs- and Zeitsoldaten). The union also claims, stretching credulity, that draftees are already represented by their previous DGB unions. This refers to an existing arrangement under which draftees who are union members prior to entering the service (approximately 50,000 out of a total of 200,000 or more conscripts) are encouraged to maintain membership in their previous union and channel complaints back to their local organizations. Such an approach divides draftee complaints among numerous civilian unions, none of which is equipped to handle military problems. Indeed, the entire system is a paper arrangement with little real substance. Despite OeTV's claims, conscripts are without any effective union representation.

OeTV's refusal to organize draftees, apart from leaving conscripts in the lurch, is a formula for certain failure. The union has cut itself off from its natural working-class base in the lower ranks while attempting to compete with the favored Verband among careerists who are essentially opposed to the labor movement. As with AFGE's preference for "career types," OeTV's recruitment efforts have aimed at the wrong audience. That OeTV has had little success in this venture should come as no surprise.

Unions and Democracy

If OeTV's horizons are so limited, why did it attempt to unionize the military in the first place? Partly the move was based on the usual bureaucratic impulses that propel any large union toward unorganized sectors of the work force: more members and more dues. But the OeTV effort was also prompted by loftier motives and was part of a larger political design. Some elements of the SPD and OeTV leadership have supported military organizing as a means of countering CDU and right-wing proclivities within the military hierarchy, as a means of gaining greater Social Democratic influence within the armed forces. It is not without coincidence that the Social Democrats' 1966 ascent to power marked the beginnings of OeTV's organizing in the Bundeswehr. Union organizing is seen as a means of assuring democratic strivings within the armed forces.

This theme was cogently articulated for us in a 1976 interview with one of OeTV's principal military activists, Master Sergeant Heinrich Linden, a lucid, engaging army careerist who was at the heart of OeTV's military organizing program for over ten years. We met Linden in a working-class tavern of Koblenz and found him to be an eloquent and passionate advocate of democratic rights for soldiers.[13] He spoke openly of the Hitler era and the dangers of resurgent militarism. Linden's point was simple but convincing: If the armed forces are to remain under democratic control, they must have democratic guarantees in their day-to-day operation. Union organizing can assure such guarantees and prevent the armed forces from becoming a state within a state. As Linden phrased it, "an army that does not practice democracy is a threat to democracy."

10

Eastern Europe and the USSR

In the late 1970s several colleagues familiar with our work objected to the Threshold Theory because it suggested the possibility of similar developments in the socialist countries. If capital accumulation is the motor element in opening the door to rank-and-file resistance, they asked, where were such movements in the industrialized countries of the East? The East European countries possess relatively large "mass" conscript armies, and their economies have become highly capitalized, so where was the GI resistance phenomenon hypothesized by our theory? The question also suggested another. Could the predictive value of our initial observations be extended into the future in relation to the "REXSO" (real existing socialism) countries?

Before looking at these countries, two qualifications must be considered. The first concerns the manipulation of economic data, which makes a strict application of the GNP/capita ranking unsuitable. Not only was preglasnost falsification of income data common, but the official exchange rates often bore little relation to real currency values. The Soviet Union, for example, is certainly less affluent than Italy, although they are ranked next to each other on the GNP/capita chart. A more realistic assessment would place the REXSO countries lower than official figures suggest. However, even with such an adjustment, we must recognize that a considerable degree of capital accumulation has occurred since 1945, and that, as in the capitalist countries, this has modified daily life and consciousness.

A further problem in our initial study was that until the advent of perestroika, information about East European armies was extremely difficult to obtain. Independent printing or the publication of GI underground newspapers were practically impossible under the previous system. What we did learn about soldier behavior in the East was almost always based on scattered personal observations, anecdotes, and interviews. Soldier attitudes seemed to be changing along lines similar to what we had observed in the West, but hard evidence was lacking.

The Other Germans

According to our hypothesis changes in soldier behavior would be most likely to appear, and soonest, in that most highly capitalized of the Eastern countries, the GDR, German Democratic Republic. In 1968, though, not only Soviet but also GDR troops, together with Polish, Hungarian, and token Bulgarian units moved into Czechoslovakia and crushed the "Prague Spring" of reform communism led by Alexander Dubcek. Although individual students in the GDR protested against the "invasion" and attempted to recall the thirtieth anniversary of Hitler's annexation of the Czech "Sudetenland" in fall 1938, we have found no evidence of any resistance or even indiscipline among GDR troops during that grim episode. The soldiers of the pre-T Nationale Volks Armee, NVA, of East Germany obeyed their orders. As Czech resister friends in Paris observed: "The GDR soldiers? They were Germans, all right, but no democrats."[1]

Eight year later, by the mid 1970s, things were beginning to change. Here is what one U.S. GI wrote about East German troops from his vantage point at "OP Alpha," a huge tower overlooking the "Iron Curtain". It comes from the second issue of *Squadron Scandal*, a short-lived U.S. GI paper published by the Fulda Soldiers' Committee in 1976:

My first experience of seeing our "mortal enemies," the communists, was a complete surprise . . . I expected the East German soldiers to look like shaved-headed robots. What did my eyes behold? Soldiers with long hair and mutton chop sideburns, many not even wearing their head gear . . . One time last winter Pvt. George Kawiki was looking through his binoculars and spotted a group of East German soldiers standing suspicously in the wood line. On closer observation he noticed they were indulging in our favorite pastime, blowing a bowl [of hash]! As they passed it along to each other, they noticed they were being watched by their "mortal enemy." They then proceeded to smile and wave.

Other anecdotes suggest similar tendencies. After the often-banned political singer Wolf Biermann was refused permission to return to East Germany in November 1976, soldiers played his music on tape recorders and guitars all over NVA bases. One soldier from Jena went from company to company playing forbidden Biermann songs in the barracks for five months, until he was arrested in April 1977.

The tide of history turned for East Germany, as for most of East Europe in fall 1989. Once the Kremlin signaled it would no longer intervene to prop up its former clients (Soviet spokesman Gennadi Gerasimov dubbed this the "Sinatra Doctrine": Let Eastern Europe do it their way), the prospects for peaceful change and democratic reform dramatically brightened. Long suppressed democratic strivings suddenly burst forth, and the corrupt and repressive dictatorships of the region were quickly swept aside.

The democratic revolution that transformed East German politics also took hold in the army. Individual NVA soldiers participated openly in the massive demonstrations in October and November 1989 that forced the overthrow of the old system. In fact, it was the unwillingness of soldiers and their commanders to use the army to defend the Communist regime that led to the government's rapid demise. In the critical days immediately after October 7, when the GDR's fortieth anniversary celebration (and a visit from Gorbachev) sparked prodemocracy street protests, Communist Party leader Eric Honecker called upon regular army units (as well as the notorious "Stasi," Staatssischerheit, state security police) to suppress the demonstrations. The NVA troops of 1989, however, were not the same as those of 1968. The soldiers wanted democracy and a better way of life just like their civilian counterparts. When the government ordered them to repress the peaceful candlelight marches then beginning in Leipzig, they refused. While the Stasi units were willing to club people in the streets, the army was not. When the government called for troops to go out into the streets with live ammunition, they balked. Instead, many soldiers joined the marchers. For the Honecker regime this was the end. Deprived of Red Army backing and now lacking even the support of his "own" troops, Honicker resigned on October 18, and the system quickly collapsed.

The overthrow of the government did nothing to improve conditions in the NVA, however, and the soldiers soon launched their own democratic reform movement. During the brief existence of the democratic GDR prior to German reunification, an active soldiers movement appeared. The GIs were demanding more free time, fewer training exercises, shorter terms of service, the freedom to wear civilian clothes, and the right to bring their cars on base. Thus as civilian demonstrations declined after November, the conscripts became more active and increasingly militant. Soldier committees began forming throughout the army, and for a brief time strikes and demonstrations became commonplace. Desertion skyrocketed, as many conscripts simply walked off their bases and returned home. Many joined the exodus to the West, and some even applied to join the West German Bundeswehr (jumping the gun, so to speak, on reunification).

One protest incident in the GDR observed by a reporter from the *New York Times* in early 1990 involved the supposedly elite 8th Motorized Rifle Division in Schwerin. When troops of a communications unit were roused at 4 A.M. to go on an exercise, they refused. After negotiating with their commanders for seven hours, the troops finally agreed to move out. Two soldiers were arrested for the incident, but an officer interviewed by the

Times admitted that nothing was likely to happen to those arrested.[2]

With soldier resistance spreading and the NVA rapidly disintegrating, the new reform government in East Berlin was forced to respond. The turning point came after an incident during the Christmas season in the city of Beelitz. A seemingly minor dispute over holiday cheer led to a sudden burst of conscript resistance. When soldiers were denied the champagne they had requested to celebrate the holidays, they simply refused to follow orders any longer and went out into the streets. As word of this strike by local soldiers spread, conscripts all over the country quickly joined in a wave of protest actions and demonstrations. In early January a group of ten conscripts appeared in uniform on primetime television to air their grievances. The next day the Ministry of Defense met with the soldiers and agreed to accept nearly all their demands. The government announced that the term of military service would be reduced from eighteen to twelve months, conscientious objection and alternative civilian service would now be permitted, and the previous barriers between military and civilian life would be reduced. And yes, the soldiers could now even wear civilian clothes and bring their cars and radios on base. As had occurred in many Western European armies fifteen years before, a GI resistance movement had emerged in the GDR and forced major changes in the conditions of service.

Soviets for the Red Army?

In the 1960s it was Vietnam, in the 1980s Afghanistan. As did their American counterparts twenty years before, Soviet soldiers found themselves bogged down in a brutal, seemingly endless guerrilla war. Initially told they were there to defend Afghan socialism against American, Chinese and Pakistani-supported "banditry," Soviet troops soon realized that they themselves were the foreign invaders and oppressors. The more they used their helicopters and modern weapons against rural villages, the more determined the native resistance seemed to become. Atrocities and war crimes were reported, and discipline deteriorated. The heroic Red Army, victorious over fascism in the Great Patriotic War, began for the first time to face internal opposition.

One of the most dramatic manifestations of the internal malaise within the Soviet Army was the prevalence of drug abuse. There is considerable evidence that Soviet soldiers sold arms to the Afghans for hashish, which was then smuggled into Tashkent where mafia-like syndicates distributed it throughout the Soviet Union. Soviet news sources reported soldiers working with gangs in Tashkent to steal televisions, stereos, and other goods, that were then traded for drugs and gold in Afghanistan. One

Afghan vet told *Moscow News* that "all the dukans (shops) were stuffed with goods stolen from Army warehouses, while drugs and gold were hidden in the coffins in which the dead were returned to their native land".[3] (U.S. Vietnam vets reported similar stories of drugs being smuggled into the United States in body bags.) Complaining of harassment by their officers and widespread racism (many of the troops were Central Asian), some Soviet soldiers deserted. A few even fought on the side of the Afghan guerrillas.[4] Returned vets began to organize "informal" groups to criticize the war and complain of their lukewarm welcome by civilians and authorities. Resistance within the ranks became more and more open as the war continued. Of course it would be foolish to say that the Soviet government's decision to withdraw from Afghanistan was due only to this internal resistance, but the spreading disaffection within the ranks undoubtedly played some role. We await the work of Soviet scholars before a definitive judgment can be made.

The Soviet General Staff no doubt hoped and expected that once the war was over, troublesome soldiers and junior officers would forget their restive ways and military life would return to normal. This did not happen in the United States after Vietnam, and it did not happen in the Soviet Union after Afghanistan.

In the United States there was an attempt, widely supported by rank-and-file GIs, to unionize the military (see Chapter 3). The attempt failed, and the very idea of a soldiers' union was outlawed in the U.S. Congress in 1977. Anyone even advocating a union in the U.S. military today could be punished with imprisonment and heavy fines. In the Soviet Union too the idea of a military union was raised after the withdrawal from Afghanistan. In 1989 mid-level and junior officers in Moscow and other cities announced the formation of a union organization called "Shield" (in Russian, "Shchit"), the purpose of which was "the protection of servicemen's rights."[5] The General Staff attacked the unionists as "subversives" and subjected them to constant harassment, but the union was not outlawed. Ironically, in the land of Stalin and the Gulag, a military union could survive, however precariously, while in the supposed land of the free, military unions are completely banned.

The emergence of a politically progressive trade union among Soviet junior officers seems to fit with our Threshold Theory. In our hypotheses in Chapter 1 we posited that the rank at which military resistance movements occur is inversely proportional to the degree of capital accumulation in the country involved. The lower the degree of capital accumulation, the higher the rank at which military resistance is likely to occur. The Soviet position in our GNP/capita chart, based on preglasnost official figures, is 27, right next to Italy. However, when the falsification of income data and inflated currency values are taken into consideration, the actual ranking of the

Soviet Union is considerably lower. Without attempting the hopeless task of computing an exact ranking, we may safely say that the Soviet Union as a whole has a level of capital accumulation below that of most European nations (including the GDR, Czechoslovakia, and Hungary) and probably ranks somewhere between Greece and Portugal. That is, it fits the model of those less highly capitalized countries where military resistance movements would be expected to appear among lower-ranking officers.

The formation of Shield is a manifestation of this tendency and reflects growing discontent within the Soviet military. Social and economic conditions have deteriorated, as they have throughout the Soviet Union. Officers and soldiers returning from Eastern Europe have been forced to billet in tents. Ethnic unrest in the republics has meant that the military must assume the dirty and thankless task of internal repression. Some officers have also criticized how the Ministry of Defense has carried out the reduction in the size of the armed forces resulting from the ending of the cold war. According to Shield representatives, union supporters and other "dissidents" have been singled out for immediate release as part of the force reduction.

All of these factors have produced record low morale and political divisions within the ranks. The general officer corps remains wedded to the old Communist Party system, opposed to democratic reform, and intensely conservative. Mid-level and junior officers demand radical reform with the military (including a volunteer force) and sympathize with nationalist and democratic political tendencies. Among military delegates to the Congress of Peoples Deputies, for example, generals side with conservatives 82 per cent of the time, compared to only 18 per cent with the democratic reform bloc. Among junior officers, the reverse is true: They vote with the democratic bloc 73 per cent of the time.[6] Rumors have circulated in Moscow of preparations for a possible military coup by those discontented with the loss of privilege and the turmoil of perestroika, but doubts exist whether junior officers and the middle ranks would follow such orders. The "reliability" of conscripts has also become questionable.

One of the reformers discharged as part of the first wave of reductions in the Red Army was Colonel Vitaly Urazhtsev. "I was the first officer to be cut" due to the ending of the cold war, joked Urazhtsev. The colonel, a former political commissar at the Defense Ministry, had committed the indiscretion of running in a supposedly free election against the commander of the Moscow military garrison. For this temerity the colonel was promptly discharged, although he carried on his fight for democratic reform as a reservist. Urazhtsev had also served during the tense years of 1980 and 1981 in Poland. Urazhtsev said that he and other officers stationed in Poland at the time were impressed by the "patriotic feelings" of their Polish counterparts, and that this factor helped deter a planned Soviet invasion.[7]

Urazhtsev and other founders of Shield thought they were the first officers ever to form a democratic military organization and were astonished to discover the existence of so many unions in West European armies. Urazhtsev attended the twelfth annual meeting of the European Conference of Conscripts' Organizations, ECCO, in Madrid in 1990 and learned of dozens of conscript organizations in the West. Several Shield members were also invited to meet with officials of the West German Bundeswehr Verband.[8]

While the Bundeswehr Verband enjoys cozy relations with the conservative Bonn government, however, the members of Shield have been denounced by the Soviet General Staff. The official Soviet army newspaper, *Red Star*, has attacked Shield and its activities. Many of the group's leaders have been summarily discharged or punitively transferred, as the following listing from a letter to Moscow's *New Times* in February 1990 indicates:

• Captain Y. I. Danileychenko, chair of Shield's Control Commission, was transferred to a base 200 kilometers away when he was also nominated to the Supreme Soviet.

• Major N. Moskovchenko, co-chair of the Moscow branch, was discharged after filing to run as a candidate for the Supreme Soviet.

• Senior Lieutenant A. T. Ozolins was discharged after being nominated for a position on the Moscow City Council.

Shield has fought back against these harassments with frequent demonstrations and pickets in front of Ministry of Defense buildings. Support for the union has grown to encompass more than one hundred varied organizations, such as mothers of soldiers, associations of sailors and officer groups. By 1990 more than 10,000 servicemen claimed to be members of Shield.[9]

The junior officers who founded Shield talk openly of the need for "new thinking" in the Ministry of Defense.[10] At the union's founding in Moscow in October 1989, Shield chair, now reserve colonel, Vitaly Urazhtsev told more than 100 active and reserve army officers: "The task of the army is to insure a reliable defense of the nation and its territory. The army must not be used against defenseless people." Shield members have warned Gorbachev and central government officials about the possibility of a coup and have vowed to attempt to prevent the use of the military against the Soviet people. The honorary president of Shield is former General Chapochnikov, who distinguished himself in 1962 when he refused orders to attack civilian demonstrators in the city of Novocherkassk. (Other commanders were more pliant, and the workers' strike in that city to protest price increases was violently suppressed.) Reflecting upon that tragedy in late 1989,

Chapochnikov wistfully declared: "If only we had had a union like this then
. . ." [11]

It remains to be seen whether Shield will survive command harassment
and grow into a large-scale union organization. Its fate will depend on the
success of the overall process of democratic reform in the Soviet Union. The
members of Shield recognize this connection and see themselves as carrying
forth the process of renewal inside the military. Shield is primarily
dedicated to bread-and-butter unionism--an improvement in the material
conditions of professional servicemen and their families--but it also pursues
a larger political goal: preventing a military crackdown against perestroika.
Ensuring the success of the democratic reform process in the Soviet Union
is thus closely linked to the future of unionism and democracy within the
ranks.

Conscripts Too?

As noted, Shield is a union primarily for officers. To date there is little
evidence of independent organizing or the formation of soldier committees
among the more than one million conscripts in the Red Army. This should
not surprise us, for as noted above, the Soviet Union is far less highly
capitalized than the other nations where resistance among low-ranking
soldiers has appeared. However, the Soviet Union is a vast country with
huge internal differences in wealth and levels of capital accumulation. A
marked north/south differential exists, with the Baltic republics and European Russia enjoying a much higher standard of living than the Moslem
republics of Central Asia. The following table from *Moscow News* on the
percentage of each republic's population earning less than the official Soviet
poverty level of seventy-five roubles per month gives a rough idea of this
differential in wealth and capital accumulation:

TABLE 10.1
Percentage of Population Earning Less Than The Poverty Level

Republics [12]	Percentage
Latvia	3.2
Lithuania	3.6
Estonia	3.9
Byelorussia	5.0
Russia	6.3
Ukraine	8.1
Moldavia	13.0
Kazakhstan	15.9
Georgia	16.3
Armenia	18.1
Azerbaijan	33.3
Turkmenia	36.6
Kirghizia	37.1
Uzbekistan	44.7
Tajikistan	58.6

Given these sharp regional differences within the Soviet Union, we might expect to find evidence of GI resistance in the Baltic republics and the more highly capitalized areas of the North. However, several factors mitigate against such a development. First is the official Soviet policy of stationing conscripts in regions distant from their homelands. To prevent conscripts from perhaps sympathizing too strongly with local concerns, the Red Army has long sought to assign troops outside their home republics. This practice is increasingly under challenge in the era of perestroika (according to *Red Star*, a group of Azerbaijani conscripts in Siberia threatened to strike in November 1989 if they were not transferred back to their home republic), but the practice remains in effect for most recruits.[13] A more important factor accounting for the lack of GI resistance in the Soviet Army is the widespread avoidance of military service by the sons of the privileged classes. Although military service is theoretically universal, exemptions are available for full-time students and for those who can invoke "reasons of state." In practice this means that the more highly educated youth from better-off urban families can manage to avoid military service.[14]

In part because the more educated and privileged youth of the North can gain exemptions, the burden of conscription falls disproportionately on poor Moslem youth from the South. Recent figures show that conscripts from the Asian republics make up thirty-seven percent of all draftees, although the Moslem share of the overall manpower pool is only twenty-four percent.[15] White youth from the European parts of the Soviet Union can thus avoid military service, while Asian youth from the poorer Moslem republics shoulder a disproportionate share of the military burden. This internal disequilibrium within the ranks is not without its difficulties for the General Staff (exacerbating language differences and problems of inadequate training), but at least it spares commanders some of the tensions that might otherwise arise from dealing with more highly educated and anti-authoritarian recruits.

Despite these limitations, however, draft resistance and internal unrest have increased, especially among recruits from the Baltic republics. Draft resistance in the Soviet Union increased eightfold from 1985 to 1990.[16] In 1989 alone there was a sixfold increase in draft evasion, resulting in a shortfall for the national quota.[17] During the fall 1990 callup, 400,000 young men failed to report.[18] Desertion rates within the ranks have also begun to rise, although they remain below 1 percent.[19]

In the Baltic republics civilian independence movements have sparked opposition within the ranks as well. Organized campaigns against military conscription have been launched in all three republics. In Lithuania, desertions by native conscripts reached massive proportions by 1990 and nearly sparked an armed confrontation between Red Army officials and local independence authorities. Of an estimated 38,000 Lithuanians in the Soviet military, 3,000 had reportedly deserted by March 1990.[20] In Estonia, the official Young Communist League (Komsomol) paper, *Noorte Ha'a'l*, in early 1989 began publishing letters and interviews with active-duty conscripts. For the first time the voice of low-ranking soldiers was heard in official Communist youth journals. (It should be noted that soldier movement campaigns in several West European armies began in similar fashion, with the publication of soldier grievances in the youth journals of political parties, usually the Social Democrats.) The youth journalist who was responsible for publishing the letters in Estonia, Madis Jurgen, was punitively drafted for his courageous and unauthorized venture into military reporting, but he deserted and as of this writing is reportedly in Canada. (History repeats itself?) Despite pressures from the Ministry of Defense, the stories from Estonian soldiers were translated into Russian and widely distributed in other parts of the Soviet Union. Other "soldier stories" have also appeared in the Soviet media, and independent publications are beginning to circulate in the barracks.

As of this writing there is still no hard evidence of autonomous soldier committees or GI newspapers within the Soviet army, but conditions are evolving. In 1989 a nineteen-year-old Soviet conscript, Armen Handkaryan, attended the eleventh conference of ECCO in Helsinki. (Two conscripts from Hungary also attended the conference.) Secretary of the Komsomol in his regiment, Handkaryan told the assembled conscripts from a dozen European countries that perestroika has reduced the Red Army's social isolation and led to greater openness and criticism about the oppressive conditions of military service.[21] (Pay is only seven roubles a month, what the soldiers call "tobacco money," and hazing and harassment of new recruits remains widespread.) Handkaryan also described the system of official "sergeants' councils," similar to the representation systems of Western armies, in which conscript sergeants (senior recruits in their second or third year of service) attempt to represent the interests of low-ranking soldiers in consultation with the command. As conscripts like Handkaryan learn about the efforts of Scandinavian and other soldiers to transform such company union systems into voices of an independent soldiers movement, similar trends may emerge in the East. It may only be a matter of time before Soviet draftees launch their own movement to protect the rights of soldiers, and defend democracy in their country and in the army.

France: Halte à la Misère Sexuelle!

May 1968 is usually seen as the peak of the New Left movement in France. The student revolt and general strike of that month truly shook the foundations of French society. A veritable revolution seemed at hand, and a nonviolent one at that. Only two people died during a thirty-day revolt and general strike that involved over 10 million people.

Much has been written about those momentous events, but very little is known about a similar, perhaps equally important upheaval that erupted six years later in the ranks of the military. In this chapter we recount the story of the French soldiers' movement and its brief flirtation with unionization.[1]

Prior to the mid-1970s, the French conscript faced a miserable and austere existence. His conditions of service were among the worst in Europe. He was expected to perform service to the nation without complaint, and without amenities. Conscript pay (if you can call it that) was a meager seventy francs per month (about fifty cents per day). Weekend passes were almost nonexistent. Civilian clothes were forbidden on base. Overnight passes were rare. Military discipline was strict and severe. When French conscripts toured Dutch army barracks in 1974 (during the soldiers' congress in Amsterdam that year), their Dutch colleagues gasped in disbelief at stories of French army life. No one could believe that such feudal conditions still existed, especially in an affluent, supposedly democratic nation such as France.

After 1974 all of this began to change. Pay was increased, conditions were improved, and reforms were introduced. This resulted not from the spontaneous generosity of the French General Staff but from the political struggle of the soldiers themselves.

Soldier resistance may have appeared late in France, but it swept through the ranks like a prairie fire. For a brief two-year period, France's

280,000 conscripts (out of a total armed forces of 500,000) came alive with protest and political action. Soldier committees were formed, newspapers were published, petitions circulated, and demonstrations held. The clamor became so great that the minister of defense was forced to resign and a new cabinet post of secretary of state for defense was created.

The climax of this upheaval came in November 1975, when soldiers in eastern France at Besançon publicly announced the formation of a soldiers' trade union. The soldiers were supported in this effort by the local branch of the CFDT (Confederation Democratique des Travailleurs), France's second-largest union. This move toward unionization was the last straw for the beleaguered French military establishment. The government responded fiercely, launching a wave of repression and arresting over forty-five soldiers and civilian unionists. These draconian measures dealt a crushing blow to the soldiers' movement, and the wave of mass resistance quickly faded.

The Silent Soldiers of 1968

A major question for students of the May 1968 uprising has been the attitude of the PCF, the French Communist party. That the "PC" had been unable to predict such a major uprising is one thing. Apart from a twenty-one-year-old sociology student leader, Danny Cohn-Bendit, everybody (including that consummate politician, the then-president, General Charles De Gaulle) was completely taken by surprise. But why did the communists so resolutely oppose the revolt, pull out all stops to end the massive strikes, the factory occupations?

In late May 1968 one of the authors participated in a stormy discussion with senior French communists in Villejuif, a "red bastion" south of Paris. The mayor, who could in no way be accused of cowardice (he had "paid his dues" fighting in the International Brigades in Spain and in the French anti-Nazi resistance) was asked: "Don't you want to see socialism come to France?" He answered: "Not at the price of 3 million dead." Who would kill 3 million Frenchmen? "The army."

When this questioner challenged the possibility of French draftees carrying out such a massacre, the communist said: "Well, if our troops won't, then the Americans coming in from Germany will."

The mayor did not know that dozens of U.S. soldiers were already fighting in France, on the side of the Paris students, of the Tours strikers, against the police, the "CRS" (Republican Security Companies, brutal antiriot squads). AWOL GIs, such as Pvt. Dick Perrin and Pfc. Terry Klug from "RITA Act" (Resistance inside the Army), and the Paris "ADC" (American Deserters' Committee), brought many soldiers who were AWOL on weekend passes or on leave from Germany to the "friday night barricade battles." It is highly unlikely that the U.S. 7th Army in Germany, already then racked by growing dissent and resistance to the war in Vietnam, could have been used to reestablish order in France if the 1968 revolt had grown into a revolution. But without communist support or, more precisely, against determined communist opposition, this could not happen. And the communists remained convinced that any revolution would be bloodily crushed by the army.

Their point seemed proved when, at a crucial moment at the end of May, De Gaulle made a sudden, unannounced visit to French army units in Germany. The generals there detested him violently. They considered him a traitor to their ranks for his 1962 "sell-out" to end the war in Algeria.* But faced with a major uprising on the left, they were willing to "forget the past" and unite against the students and strikers. De Gaulle pardoned the imprisoned leaders of the OAS (Organization of the Secret Army), including some generals who had repeatedly attempted to murder him; the French generals in Germany publicly assured him of their support. Little or nothing was heard from the mass of French soldiers, restricted to their barracks. "La grand muette" (the big dumb one) as the French army was long called, had still only one voice, that of its top officers.

Six years later the scenario would have been very different.

From the Appeal of the 100 to the Incident at Draguignan

Theoreticians of the lunatic right, such as Allen de Borchgrave, search for a hidden hand, preferably Moscow's, controlling and coordinating the GI resistance that has appeared in more than a dozen countries during the past twenty years. This cannot help but produce a somewhat fantastic view of the world. In fact, "Moscow" (and most established communist parties) are puzzled and distressed by the uncontrollable, spontaneous nature of GI resistance.

The rise of soldier resistance is caused fundamentally by internal social change. Once the social preconditions exist, once youth have acquired a greater autonomy, independence, and self-confidence, then a relatively small spark may start that mass concentration of young people, the rank-and-file soldiers, thinking, and more importantly, acting for themselves.

---

* Brought to power by a right-wing military coup in May 1958, De Gaulle bitterly disappointed his colonialist, semifascist supporters when, after three more years of bloody, unsuccessful attempts to keep Algeria "French," he accepted the inevitable and began the "Evian negotiations" with the Algerian revolutionaries. These ended the war and 130 years of French colonial dominion in North Africa.

Such sparks are usually lit not by "Moscow" but by the local version of the Pentagon, the military establishment.

Perhaps the best example of this phenomenon was in France, where the draftee army remained quiescent during the 1968 storm but began to move about five years later, at a time when red flags over the factories and the universities were but a distant memory.

The first sign of trouble for the French military appeared in 1973. The immediate cause was the government's abolition of student deferments. Under the new law all young men were forced to serve army duty when they reached draft age, nineteen, not when they completed university studies (or sometimes never for the resourceful). The end of student deferments touched off a wave of youth protests, with hundreds of thousands of students demonstrating in the streets of Paris and other cities.[2] Although most young people and all major political parties continued to support the concept of universal conscription, criticisms of military service and the role of the army became more frequent.

As deferments ended, many of the students who protested military service soon found themselves in the army. Some brought with them a spirit and experience of resistance. They began to organize in the barracks. Outside the army, civilian political activists began to support these efforts. While the established communist and socialist parties remained silent, the far-left Trotskyist Ligue Communiste Revolutionnaire, LCR, recognized the importance of resistance inside the army. Two major support groups were formed: the Committee for the Defense of Conscripts, and the Comite Anti-Militariste.

The sudden death of President Georges Pompidou in early 1974 sparked intensive political debate and activism throughout society, including in the army. During the presidential election campaign, soldiers began to circulate a petition addressed to the major presidential candidates, Valéry Giscard d'Estaing and François Mitterrand. Such petitioning had to be done clandestinely, of course. Called the "Appeal of the One Hundred," L'Appel des Cent, the document demanded a radical overhaul of the terms and conditions of service.[3] The soldiers demanded not only a major pay boost, improved barracks conditions, freedom of speech, and an end to repressive surveillance and military courts; they also cried: "Halte à la Misère Sexuelle!" (Stop the Sexual Misery!) They were, after all, French.* The appeal

---

* This point was often picked out by the media, and sometimes used to ridicule the soldier movement. This incomprehension again illustrates the gulf between civilian life and even a mass army. For the French draftees, particularly the 50,000 then stationed in southwest Germany, sexual misery was and is a very serious matter. However many problems American soldiers in Germany have had, they at least had twenty times more money than the French's $15 a month. German girls,

circulated rapidly within the barracks and was eventually signed by more than 5,000 soldiers.

One of the posts where the appeal found strong support among local soldiers was the small southern garrison town of Draguignan. In the second half of 1974 it became the center of a major national controversy.[4] When copies of the petition fell into the hands of local commanders, soldiers were questioned and harassed and threatened with heavy punishment. This episode at Draguignan came after a long period of mistreatment and racial discrimination (a number of the soldiers were of Antillean descent). The troops responded with drastic action. On September 10, approximately 200 soldiers gathered in uniform at their military post and marched en masse to the local city hall. Among their slogans were "Make Love, Not War" and "No to Racism." They sat down in front of the local government office and demanded to speak with "higher authorities." After about two hours, a colonel finally agreed to come out and speak with them, after which they returned peacefully to their barracks.

The incident was widely reported in the French press. It created an instant political sensation and brought swift repression against those involved. The Military Security Service (a special intelligence branch for the armed forces) conducted a major investigation at Draguignan and identified three so-called "ringleaders": privates Serge Ravel, Robert Pelletier, and Alex Tares. The three were brought before a military court-martial in Marseilles for "incitation to commit acts contrary to duty and discipline", and were faced with the prospect of lengthy prison terms. As the confrontation over the "Draguignan 3" intensified, press attention and controversy grew. The army's heavy-handed methods prompted increasing calls to free the imprisoned soldiers. As the January 1975 trial of the three leaders approached, the eyes of France were focused on the courtroom in Marseilles.

The trial of the "Draguignan 3" became a *cause celebre*.[5] The League for the Defense of the Rights of Man took up the case of the soldiers (the league had been formed seventy years earlier at the trial of another famous victim of military injustice, Captain Alfred Dreyfus). *Le Monde* and other French

---

who were already cool towards "rich" American GIs, would not be seen dead with a French draftee. And when the French soldier who by the 1970s usually had a "permanent" girlfriend before he was drafted finally did get "home leave," he often took the tensions of his horrible barracks life out on his "amie"; French underground GI papers quite seriously discussed the problem of the "third month" (of service) for in this month many soldiers found existing relations with their women friends under great strain, often permanently disrupted. Previous generations of French soldiers had visited the "BMCs" (Military Field Bordels) organized by the army; by the 1970s these no longer corresponded to the tastes and wishes of more enlightened young Frenchmen.

newspapers attacked the army for its bungled handling of the affair. The Socialist Party, the Communist Party, the major unions, all testified in defense of the soldiers. The trial became a farce as the government witness retracted previous statements and publicly announced his support of the defendants. Other soldier witnesses accused the Military Security Service of trying to force false confessions against the soldiers. For their part, the three defendants performed brilliantly, turning the trial around and using the courtroom as a platform for condemning military repression and racism.

In the end the government backed down. Ravel, Pelletier, and Tares were given very light sentences and were quickly discharged back to civilian life. The trial was widely seen as a victory for the soldiers and a significant advance for the resistance movement.

The Revolt Spreads

The drama at Draguignan was closely followed by soldiers in their barracks. Throughout the trial, conscripts expressed strong and vocal support for the accused activists. Among the French troops stationed in the southwest German town of Karlsruhe, this support boiled over into mass protest. A few days before the end of the trial, approximately 300 troops, mostly transportation corpsmen, took to the streets, blocking downtown Karlsruhe during the morning rush hour in an unprecedented demonstration: "Halt to the Army's Repression!"[6] After marching through town, some of the troops made a dramatic appearance on television (with stockings over their faces). In addition to freedom for the Draguignan defendants, the protesters demanded better pay, free rail passes, an end to harassment by the military police, and the right of draftees to choose when and where they must serve. The Karlsruhe demonstration stunned the nation. Only a few days before the army had termed Draguignan an "isolated incident."

Still reeling from the shock of Karlsruhe, military commanders were confronted with two additional demonstrations a month later. On February 17, 1975, more than 100 soldiers took to the streets in the eastern French town of Nancy. Two days later, a similar protest march occurred in the historic northern fortress town of Verdun.[7] Suddenly the ferment appeared to be everywhere. The army seemed to be coming apart.

At about this same time, the press "discovered" that numerous underground soldier newspapers were being circulated in the French army. Young soldier editors in France and Germany were publishing such barbed titles as *Les Boeufs Voient Rouge (The Grunts See Red)*, *Arrete Ton Char (Stop Your Tank)* and, perhaps the most famous, *Spirate Rouge* (an almost untranslatable triple pun on the French name of their Rhine garrison town, "Spire" [in German: "Speyer" or "Pirate"] and on "Spirou," a French comicbook hero).[8] Leftist political agitation became combined with sharp attacks on military discipline and command authority.

The panic among the French establishment grew as they realized the breadth of the movement and its extension to "elite" combat units. Initially they had discounted the resistance, assumed it limited to second-line service or transportation regiments, where morale was chronically poor. But *"Les Bouefs"* was the voice of a strong soldier committee in an Atomic Artillery unit, and the *"Spirate"* that of an elite "Spahi" reconnaissance regiment. Perhaps most embarrassing, the tanks of the Kaiserslautern armored regiment, whose drivers were now publishing *Arrete Ton Char*, were those which in 1968 had been destined to roll toward Paris.

To a degree, the alarm of military commanders in early 1975 was justified. During this period tens of thousands of active-duty soldiers were organizing in the barracks and demanding improved pay and conditions. Conscript grumbling had turned into active political opposition. In less than two years the French armed forces had gone from placid somnolence to what seemed like a virtual revolution.

Reforms to the Rescue

After May 1968, the French government escaped further threats to the civilian social order through a judicious application of reform combined with a defense of essential interest. The government made partial concessions through such steps as increased salaries, worker councils in factories and offices, and reforms of the educational system. At the same time the Gaullists and other center-right forces heightened their control over the central government. Key leftist militants were investigated and harassed.

Seven years later a similar formula was applied. The army made limited concessions to the demands of the protesting soldiers, while ensuring that command authority remained absolute and unquestioned.

The first task was to clean house organizationally. Soon after the trial of the "Draguignan 3," Minister of Defense Jacques Soufflet announced his "retirement" (he had served only one year). He was replaced by the hard-liner Yvon Bourges. The government also created the post of secretary of state for defense. The appointee for this new cabinet position was the notorious, straight-talking former general, Marcel Bigeard. A veteran of both Dien Bien Phu and the Algerian War, Bigeard quickly established himself as the mortal enemy of the soldiers' movement. Upon taking office he vowed he would "destroy those who openly advocate the destruction of our society through our army."[9] The appointment of Bigeard was hailed by the right. They hoped that the government would now regain firm grasp of the army. For their part the soldiers vilified Bigeard. They carried on a publicity campaign against him, reminding French citizens among other things that Bigeard had approved the use of torture during the Algerian War.

The government next moved to cool the situation in the barracks by offering a wide range of reforms and improvements. Conscripts' pay was immediately tripled (although the raise to $1.80 per day still left conscripts abysmally underpaid). The wearing of civilian clothes was allowed. Haircut standards were relaxed. Evening formation (roll call) was abolished. Bonus payments were instituted for soldiers to return home from Germany on weekend passes. More money was made available for recreational facilities. A new Regulation of General Discipline was announced. Command-sponsored soldier committees were established (these representation councils, theoretically similar to the Scandinavian system, provided a forum where grievances could be aired, but without conceding any genuine power).

Although soldier activists criticized the government's reforms as too limited, they recognized them as a major improvement over previous conditions. The material changes in the soldier's day-to-day life were quite sweeping. These alterations represented a major victory for the conscripts and showed that mass protest could bring real change. Although much remained to be done, the conditions of service had definitely improved. French conscripts had succeeded in wrenching their army out of its feudal past.

To Form a Union

Over the long term, the government's reform program had the result of weakening soldier resistance. But the immediate effect in 1975 was to inspire even greater activity in the barracks. The soldiers were intoxicated by their success. Some were emboldened to press for their ultimate goal: a democratic soldiers' union.

Although no additional street demonstrations or mass protests occurred during 1975, the overall level of political activity remained high. Nearly 100 soldier committees were active at the local level, according to our estimates. General Bigeard himself estimated that there were sixty of what he termed "revolutionary cells" in the army.[10] Although the majority of soldier committees were spontaneous and independent of any political group, the Trotskyists continued to have a considerable following. In addition, the small Parti Socialiste Unifie (PSU), the United Socialist Party, a new-left offshoot of the Socialist Party, was also supporting the soldiers' movement. PSU had established a new civilian support organization, Information pour les Droits des Soldats (IDS), Information on the Rights of Soldiers, with a national newspaper, *Le Soldat*.

Throughout this period the semiclandestine soldier committees became increasingly interested in the possibility of an open, mass conscripts' union. The soldiers were influenced not only by the strong trade union tradition of France itself but also by the successful example of the nearby Dutch conscripts' union, VVDM. Several French soldiers and recent veterans had attended the 1974 soldiers' congress in Amsterdam, and articles extolling the successes of the VVDM appeared frequently in French GI newspapers.

The advocates of unionization in the French army argued that it would bring the movement many benefits, both organizationally and politically. The creation of a national structure would strengthen the overall movement and make it more difficult for the command to isolate or repress individual soldier committees, they argued. If a soldiers' union could be linked to the country's civilian labor movement, soldiers would gain valuable allies in their fight against military repression. Linkage with the labor movement was also seen as a way of preventing use of the army against workers.

Throughout 1974 and 1975, soldiers sought ways of showing their solidarity with labor. Strike support campaigns were organized by several local committees. One example of this labor support occurred during the 1974 postal strike in Paris. The army was called in to replace striking postal workers. Some of the soldiers organized support petitions, collected money for the striking workers, and publicly demanded an end to this quite-frequent use of the army for strikebreaking. There were also many reports in the tradition of the Good Soldier Schweik. Various "irregularities" were reported in the delivery of mail, especially in Paris' wealthier neighborhoods.

The Besançon Affair

It was highly appropriate that the demand for a soldiers' union in France should surface first in Besançon. This watchmaking city in eastern France had been a hotbed of labor radicalism for several years and, in 1975, was the site of one of the most unusual and dramatic strikes in all of French industry. For nearly two years, workers of the LIP Company had been on strike and were operating the famous watchmaking firm completely without the owners, as a workers' collective. The LIP workers had taken the May 1968 slogan of "self-management" and made it a reality. Many people throughout France supported the LIP strikers and purchased their "worker-made watches'"* as a gesture of solidarity. The local union at Besançon was affiliated with the CFDT and was headed by Gerard Jussiaux, a member of the new-left PSU.

All during this time, Besançon also boasted an active soldiers' committee in the local Engineering Regiment. The civilian unionists were sympathetic to the soldiers' movement, and relations between the union and soldiers' committees were friendly. Ties between the strikers and soldiers became even closer after a May 1975 incident in which a conscript was kicked and brutally beaten after complaining to his commander about frequent assignment to kitchen duties. Such incidents helped move the committee and the union toward a fateful decision to declare the creation of a soldiers' union.

On November 5, the soldiers of Besançon held a press conference to announce to the nation that their committee was affiliating with the CFDT as the country's first soldiers' union. They declared that the time had come for unionization and urged soldiers in other garrisons to come forward and join their conscripts' union. The Besançon announcement, widely covered in the French press, sparked intensive controversy. When a soldiers' committee at Chaumont also announced the formation of a soldiers' union and other soldier committees followed suit, the government and military establishment went into a state of shock. It appeared that a wave of unionization was about to sweep through the ranks.

The government's reaction was quick and severe. General Bigeard fulminated, "We are at war, a subversive war." He branded military unionism "an illegal and unthinkable act."[11] Government security services announced an immediate investigation into this so-called "enterprise of demoralization." In late November, the government referred the case to the long-dormant Court for State Security. The Court had been created during the Algerian War to try the four generals who had attempted, once again, to overthrow France's civilian government. The first such coup in 1958 had succeeded and had brought De Gaulle to power; the second and a more determined third, in 1961 and 1962, collapsed in the face of rank-and-file passive resistance. In 1962 French soldiers simply did nothing; by 1974 a similar attempt would have met active opposition. The court was no longer prosecuting semifascist generals in 1974, however; now it was invoked against soldiers attempting to form a trade union. The resurrection of this special court was combined with claims that the soldiers and their union supporters were seeking to overthrow the state in cooperation with foreign powers. At one point the government alleged that French conscripts were linked to the leftist soldiers' movement in Portugal. To underscore the

---

* Of course *all* watches are "worker-made"; what distinguished the LIP watches was the absence of a boss, a factory owner, collecting surplus value on the products.

point, a group of twelve Portuguese soldiers who were in the country at the time were deported.

A few days later, government security forces struck swiftly and decisively. The police and investigative agencies descended on Besançon and other locations, arresting some forty-five soldiers and civilian activists.[12] Among those arrested were fourteen active-duty soldiers as well as many local trade union leaders, including Gerard Jussiaux. Those caught in the dragnet were indicted under Article 84 of the French penal code, which reads, "Anyone who, in time of peace, knowingly participates in an attempt to demoralize the army with a view to weakening national defense, will be punished with from five to ten years of criminal detention." On December 15, French police and security officials conducted additional raids on the apartments and offices of civilian left-wing political organizers. Principal targets of these later raids were the PSU, the Trotskyist LCR, and other far-left groups. The raids occurred in Paris, Lyons, Montpellier, Clermont-Ferrand, Cherbourg, Bordeaux, and Amiens. Files were seized, offices were overturned, and political leaders, such as former LCR presidential candidate Alain Krivine, were detained for questioning.

The government's campaign did not stop with parties of the far left, but attempted to attack the socialist and communist parties as well. This was ironic and ultimately unsuccessful, for these parties of the establishment left had never supported the soldier committees and had disavowed the soldiers' union at Besançon as soon as it was announced. Nonetheless, Prime Minister Jacques Chirac denounced the Socialist Party in November as a threat to "the organization of our defense." At the same time, Interior Minister Michel Poniatowski blasted the Communist Party as "the party of disorder and illegality."

The socialist and communist parties responded by expressing their support for "the defense of liberty," but they took no steps to aid the imprisoned soldiers and their backers. Socialist leader Mitterand criticized government repression but also blasted what he termed "irresponsible scheming of small groups that the government is using to get to the left." Communist party officials also condemned "antimilitarist agitations," as did the party's trade union affiliate, Confederation Generale de Travail (CGT), the General Confederation of Labor. Even the CFDT disowned its union locals in Besançon and elsewhere. Edmond Maire, general secretary of the CFDT, had initially endorsed the notion of a soldiers' union at Draguignan, but he now stated that the CFDT could not support this effort to create such a union.

The imprisoned defendants at Besançon and elsewhere did not stand alone, however. Although it condemned the "antimilitarism" of the left, the CFDT national leadership was compelled to fight the government's repressive crackdown. After all, several CFDT leaders had been arrested and were under indictment. A National Committee for Release of the Imprisoned Soldiers and Militants was formed with CFDT backing and strong leadership from the PSU and Trotskyist groups. It sponsored rallies, strikes, and demonstrations all over France. A CFDT demonstration in Paris on December 5 drew approximately 20,000 people (the CGT did not participate).[13]

Perhaps the most eloquent and impassioned defense of the indicted activists came from soldiers themselves. Throughout the French army, conscripts expressed immediate support for the soldiers of Besançon. At Mont Beliard, Bordeaux, Casaux, Landau (in Germany), and elsewhere, the soldiers organized defense campaigns, signed petitions, collected money, and held protest meetings to condemn the government's indictments.

Meanwhile, in the courtroom, the government's legal case fell apart as it had at Marseilles against the "Draguignan 3." A team of fifteen prominent lawyers was assembled to defend the soldiers, and the attorneys quickly found many loopholes in the government's legal case. As political criticism and press controversy mounted in early 1976, the government decided to drop the indictments and dismiss the Security Court. Most of the imprisoned soldiers were released after forty-five or sixty days detention and were returned to civilian life.

While the government's legal case may have been a farce, its campaign of repression and intimidation in the barracks worked all too well. Harassment and threats against local organizers increased, and interrogations and searches became more frequent. Dozens of local soldier leaders suddenly found themselves facing thirty- and sixty-day disciplinary arrests. Repression had always been tight in the French army, but now it was even worse. Anyone suspected of working with a soldiers' committee was threatened with immediate punishment or arrest.

Postscript

The government's crackdown after Besançon had a crushing effect on the French soldiers' movement. Soldier committees were hit hard by arrests and imprisonment, and many did not survive. Throughout the army, soldier activists decided to "pull down the covers" to let the storm pass. Their activities became even more clandestine than before, and their efforts to attract new supporters thus became more difficult. In their postmortems after Besançon, many soldier organizers recognized that the call for a national union had been premature and adventurist. All agreed that unionization remains desirable, but most admitted that this goal is for the future.

Beginning in 1976, the French soldiers' movement entered a period of decline and reduced activity that has continued until the present. The combination of repression and reform weakened the resistance impulse. No large-scale soldier demonstrations or mass actions occurred after 1975. The number of soldier committees dropped from a high of approximately 100 in 1975 to less than 25 in the 1980s.

Although greatly reduced, the soldiers' movement still continues. Soldier committees and newspapers remain active in several garrison towns and among army units in Germany. French soldiers can still be observed in annual May Day demonstrations in Paris and elsewhere, often in uniform, huddled in with the contingent of unionists from the CFDT, sometimes with masks to hide their identities. General resistance to the military continues in the French army, as it does in the armies of many highly capitalized nations.

Italy: Conscripts and NCOs Unite!

Marcello Bettin is at first glance an unlikely representative of the soldiers' movement. Forty-three years old, a career warrant officer, married, with two teenage daughters, Bettin bears little resemblance to the youthful draftees who make up the soldier committees of France and other European armies. Yet Bettin and his organization of noncommissioned officers (NCOs) are important players in the movement to democratize the Italian military.

A veteran of twenty-six years of service in the Air Force, Bettin was a radar repair and maintenance man on Nike Hercules missiles when we interviewed him in 1976 in the town of Mestre, near Venice.[1] He had the unusual distinction at that time of being a candidate for the Italian parliament on the ticket of the Socialist Party. He was running for office not with a realistic chance of winning but to use the occasion to speak up for democratic rights within the military. We found him to be a most remarkable and personable man. He spoke excellent English, the result of having spent three years of duty in the United States, mostly at the airbase in Redstone, Alabama. During a long evening of discussion with Bettin and three of his NCO colleagues, lasting in the inimitable Italian fashion well into the morning over several bottles of wine, we gained a fascinating, first-hand glimpse into the diverse and widespread soldier resistance movement of the Italian armed forces.

The Draftees Stand Up

When we first heard about this movement of noncommissioned officers in Italy, we were interested but also a bit puzzled. We knew about a strong and very active movement among Italian conscripts and had met representatives of the soldiers' committees on previous trips to Italy and at the international soldiers' congress in Amsterdam in 1974.[2] But we had not heard of NCO organizing and indeed had not seen such activity in any other army.

When we asked Bettin and his colleagues about the origins of their movement, they pointed to the earlier efforts of conscripts as a decisive influence. The political activities of the draftees sent shock waves through the normally soporific Italian armed forces and paved the way for similar efforts by the NCOs.

The first stirrings of soldier resistance in Italy appeared in 1970 soon after the "Hot Autumn" protests and strikes that swept Italian society the year before (a wave of revolt in many ways similar to the events of May 1968 in France). As in other nations, these new-left upheavals were soon echoed in the lower ranks of the army. Many of the draftees entering the army were already politicized and were accustomed to speaking out and expressing their opinions. Spontaneous mass-resistance actions began to occur, usually prompted by harsh conditions and acts of repression. These initial actions were isolated, though, and protests against poor conditions in one barracks were not connected to similar efforts in other barracks. It was not until 1974 that a more coherent and well-organized soldiers' movement appeared.

The soldier committees and organized protests that emerged in the Italian armed forces were similar to those in France. Both resulted from abominable and archaic conditions of service: in the case of Italy a disciplinary code dating back to the Fascist era, restrictions on personal freedom and democratic rights, low pay, and serious health and safety problems.

Also as in France, the Italian soldier committees received little or no support from the Communist Party, and had to rely instead on small new-left parties. In Italy these were the Partito Radicale (Radical Party), Lotta Continua (the Struggle Continues), and Avanguardia Operaia (Workers' Vanguard). Some of these groups formed an electoral coalition in the mid-1970s called Democrazia Proletaria (Proletarian Democracy) which accepted a number of low-ranking soldiers as candidates for parliament. (Although the Communist Party found a safe place on its slate for a retired general, Nino Pasti, it could not find even token seats for the soldiers and NCOs who wanted to run.)*

---

* General Pasti was nominated to a high-ranking position on the Communist Party ticket and was duly elected to Parliament. The soldiers and NCOs merely requested bottom-of-the-list candidacies with all antifascist parties. They knew that they stood no chance of being elected but wanted to use their candidacies to speak out about military conditions. After the election, Bettin and his companions returned to the barracks.

Another similarity between the movements in Italy and France is the strong connection soldiers have drawn between their struggle for improved conditions in the barracks and the defense of democracy in the larger society. In Italy, these broader concerns took on special urgency in 1973 when it was revealed that General Miceli and other top military officers were implicated in an alleged neofascist plot to take over the country by military coup. Following these revelations, soldiers strengthened their relations with local trade unions (often participating in worker-sponsored demonstrations) and campaigned against the use of the military for repressive purposes at home. As we shall see, this has been a major concern of Spanish soldiers as well.

One area where the soldiers' movements of Italy and France differed was in their outlook toward soldier unionism. Union tendencies are not as strong in Italy. There have been no Besançons, despite close links between the soldier committees and local trade unions. Many Italian soldiers favor unionization and know that it could bring important gains, but they have apparently decided not to risk the certain wrath that an open union drive would unleash. The fierce crackdown of the French government on soldier unionists did not go unnoticed to the South.

The Mass Movement Emerges

The Italian soldiers' movement reached its peak in the mid-1970s. For a brief two-year period, the Italian armed forces witnessed one of the largest and most extensive waves of protest action seen in any army in recent years. One of the first nationally coordinated actions occurred in September 1974 when uniformed soldiers participated in labor-led demonstrations throughout the country. In Rome, 200 soldiers marched in uniform in a demonstration of 80,000 civilians, while similar delegations of uniformed troops joined rallies in Turin, Milan, and other major cities.[3]

In April 1975, soldiers again participated in a series of nationally coordinated demonstrations. These were called to commemorate the liberation of Italy from fascism thirty years before. Such antifascist demonstrations had occurred in the past in Italy, but this was the first time they were marked by significant soldier participation. In Rome, 600 soldiers marched in uniform (wearing masks) to the Gate of St. Paul, where they laid a wreath in memory of those who died fighting the fascists. In the weeks prior to the demonstration, thousands of soldiers in barracks in the Rome area had signed petitions protesting the rise of neofascist activity in Italy.[4]

Elections occur so frequently in Italy that it is risky to place too much importance on any one contest, but it is probably safe to say that the campaign of June 1976 marked a major turning point for the left, in the nation as a whole and in the army. This was the election where the Communist Party polled a postwar high of 34 percent of the vote and where the concept of the "historic compromise" (in which the Communist Party informally agrees to help govern and stabilize the society in exchange for recognition of its political power) began to emerge.

In the army as throughout society, the 1976 electoral campaign sparked a tremendous mobilization of political energy. The soldiers faced special problems, though, for disciplinary restrictions and command harassment often made it difficult to vote. A major campaign of demonstrations and petitions was therefore launched to demand that soldiers be allowed to return home to vote. At the Transmission School in Cecchignola near Rome, a lively center of soldiers' movement activity, hundreds of conscripts conducted a mess-hall boycott to protest command repressions and demand the right to vote. Similar actions occurred in the garrison town of Mestre. Soldiers also participated frequently during this time in civilian political rallies throughout the country.

At first glance it would seem counterproductive for military officers to place obstacles in the way of soldiers voting, since members of the armed forces traditionally vote right and support promilitary candidates. In the case of the Italian conscripts, though, the commanders were justified in their actions, for the evidence suggests that the soldiers voted strongly for the left in the 1976 elections. Low-ranking soldiers participated prominently in the preelection rallies of the Democrazia Proletaria and the Communist Party. The authors conducted an unofficial and informal analysis of election returns from seven voting districts in the northeastern region of Udine (where much of the Italian army is concentrated) and found a strong preference for the left. In the districts where many soldiers voted, the tally for the new-left Democrazia Proletaria was six times the national average (9 percent compared to 1.5 percent nationally) and support for the Communist Party was 50 percent above their nationwide total.[5]

"Sometimes You Get More Done Without Officers"

In Chapter 6 we discussed the relation between efficiency and effectiveness, whether organized soldiers would be able to operate effectively and carry out "their mission." The Italian army is not usually considered either highly efficient nor (if we except the partisan formations fighting the fascists in Northern Italy between September 1943 and May 1945) particularly effective. The following episode might, however, cast light on the general problem as to whether soldiers can "do their thing" better under stress if they have some degree of auto-organization.

In spring 1976 a major earthquake struck the northeastern provinces of

Italy where the army is concentrated. One of the authors spoke with the twenty-year-old draftees there shortly afterwards:

The barracks were built in the middle ages, stone roofs; they fell in, people were hurt, panicked. Often the officers just disappeared. Ran away. Where our Co-ordinazi-ones [the Italian term for their soldier committees] were strong, we took over, got our own people out from under the ruins. Then we organized help for the civilians nearby. Sometimes, when you have a real job to do, you can get much more done without officers.[6]

Mass Mobilization

By mid-1975 as many as 100 soldier committees were active in the Italian armed forces. Dozens of soldier newspapers were being circulated in the barracks. Local protest actions and petition campaigns were occurring frequently. A truly massive national movement had developed within the ranks.

In the summer of that year the government reacted to this growing movement by announcing a new law on military discipline. This so-called Forlani law (named after the minister who introduced it) was a clumsy attempt to replace the old fascist-era military code with a new law while merely reinforcing some of the previous restrictions. Instead of calming passions within the ranks, the new law provoked an outcry of protest and prompted one of the largest soldier mobilizations seen anywhere in recent years. For the first time soldiers everywhere in Italy joined together in a united, nationally coordinated day of struggle.

The protest campaign began with a remarkable soldier assembly held on November 22. On that day over 200 soldier delegates met in Rome to denounce the Forlani law and call upon soldiers throughout the country to join in demonstrations called for December 4. This first national assembly was the product of extensive organization and preparation at the barracks level and reflected a very widespread, highly structured soldiers' movement. The 220 delegates represented soldier groups in 133 separate barracks. Sixty of the delegates had been elected in company or barracks meetings. This national assembly clearly illustrated the breadth of the Italian soldiers' movement at the time.[7]

The national protests that followed on December 4, 1975 were also impressive. An estimated 30,000 active-duty soldiers and NCOs took part in a variety of actions: mess-hall boycotts, minutes of silence, petitions, barracks "discussions." Many soldiers also took part in street demonstrations. In Rome a rally of 10,000 was led by a contingent of nearly 1,000 uniformed soldiers. The December 4 protests were the highwater mark for the Italian soldiers' movement.[8]

The NCOs Organize

The campaign against the Forlani law also marked the beginnings of formal cooperation between draftees and noncommissioned officers. Many of the delegates at the November 22 assembly were NCOs, as were many of the participants in the December 4 action. For the first time in the history of the soldiers' movement, draftees and careerists were working side by side in a common campaign for democratic rights. Initially some of the soldiers and their leftist supporters had been skeptical about their ability to work with their "superiors," but they soon found the noncommissioned officers to be valuable if unaccustomed allies.

The beginnings of an organized movement among Air Force NCOs began only a few months earlier. Their first known action was a small and relatively innocuous rally held in Rome in July of 1975. Approximately 100 airmen gathered in a square to demand improved pay and better conditions of service. During the rally Sergeant Guiseppe Sodgu was harassed and harshly questioned by an officer of the Carabinièri (Italy's militarized police). Soon after the rally Sodgu was arrested and sentenced to a jail term of two years and eight months. This severe punishment caused a furor within the ranks of the NCOs and provided the spark for the creation of an active political movement.

It was the campaign to free Sodgu that helped to motivate Marcello Bettin and his colleagues. They collected money for the accused sergeant and went around to other air force NCOs asking them to help in the defense campaign. In our interview, Bettin described it this way:

We founded a movement. We went to many other air bases and contacted the NCOs there. In the beginning we met with five or ten NCOs in the "ostias" [snackbars]. But soon we had fifty or more people and would have to meet elsewhere. We planned protest actions to free those arrested and call attention to our legitimate demands for improved conditions. Our usual action was the one-day hunger strike. We would gather at the mess halls but would stay outside, speaking among ourselves but not going in to eat. The officers were furious and would try to stop us by arresting some of the "leaders," but their actions only strengthened our determination, and so our movement grew.[9]

In the months that followed, the government made new arrests and the actions of the NCOs escalated in response. In October 1975, 200 NCOs marched in uniform in the city of Treviso. A month later they responded with another rally, the largest yet. In an awesome display of their rapidly growing collective strength, over 1,000 air force NCOs demonstrated in Mestre in November 1975. The sergeants and warrant officers wore their uniforms throughout the three-hour demonstration and were joined by their wives and children, and by workers and students from the nearby area.

After the December 1975 protests, the NCOs held numerous other assemblies and demonstrations. In February 1976 nearly 1,000 warrant officers and sergeants were joined by thousands of civilian supporters (including members of parliament and the local communist mayor) in a rally in the city of Pisa. Similar large demonstrations were held a month later on March 27 in Milan, Rome, Cagliari (in Sicily), and again in Pisa. The Milan demonstration had perhaps the largest turnout of all--nearly 2,500 NCOs and 500 draftees joined a crowd of approximately 20,000 civilians.[10]

"A Job Not a Ghetto": Why NCOs Protest

During our interviews with Bettin and his colleagues we tried to probe why these military careerists had become such militant supporters of the soldiers' movement. We were particularly interested in hearing their reaction to the labor movement and the leftist groups offering to help them. We asked, "Weren't you scared of these leftists and all those hammer and sickle posters?" The noncoms responded all at once, heatedly: "Yes, we had been taught for years that these reds are our "enemies," but they were willing to help us, so we were no longer afraid." Sergeant Bettin traced his political thinking to his seventeen and fifteen year-old daughters. "I learned a lot from my girls, that these people (the left) are okay. I have changed a lot too."

We wanted to learn more about the backgrounds and motivations of this unlikely group of protesters. All of the sergeants we met had enlisted in the air force at the age of seventeen. At the time when they joined, in the 1950s, air force technical jobs were a highly desirable plum in an otherwise war-torn and underdeveloped economy, and hundreds of applicants applied for each opening.

Many of those who traditionally volunteer for an air force or military career in Italy come from the economically underdeveloped South. They enlist in the military to improve their social and economic status. As the overall standard of living has improved in recent decades, however, the relative status of these previously attractive air force jobs has declined. Also, as civilian society has become more liberal and relaxed, the restrictions and harassments of military discipline have become less tolerable. The NCOs now want greater recognition of their importance to the military. They want better pay and conditions of service, and more modern forms of authority and discipline. When their demands for these right were met with arrests and repression in 1975, political mobilization followed.

Unlike the conscripts, the air force NCOs have organized themselves into a trade union-like association. From this point of view, their organization has some similarities to the professional military unions examined in Chapter 4. However, they are more open to the left politically. After 1976 the NCO groups began to change their tactics. They decided to "go beyond" street demonstrations and focus instead on lobbying and direct persuasion of politicians and other "important people." They concentrated on building up their organizational structure and sought to cooperate not only with committees of soldiers but with civilian labor unions (especially public employee federations) and with union-type groups among the police.

The Italian NCOs are fully conscious of the political importance of their campaign for greater democratic rights. They know that the struggle of the soldiers' movement has important implications not only for their own welfare but also for the future of Italian politics. They have become a vital democratic influence within the military. In the words of Marcello Bettin:

We don't want Italy to become another Chile. We are the guarantee that this will never happen. We want to be part of society, to be citizens and soldiers at the same time. We are workers in uniform. We want the air force to be a job, not a ghetto.[11]

The Decline

While the Italian NCOs maintained their organizing efforts, their draftee colleagues became suddenly quiet. By the late 1970s and 1980s, the once-active movement among Italian conscripts all but disappeared. When Spanish soldier organizers visited the country in 1978 they could hardly find the conscripts' movement. Where once there had been more than 100 soldier committees, only a handful remained. Italians had been vocally present at the first international soldiers' congress in Amsterdam in 1974, but they were absent at the soldiers' conferences held five years later. After a brief but spectacular rise, the Italian soldiers' movement abruptly faded away.

There are no simple explanations for this dramatic decline. Many of the soldiers who participated in the demonstrations and mess-hall actions suffered disciplinary punishment, and this may have had some dampening effect, but such repression had been present throughout the rise of their movement. At that time, as has happened in other countries, repressions angered many more soldiers than they intimidated. From the command's point of view repressions were often highly counterproductive, effectively spurring the resistance.

The reform measures that were introduced in response to the soldier demonstrations may have had an effect, but here again the changes were relatively minor, with one exception. In 1979 the government and Ministry of Defense introduced elected representation councils in the Italian armed forces. These now-familiar consultation systems allowed soldiers the forms of democracy in the ranks without any of the substance. As in the Scandinavian countries, Italian conscripts were now permitted to elect delegates who could represent them and present their grievances to the command. As in other countries, though, these delegates had no power and no legal means of enforcing their demands. Nonetheless, the introduction of these elected councils may have had some impact in diverting the energies of would-be soldier activists.

The decline of the Italian soldiers' movement came shortly after the adoption of the "historic compromise" policy of the Communist Party. Not just the soldiers movement but also other mass movements in Italy went through a period of similar decline while the Communist Party increased its electoral standing. In the case of the soldiers' movement this was not because the party consciously tried to quash conscript organizing. The party's position was the same after the 1975 election as before: They opposed the soldiers' movement and would have nothing to do with it. Rather, the effect of the Communist Party success may have been more indirect, through a diversion of political energies from mass action toward legalistic and electoral forms of action. At the same time, those civilian groups to the left of the Communist Party that had supported the soldier resistance, such as Avanguardia Operaia and Lotta Continua, declined. Whatever the cause, there is an unmistakable and ironic association between the strengthening of the position of the Communist Party in Italy and the decline of the soldiers' movement.

13

Spain: From Massacres to Mess-Hall Strikes

The last big war fought by the Spanish army was against its own people. In July 1936 the late, unlamented Generalissimo Francisco Franco led a group of fascist generals in a military putsch against the elected Republic. With the help of Adolf Hitler and Benito Mussolini the Francoists managed to defeat the Republic in a bloody three-year war that took nearly 1 million lives. For almost forty years Franco and his army ran Spain on behalf of a small clique of rich landlords and industrialists. Of course, the generals did not run the country themselves. They ordered their soldiers to do it. And like nearly all such soldiers in previous circumstances, Spanish troops followed orders.

Gradually conditions began to change. The generals, as many a soldier will testify, tend to run things badly. By the mid-1970s, not only Franco but his fascist system were dying. The regime was coming apart at the seams. Workers were striking for better wages, farmers were agitating for lower rents, students were demanding academic freedom, and the national minorities (especially the Basques and the Catalonians) were in sometimes armed revolt against the central dictatorship in Madrid. The diehard fascists and generals tried to prevent political change, but by the mid-1970s the pressure for reform became overwhelming. The dictatorship steadily unraveled. By the time Franco finally died in 1975, his regime could count only on the Falangist Party, the special police (Guardia Civile) and, perhaps, the army.

Here, too, conditions were changing. When the regime began to unravel, Spain's fascists had hoped to turn to the military for relief from the rising tide of democracy, but the army was not what it had once been. The changes sweeping society had also taken root in the country's largely draftee army (over 75 percent conscript, a very high proportion). Spanish soldiers became "infected" by the atmosphere of reform, and like their colleagues in France, Italy, and other industrialized nations, began to speak out for improved conditions and democratic rights.[1]

Union groups were formed in the army in 1974 and 1975 to nurture the flower of democracy just beginning to rise from the ashes of Franco's dictatorship. The soldiers spoke out strongly against the possibility of a military putsch, and they insisted that the army not be used against the people. Thanks in part to these democratic strivings, the army was in fact not used, and the dictatorship was replaced by a constitutional monarchy and parliament. Democracy blossomed again in Spain.

Democratic Soldiers

The first sign of organized political opposition within the barracks emerged in 1974, even before the death of Franco. That summer clandestine draftee groups formed in the barracks of Madrid, Barcelona, Seville, and other cities. Soon these groups established contact with one another, and in late 1974 they began publishing the newspaper, *La Voz del Soldado*, "The Voice of the Soldier."[2] It disappeared soon after its founding, but it was followed by dozens of other clandestine soldier newspapers read by tens of thousands of Spanish conscripts.

When soldier newspapers began to appear, the military command immediately saw red and imposed a harsh crackdown. Dozens, perhaps hundreds of Spanish soldier organizers were sent to jail. It was not necessary to join a committee or advocate soldier unions to be locked up; a soldier could be imprisoned simply for being caught reading an underground newspaper.

Of course, thirty-five years earlier officers had simply shot soldiers for being "republican." At that time, putting out a soldier newspaper inside the Franco barracks would have been unthinkable. But although old Francoists no doubt much regretted this and fulminated against the collapse of society, the times and the army had changed. Shooting draftees for "red subversion" just was no longer "in." The best (or worst) the generals could do was to put them in the stockade, and that, too, proved counterproductive.

Despite the command's best efforts, the new movement could not be crushed. This is how the situation was described to us by Miguel Durin, a former army private who himself spent several months in the stockade and later became president of the Union of Democratic Soldiers:

For every one of our members who went to prison, ten new soldiers took his place and joined the movement. The more the brass tried to crush us, the more soldiers saw the need for a union, and the more we spread--from barracks to barracks, city to city, region to region. The Spanish army became "corrupted" by democracy, no longer a useful tool for dictatorship.[3]

As additional soldier committees began to form in 1975, especially in the Madrid and Barcelona regions, several of the groups came together and formed the first real organization, the Assemblea Democratica de Soldados, the Democratic Assembly of Soldiers. Gradually the soldiers began to call their groups uniones, or unions. By 1977 the Assemblea was merged with other groups to form a national soldiers' organization, the Union Democratica de Soldados (UDS), the Union of Democratic Soldiers. UDS remained active into the early 1980s and for several years was one of the largest, most-cohesive soldier organizations in Europe.

It is particularly striking that such a strong, unified organization could prosper in Spain, with its sharp regional diversity and tradition of political divisions within the left. For the draftees in the barracks, the enemy was the army. They had little interest in the disastrous splits that had divided communists, socialists, anarchists, and trotskyists during the Republican years and afterwards. At its height in the late 1970s, UDS claimed to have 10,000 soldier members. Its influence went far beyond these numbers, though, and at times reached a majority of Spain's 300,000 conscripts. Because of the continuing repression in the Spanish military, UDS had to operate in a semiclandestine underground manner. Initially the group had formal membership cards and files, but a wave of repression following the national protest actions of 1978 forced the organization to adopt a less formal, more clandestine mode of operation.

Operation Eat-in

Although the initial focus of the Spanish soldiers' movement was very political, UDS and the soldier committees also worked on the "normal" problems of enlisted life: poor conditions, low pay, and command harassment. The passing of Franco had brought no immediate relief to conscripts in the barracks. Soldier organizers continued to face arrest and punishment, and the oppressive conditions inherited from fascism remained unchanged. Some generals even tried to tighten discipline. Forced to relax their clutches on the civilians, they tried to tighten the screws on the soldiers. Such efforts usually backfired, though, and led to protest actions among the troops.

The first such mobilization occurred in Madrid in March 1976 after soldiers learned that local commanders were planning to cancel overnight passes.[4] This would have meant that the 20,000 soldiers of the Madrid military district would be forced to sleep inside the barracks. The soldiers panicked because such a restriction would have been a heavy blow financially. With a base pay for draftees of only $4 per month ("Just enough to pay for the shoe polish," according to Miguel Durin), many draftees moonlighted evenings and weekends to make ends meet. Barracks restriction would have eliminated this outside income and plunged the conscripts into miserable poverty.

When the Madrid UDS heard of this planned restriction (it was supposed to be secret, but the conscripts who typed the orders apparently had different ideas), they published it in their local soldier newspaper. The soldiers also planned a "show of force." By word of mouth and clandestine leaflets they organized "Operation Eat-in."

Normally in urban garrisons such as Madrid, only about a quarter of the soldiers show up in the mess halls to eat army chow. On the appointed day, however, all the soldiers suddenly showed up to eat, and just to make a point, they left their dessert untouched. In Memorial Regiment 1 in Madrid, the normal mess hall crowd of 200 soldiers swelled to nearly 900. The UDS's inventive protest action created total disorganization and chaos in the kitchens and mess halls. The command was incensed, but who could they punish? And for what, the "crime" of leaving dessert? The conscripts' message came across loud and clear. The officers were forced to retreat and the nighttime passes were preserved.

Heartened by their victory in Madrid, Spanish soldiers began to see that they had power. The movement grew rapidly, and UDS developed a substantial national following. By 1978, with 10,000 members, the organization felt strong enough to attempt a nationwide protest action to improve the conditions of military service. The UDS decided to focus on two basic demands: weekend passes and free rail travel home. To enforce their appeal they made preparations to repeat the Madrid action on a national scale. UDS called on soldiers everywhere in Spain to "leave dessert on the table" and observe a minute of silence to show their support for the demands.

When the day of protest arrived in March, the results astonished everyone, including UDS. Soldiers everywhere in the country participated in the action.[5] Even in barracks where there had been no previous UDS organization, large numbers of soldiers showed up in the mess hall and refused to touch dessert. According to the estimates of UDS, approximately 60 percent of all Spanish conscripts participated in the mess-hall protest. Over 150,000 uneaten desserts.

Retrenchment

The March 1978 mess-hall protest was one of the largest coordinated actions by soldiers anywhere in recent years. It was also a high point for the Spanish GI movement and was followed by a period of decline and retrenchment. As in France and Italy, soldier resistance in Spain had grown rapidly and reached a sudden and dramatic peak, only to fall back to a lower level of activity. The familiar combination of repression and reform led to a weakening of the organized movement, although spontaneous forms of resistance continued into the 1980s.

An incident in November 1978 graphically illustrated the continuing importance of the soldiers' movement to Spain's fragile young democracy. "Operation Galaxy," a coup d'etat planned by several Spanish generals, was uncovered and stopped before it could start. The generals had apparently planned to move against the state during a trip abroad of King Juan Carlos and to return Spain to a more authoritarian form of government. Their plans never got off the ground, though, in part because they were discovered and exposed by Spanish soldiers.[6] When UDS members heard of the plans, they obtained some of the key documents involved and delivered them to the civilian government. The generals were then quietly arrested and their plan collapsed. While UDS leaders were glad to have helped stop the coup, they felt that they should have received more credit and recognition from the government. They also complained that the military plotters were allowed to retire on generous pensions, while many UDS members continued to face harassment and imprisonment.

Officers Too--Patterns of Military Resistance

The first publicly known organizing efforts in the Spanish army were not those of the conscripts but of low-ranking officers. In the last year of the Franco dictatorship, a group of more than 1,000 junior officers--mostly lieutenants, captains, and majors--formed the Union Democratica de Militares (UDM), the Democratic Military Union. The activities of UDM were widely covered in the press, while the concurrent beginnings of protest among conscripts were largely ignored.

When this movement of junior officers emerged, it seemed natural to draw analogies between events in Spain and similar developments in Portugal (where the "captain's movement" had helped to overthrow fascism and move the government leftward). In both countries, military resistance movements had appeared among lower-ranking officers in the waning days of fascism . Spain's UDM and Portugal's "captain's movement" seemed to be cut from the same cloth. Spain and Portugal apparently belonged to the class of less-developed nations where military resistance occurs not among low-ranking soldiers but in the ranks of noncommissioned officers and junior officers.

As we look at the two countries more carefully, however, we notice substantial differences. Spain and Portugal may be close in geography and cultural tradition, but their economies and standard of living differ substantially. Although economic development in Spain is uneven, the nation as a whole has a considerably higher level of GNP per capita than Portugal. Its standard of living is closer to Italy's. Using 1974 figures, Spain ranks 29th among the nations of the world in GNP per capita, while Portugal ranks 42d. Economically, Spain more resembles Italy than Portugal (see Table 13.1).

Table 13.1

| Country | GNP/Capita (1974 figures) | |
	Rank	US$
Italy	28	2632
Spain	29	2388
	(Threshold)	
Portugal	42	1693

These differences in standard of living and economic development are paralleled by differences in military resistance movements. The developments in Spain more closely resemble events in Italy than in Portugal. Italian and Spanish privates built widespread, well-organized, independent conscript movements separately from their "superiors." In fact, the initial resistance of the Italian NCOs was inspired by the successes of the earlier draftee movement (see Chapter 12). By contrast, the short-lived Portuguese soldiers' movement (SUV, "Soldiers United Will Win") appeared only well after the captains and majors of the MFA (Armed Forces Movement) had successfully overthrown the fascist Caetano dictatorship (see Chapter 14).

While Italy and Spain had similar military resistance movements, there were slight differences between the two that help shed additional light on the interrelation of capital accumulation levels and political movements inside the army. Like Spain, Italy experienced leftward military movements not only among conscripts but also among somewhat higher-ranking professionals. In Italy these were sergeants, NCOs, and warrant officers. The Spanish UDM, by contrast, occurred among officers of a slightly higher rank, predominantly captains. Thus, in the country with a slightly higher level of capital accumulation, Italy, military resistance occurred at a slightly lower rank, among warrant and noncommissioned officers. In the country with a slightly lower level of capital accumulation, Spain, military resistance occurred at a slightly higher rank, among captains and majors. These developments tend to confirm our hypothesis: The rank at which military resistance occurs tends to be inversely related to the degree of capital accumulation in the particular nation. We explore these interrelationships in more depth in the following chapters.

Portugal: The Revolution
of the Carnations

As we have noted throughout the book, resistance movements among low-ranking soldiers occur almost exclusively in highly developed nations. Such movements do not normally appear within the armies of less capitalized countries, in nations whose gross national product per capita is below a certain threshold. Where military resistance movements do occur in nations below the threshold, they are usually led by officers.

In this chapter and the three that follow we explore patterns of military resistance in four countries below the threshold: Portugal, Chile, Iran, and the Philippines. We find in these countries not only that resistance movements occur within the higher ranks (usually career NCOs and mid-level officers) but also that this resistance tends to be more frequent in the technical branches, especially the navy and the air force.

In Chile it was career petty officers of the navy who tried to stop the putsch against Allende. In Iran the Shah's regime collapsed when air force officer cadets sided with the Ayatollah and distributed arms to civilian demonstrators. In both countries regular army soldiers and sergeants continued to "follow orders" and fired into the streets. Only in Portugal, where we turn now, did a revolt initially propelled by captains and majors spill over into a short-lived but dramatic uprising among low-ranking soldiers.

A Coup for Freedom

In the early morning hours of April 25, 1974, Lisbon's Catholic radio station Renascensca played a special, prearranged folk song. On that signal officers in the clandestine Armed Forces Movement, MFA, took their troops into the streets, officially on maneuvers but in fact on a mission to overthrow the Caetano dictatorship. There was no effective resistance, and by evening all was over; fifty years of fascism crumbled into dust.[1] A poor street flower vendor, who realized that the soldiers were for once on the side of the people, gave the advancing troops his entire stock of carnations. The soldiers stuck the flowers into their rifle muzzles, and the revolution thus acquired a symbol and a name. General Antonio de Spinola, who had earlier acquired an antifascist reputation for his book against the African wars, was installed as president.

The revolution quickly ended the decade-long wars in Mozambique, Angola, and Guinea-Bissau and brought a refreshing wave of democracy and freedom to Portugal after fifty years of repression. For a brief eighteen-month period Portugal experienced a revolution of rising empowerment for the poor and dwindling authority for the rich and powerful. The armed forces were the driving force for this revolution--led first by the generals, who tried to control the revolution; pushed to the left by lower-ranking officers, mostly captains; and later invigorated by a short-lived movement of rank-and-file soldiers.

A Little History

Despite (or perhaps because of) a huge overseas empire, Portugal had long been the poorhouse of Europe. The wealth and benefits of Portugal's overseas holdings and domestic resources were concentrated in the hands of a tiny minority. A military dictatorship under Salazar was established in the 1920s, and it dutifully protected the privileges of the wealthy. Unlike the military of neighboring Spain, where the armed forces fought a bloody civil war against their own people, the Portuguese military did not face major revolt until the 1960s. The challenge came from abroad, where African people of Mozambique, Angola, and Guinea-Bissau rose up against centuries of Portuguese domination. The Portuguese army attempted to suppress these uprisings, but the military soon faced a protracted guerrilla war.

Within the Portuguese military, officer life had always been a comfortable sinecure. Until the early 1960s, the officer ranks were filled mostly with the sons of the landed gentry. A military career was a stepping stone to the aristocracy and political elite. But as the wars in Africa developed, the Portuguese army soon found itself facing three not-so-mini-Vietnams. As a result the armed forces were rapidly enlarged. The social composition of the officer corps began to change, and middle-class high school graduates, college students, and intellectuals now entered the officer ranks in greater number. These new, noncareer "militia" captains (they rarely rose to higher rank) were quite unlike the old regulars, the colonels and generals. They were not from the leisure class but from the rising middle classes. Fighting in Mozambique and Angola and against the highly politicized guerrillas of Guinea-Bissau, the captains began to wonder about the cause they were serving.

As the costs of the war grew, as atrocities and massacres became more frequent, as discontent multiplied at home, officers of all ranks began to question the regime's policies. Even leading generals began to argue, as did Antonio de Spinola, that the war could not be won. Some officers hoped for support from NATO, particularly the United States, but U.S. action was precluded by the "Vietnam syndrome" and rumblings of revolt among the substantial black segment of the army (see the story of Pfc. Larry Johnson in Chapter 2). Unwilling to pull out of Africa but unable to sustain the wars on their own, the Salazar/Caetano dictatorship soon lost political support. Portugal's officers prepared to do something new, to putsch for freedom.

There were different sectors and political interests within the Armed Forces Movement, and the political complexion of the revolution depended upon which sector was most active. The course of events depended greatly on whether generals, captains, or privates played the leading role. We distinguish four distinct sectors within the military at that time:

Group 1-- The Generals: older, career officers.
Group 2-- The Captains: the non-career militia most identified with the Armed Forces Movement.
Group 3-- The NCOs: usually career men, but with some left leanings.
Group 4-- The Soldiers: draftees who became politically active in the last months of the revolution in 1975.

Spinola and other generals from Group 1 no doubt took part in the then-unavoidable revolution in order to keep an eye on things, to see that "the more things change, the more they stay the same." The generals wanted a democracy that guaranteed their rule, and a negotiated settlement in Africa that would keep a close rein on the ex-colonies and protect Portuguese investments. Spinola's model was de Gaulle, and a neocolonialist system such as France had established in West Africa.

For the captains of Group 2, who formed the bulk of the MFA, their interests were different. The junior officers were more optimistic; some might say naive. They wanted independence and friendly relations with the former African colonies. At home they wanted rapid change and reform. They promised to introduce "democracy, liberty, and socialism." Some were greatly impressed by the political program and methods of mobilization of the African guerrillas against whom they were fighting, particularly the PAIGC, the African Party for the Independence of Guinea and Cape Verde.

Among the career NCOs, Group 3, sergeants and particularly navy petty officers, the long illegal Portuguese Communist Party had been able to maintain some influence. To the best of our knowledge, though, the sergeants, and indeed the Communist Party itself, were not directly involved in the planning of the April 25 revolution.

As for the draftees of Group 4, they were not even informed. As an MFA leader Captain Matos Gomes told the authors:

We did not tell our soldiers anything. We were afraid that if we did, the PIDE (the fascist secret police) would get wind of our plans. Not so much that there were spies among the kids, but that these "unpoliticals" would simply talk too much. And we didn't think they'd understand what we were doing. And in any case, we did not consider it necessary. They would obey our, any orders.[2]

This elitist attitude toward the soldiers was realistic, at least initially. The soldiers did indeed follow orders. They were told by the captains that they were going on maneuvers. It was only during the actual operation that they learned they were making an antifascist revolution. They were, as one of them later told the authors, delighted but surprised, or as another said, surprised but delighted. They enthusiastically obeyed the orders to revolt, to disobey orders.[3]

An Uneasy Revolution--The Soldiers Awaken

Spinola and the generals assumed that they were going to run the country and that the captains who had helped make the coup would, as captains normally do, obey their superiors' orders. Matters came to a head very quickly, though, over the issue of political prisoners. No sooner had the dust settled from the revolution than demands were raised for the release of all "politicals" imprisoned in Caixas, a prison near Lisbon. General-President Spinola said no, but the Armed Forces Movement captains said yes. The prisoners were freed.

For five months the captains and the generals shared power in an increasingly uneasy alliance. Then on September 28, 1974, General Spinola made a determined attempt to end the revolution and restore order. His attempt to eliminate the political influence of the MFA captains failed completely, and the general was abruptly forced into retirement. Once Spinola was removed, the Portuguese government quickly moved to accept the independence of the African colonies and that of East Timor as well.

In order to defeat General Spinola's attempts at counterrevolution, the captains had sought the active support of the noncommissioned officers and had even begun to accept, hesitantly, the participation of soldiers. More to the point, the repression that Spinola had attempted to maintain inside the barracks now almost completely ceased. For the first time Portuguese soldiers were able to discuss issues openly.

Particularly in the Lisbon region, there were growing contacts between soldiers and politicized civilian youth. In several regiments soldiers now elected their own delegates and began to hold meetings in the barracks. One of the most developed of these units was, surprisingly enough, the military police regiment in Lisbon. In fact these MPs were a new unit, specially formed to take the place of the old "national police" (GNR), which had remained loyal to the fascist regime to the bitter end. Another activist unit was RALIS 1, a light artillery regiment based in a suburb of Lisbon.

On the morning of March 11, 1975, an extraordinary event occurred at the RALIS 1 barracks--all of it recorded live on television and preserved for posterity in the film *Viva Portugal in the Barracks*. The soldiers of the RALIS 1 regiment, to their complete surprise, suddenly found themselves under aerial and ground attack. Planes and helicopters were strafing and bombing their barracks. The generals had launched a preemptive strike in an attempt to quell further leftist developments within the ranks. Parachutists from the Tancos air force base were activated by the generals, ferried to Lisbon by helicopter, and ordered to overrun the base. The RALIS artillery men resisted, though, and an uneasy stalemate ensued.

As the television cameras continued to roll, a crowd of local citizens gathered to taunt and heckle the parachutists. The captain in charge of the parachutists held his ground and shouted to the RALIS barracks: "We have our orders. Surrender!" Suddenly, however, a Pfc in the parachutists' unit jumped up on a truck and yelled to his mates: "Hey, let's go, let's stop this now." Quickly and in mass the paratroopers put their guns down, kept the sheaths on their bayonets, and walked toward the barracks to greet their would-be enemies. The paratrooper officers cried out: "Where are you going?" The soldiers replied: "Over to the RALIS, to discuss this mess with them." The RALIS soldiers watched uneasily as the paratroopers approached, but when they saw that the Tancos troops no longer had guns, they jumped from their armored personnel carriers and jubilantly embraced their fellow soldiers. Another right wing putsch had failed--this time on camera.[4]

The unsuccessful attack on the RALIS barracks had been part of another attempt by the right-wing generals to cancel the revolution. The generals had expected the soldiers to follow orders dutifully, but their assumptions were wrong. They had not realized to what extent the example of independent thinking had taken hold among privates, and how the revolution had changed the balance of power within the ranks.

Once the Tancos parachutist privates had fraternized with the RALIS soldiers and stopped the second counterrevolution, the balance of forces within the military swung sharply toward the lower ranks and toward the left. It became apparent that the privates of Group 4 not only could think for themselves but could also act for themselves. Initially the revolution had been made by the captains and the generals, then by the captains alone. Now, after March 1975, the privates would have their say as well.

Spring 1975: The (Brief) Flowering of Socialism

Until now the revolution of carnations had indeed brought much liberty and even some democracy to Portugal. After the unsuccessful coup of March 11, the third aspect of the original MFA program, socialism, began to come to the fore. Portuguese capitalists, particularly the "100 families" who controlled big business and agriculture, came under increasing attack for their close associations with fascism. They were blamed for the two botched attempts to overthrow the revolutionary government and were discredited.

For the first time in Portugal some owners of industry and large landed estates lost control and for a while even ownership of "their" property. Sometimes it went directly to the people who did the work, sometimes to the government. Private banks, insurance companies, and major industrial concerns were taken over by their employees and often nationalized. The homeless squatted in empty urban housing. In southern Portugal landed estates were occupied and run by the agricultural workers. When the bosses appealed to the police to protect their property, the workers began calling on "their" soldiers--soldiers who had been told for the last year that it was their duty to defend "the people." And now they believed it. Often the police found it safer not to interfere.

On April 25, 1975, one year after the revolution, the freest election in Portuguese history gave a clear majority to the left. Between them the socialists, communists, and the various groupings of the new left, polled almost 59 percent of the vote. A further 7 percent of the voters cast blank ballots, as some of the most radical MFA had urged.[5] All the left-wing parties were officially anticapitalist, indeed Marxist. They were agreed, at least on paper, with the three MFA slogans: liberty, democracy and . . . socialism.

Although the socialists, who obtained 38 percent of the vote, officially stated that "capitalism is an oppressive and brutal force" and claimed to be "fighting for its total destruction," in reality their leader, Mario Soares, was now maneuvering to stop all further revolutionary change. For Soares and other socialist leaders, liberty for the people had been an acceptable slogan, and democracy was fine as long as only "responsible" people, such as themselves, were elected to office. But socialism in the form of attacks on the ownership of capital was taking freedom too far. Behind his anticapitalist verbiage, which brought the party many votes, Soares began to enter into de facto alliances with counterrevolutionary forces. A curious amalgam was mobilized to slow down any further development of the revolution.

Socialists, fascists, clerical reactionaries, and maoists found themselves united against the revolution.

Soares concentrated particular attention on splitting the MFA. Attempts to defeat the captains head on with right wing coups had failed, so the counterrevolutionaries now focused on exploiting the movement's internal differences. The MFA had long included three different tendencies: the radicals, led by Otelo de Carvalho; a middle group, then running the government (also called the Goncalvists); and the right, the so-called group of nine around Maelo Antunes. By summer 1975 the rightist group was fed up with socialism and the revolution, but by themselves they were a tiny minority within MFA. So the group skillfully maneuvered to take a prosocialist but anticommunist position as a means of attacking and isolating the Goncalvists, then in control of the government. The Antunes opposition claimed that the Goncalvists had become "tools of the Stalinists." At a critical moment in August these officers were able to win support of some of the naive radicals around Otelo, who had been antagonized by the bureaucratic and superior attitude of the Communist Party. The rightists and radicals together had a clear majority within the MFA, and the Goncalvist group was thus defeated and forced to withdraw from the government. The right then turned on the radicals and removed them from positions of power. As a result a new right-wing government was installed in early September.

A belated, last-minute attempt on August 25 to unite the various left forces in a "united revolutionary front" failed within two days. The accumulated hostility between the Communist Party and other revolutionary groups was simply too great. The communists felt threatened by the new left groups, while the leftists could not accept the bureaucratic approach of the communists. Possibilities for unity were further reduced by the still strong influence of maoists, who considered the pro-Soviet Portuguese Communist Party a greater enemy than Portuguese reaction. Divided among themselves and outmaneuvered by the right, the Portuguese revolutionaries both within the army and without were in retreat.

The SUV: Soldiers United Will Win

Just when the revolution seemed lost for good, a quite unexpected development occurred. An independent rank-and-file movement arose among low-ranking soldiers. For three months in the latter half of 1975 a few thousand nineteen-year-old recruits, abandoned and reviled by their superiors, kept the revolution alive.

Who were these soldiers who thought and acted as if they could change history? How and why did they challenge the power structure?

The facts are easy to summarize. In early September 1975 some soldiers in the northern city of Porto issued manifestos and demonstrated in the streets. They called themselves Soldados Unidos Vencerao (SUV), Soldiers United Will Win. Within days rank-and-file soldiers in Areman, Lisbon, Coimbra, Ambrantes, Beja, and towns all over Portugal also began meeting and organizing under the name SUV. Within weeks these soldiers were in the streets, blocking the efforts of the new counterrevolutionary government to restore and protect capitalism and the established order. When the government sent commandos to disperse demonstrating strikers and farmers, the SUV protected the people.[6]

SUV is forgotten now, but for three months in 1975 this independent rank-and-file movement prevented an apparently already victorious counterrevolution from taking power. The story of the SUV shows what can happen when previously passive soldiers finally move and take matters into their own hands.

The Battle of the Driving School

Before the revolution of the carnations tens of thousands of young Portuguese youths refused the draft or deserted military service rather than perform two and sometimes four years of duty defending the Portuguese empire. They realized, quite correctly, that it was not their army, nor their empire, and that they had no interest in protecting these institutions. The common thread among low-ranking soldiers in the days before and immediately after the revolution was to avoid or get out of the army. But as the Armed Forces Movement developed and the revolution it spawned showed promise, a new feeling of belonging emerged. In this new stage many young soldiers now wanted to stay in their unit, their army. It was now the military establishment that wanted to get rid of troublemakers in the ranks and assure absolute, unquestioning discipline.

This was the state of things in September 1975 as SUV began to exert influence. The soldiers of SUV no longer wanted to desert. Instead, one of their main demands was the right of soldiers to remain in their units in the army.

This is well illustrated in the incident at the army driving school, the CICAP, in Porto. As so often with soldier resistance, events started with a minor incident. On September 11, 1975, the soldiers had stood in silence for one minute during the morning formation. Silent standing, of course, is hardly unusual for morning assembly. It is what the soldiers are expected to do, while officers give them orders. But this minute of silence was different: It was to commemorate the second anniversary of the Pinochet putsch in Chile. And also to demand better food. (Here again the linkage of the small and the great, the demand for food and opposition to military dictatorship. This is a constant hallmark of effective GI resistance.) A month earlier, before the MFA turned right, this minute of silence might have passed unnoticed. But now, in September, the officers were out to reestablish discipline and order. Ringleaders were sought and found and were later expelled, sent home. Instead of gladly accepting the return to civilian life, though, these soldiers wanted to stay in the army. They appealed their discharge, not to the commanding officer but to their peers, the other CICAP soldiers. These troops voted 312 to 6 that the dismissed men be allowed to stay. The issue escalated. The command gave everyone a three-day pass over a holiday weekend, but when the soldiers returned, they found the entire unit disbanded, the barracks closed. Several hundred draftees now faced early discharges.[7]

Instead of rejoicing and going home, the fired soldiers insisted on staying in the army. They moved in with a neighboring artillery regiment, the RASP. Together the drivers and the artillerymen ran their barracks democratically. An "open-door festival" was organized. Civilians were invited in, films shown, and a good time had by all. The local commanders, dominated by the now counterrevolutionary leadership of the MFA, went berserk. One general wanted to starve the soldiers out, while another, Pires Veloso, wanted to bomb the barracks. Right-wing demonstrators attempted to storm the barracks, but the soldiers easily dispersed them. After a series of dramatic confrontations the command backed off. It accepted the "volunteers" and reopened their unit.

Freedom or Exile

While SUV soldiers fought to stay in their units, they did not want to stay inside the stockades. On September 26 over 3,000 Lisbon-area soldiers, followed by twice as many civilians, marched on the Caxix prison. They were peaceful but determined. They demanded that two GIs, jailed for participating in SUV, be freed. By 3 A.M. they were.

When the command could not disband a SUV-infected unit, they tried to transfer it away, out of Lisbon, and if possible out of Portugal. This was the case of airmen at Beja, who were ordered to the Azores. The airmen and their civilian supporters responded by marching through the streets; four were arrested and jailed. As the situation escalated, the supposedly "unpoliticized" parachutists from Tancos were flown in to reestablish order. The airmen refused to be intimidated and staged a sit-in and occupation of their barracks, daring the parachutists to open fire.[8]

In another incident the Lisbon military police regiment, a stronghold of the SUV, was to be transferred to Angola. The MPs discussed the transfer, noting that other units, not yet "infected" by the SUV, were being brought back from Africa. They voted not to go. And they stayed in Lisbon.[9]

Soldiers For the People, and For Themselves

In almost every army the soldiers swear to "protect the people." In practice this sometimes means shooting them. In Portugal, as SUV grew in strength, this was no longer the case.

Consider the incident of the veterans' march in September 1975. Thirty soldiers who had been maimed and permanently injured during the African wars precipitated a near-fatal confrontation. Their pensions were miserably low, approximately $80 per month. Since November 1974 the disabled veterans had been asking for more, but nothing had changed. In September the veterans took to the streets and marched near the parliament. A commando unit was called in to disperse them, a unit where all leftist soldiers and officers had been replaced by "trusted" troops. When an armored car bore down on a crippled vet in a wheel chair, ready to run him over, SUV soldiers from another unit intervened, firing over the heads of the commandos. The commandos withdrew, and the vets stayed. They took over the bridge on the Tagus River, abolished tolls, and then collected them one night in order to give the money to *Republica*, an independent newspaper run by its printers and journalists. The government sent additional troops to chase the vets from the bridge, but again the soldiers intervened on the side of the vets. In the end the pensions were increased.

Another incident occurred at the Spanish embassy on September 27. The dying Franco dictatorship had murdered, through garroting, five political prisoners. Antifascist demonstrators stormed the Spanish embassy in Lisbon, setting it on fire. Soldiers were called in and told to shoot to disperse the crowd. They refused. Instead they helped the firemen control the flames and then sang songs and picnicked with the crowd.

On November 12, building workers went on strike and marched on the parliament. They wanted better pay and collective bargaining. The government said: "Later." The workers said, "We can wait," and on the spot they staged a giant sit-in. To help speed up the debate they blocked food vans delivering supper to the members of parliament. Troops were called out to save the legislators from starvation. The soldiers laughed and sat down with the strikers to share the officials' dinner. Parliament quickly granted the workers' demands.

Of course the soldiers also had demands of their own. They marched in Porto, Lisbon, Coimbra, and elsewhere not only for "revolutionary unity between workers and soldiers", but also for free transport and more pay (they were getting only $20 per month). They also wanted better food and insisted upon the revolutionary demand that soldiers, officers, and NCOs be fed alike. Like soldiers elsewhere they also demanded freedom for their heads, to wear their beards and hair as long as they pleased. They also wanted to speak out, not only in their own newspapers, but also on the radio.

The Beginning of the End: Armed Intervention Groups and the Commandos

The right-wing officers who took control of the government in September were bent on stopping this revolution in the ranks. But as long as the politicized soldiers of the SUV remained in their barracks, armed, the officers were hampered. The only answer was to start a new army. Its core were the Armed Intervention Groups (AMI). At first these were to be formed from normal army units, with draftees commanded by right-wing officers. This did not work, because the soldiers organized SUV groups and refused to follow counterrevolutionary orders. Then commandos were used to form entirely new groups. These commando units included ex-fascist NCOs and officers brought back from the previous year's early retirement, uncontaminated troops freshly returned from Africa and free of the revolutionary influences of the past year, and the reactivated GNR, the hated fascist police force from the period of the dictatorship.

The formation of these commando units posed a serious problem for the leftist officers, who had to make a choice between obeying their superiors and charting a new, independent political course. In July 1975 one of the MFA commanders, Colonel Jaime Neves, began to convert his unit by bringing in right-wing commandos. Some of the other captains of the MFA opposed this trend and tried to stop the colonel. Together with a group of soldiers they barred the colonel from his unit. Colonel Neves then appealed to General Otelo de Carvalho, leader of the radicals within MFA. Officers stick together. In the name of discipline and hierarchy, Otelo ordered the leftist captains to obey the colonel, who, once back in command, quickly got rid of them and any other soldiers considered unreliable. Four months later the purged commando units played a major role in defeating the SUV, and then in arresting Otelo and other radical officers.

The "Soldiers' Coup?"--The Incident of the Tancos Parachutists

The Tancos parachutists were a key regiment of some 1,600 men and 150 officers stationed 60 kilometers from Lisbon. As we have noted, during the March 11 coup attempt they fraternized with their soldier brothers at the

RALIS barracks. The SUV as an organization was not strong in this unit, but among the NCOs there was an important group of the left-wing National Sergeants' Committee. The privates had previously been relatively unpoliticized, but they were becoming more aware and were dissatisfied with their use for counterrevolutionary purposes.

The final straw for the rank-and-file parachutists came on the night of November 7 when they were used for the destruction of radio Renascenca. This Lisbon radio station had been a center of controversy for some time. The station gave prominent coverage to SUV and allowed rank-and-file soldiers to speak on the air. On September 29, progovernment commandos had taken over the station and silenced it. The radio station then resumed broadcasting for a brief time, but on the night of November 7, the offices and broadcast facilities of radio Renascenca were destroyed in a fiery explosion. A company of the Tancos paratroopers had been used as cover for the operation, but a group of five officers actually did the dirty work.[10] The parachutists did not know why they were being called into action and were shocked to find out how they had been used. By the time they realized what was happening, though, it was too late: Radio Renascenca, the voice of the GIs, had been destroyed.

When the Tancos men realized they had been tricked, they contacted their home unit and quickly returned to explain what had happened. The sergeants, meeting apart from the GIs, condemned the destruction of the radio station and voted to ignore any future orders that went against the interests of the working class. They issued a press release to this effect. Air force Chief of Staff Silva immediately went to Tancos and demanded a meeting with all the officers and men. The majority of the NCOs boycotted this meeting. The air force chief tried to explain that the destruction of radio Renascenca had been ordered by the Revolutionary Council (which since September had passed into the hands of right-wing officers). Silva insisted to the men that "orders are orders."

The soldiers were not interested, though. Some privates and sergeants came to the "official" meeting and explained what had happened in Lisbon. General Silva was surrounded by angry paratroopers. One of the soldiers who had participated in the raid on radio Renascenca shouted to his colleagues: "We have no business here, comrades! Let's get out of here and go to the meeting of soldiers and sergeants." Most of the soldiers promptly walked out and went to the other meeting. There they voted to support the resolution of the sergeants. Confronted with such a revolt, the officers held their own meeting. Deciding that they had been "marginalized" and that they no longer could effectively command their troops, over 120 of the officers stationed at the base walked out of the barracks gates and abandoned their units.

Although some soldiers were jubilant that the officers had abandoned the regiment, the government was outraged. The Tancos parachutists were told that they were being discharged. The paratroopers refused to accept this solution, for they had developed a keen sense of pride in their unit, a high esprit de corps. The paratroopers promptly left Tancos and headed for Lisbon. There they occupied four air force headquarters stations and staged a sit-in strike. Their aim was merely to rescind the dissolution order, not to take state power as was later charged.

The Tancos soldiers had taken no heavy arms and very little ammunition on their march to Lisbon. They had made no attempt to coordinate with the other units where SUV was strong, nor with the few radical officers who still remained at command headquarters. They were in no way prepared to seriously defend themselves or engage in combat. At the Monsanto air force base they took the commanding general into custody, but they did not intend to harm him. In fact they allowed him to use the telephone freely, which turned out to be a big mistake. The general used the occasion to put into motion the counterrevolutionary coup that had been planned weeks earlier at a secret officers meeting in Laranjeiras.

The rightists now moved in for the final defeat of the revolution. Rearmed GNR police, commandos, and other AMI units were concentrated against the soldier strikers. Confronted by heavily armed troops who were prepared to shoot them even as they sat, the paratroopers broke off their strike and returned to Tancos. They had demonstrated for the right to remain in the military, not to engage in armed revolution. Nonetheless, the government, now in complete control of all radio and television stations, broadcast reports of an alleged "communist coup." The SUV soldiers supposedly engineering this coup were utterly confused. With no prearranged plan and no communications to the outside, they simply stayed where they were in their barracks. Regiment by regiment they were rolled up by the commandos. Only in the military police unit did SUV soldiers fight back, killing four commandos and losing two or three of their own men.[11]

By the evening of November 25 all was over. A few civilian leftists came to the barracks to ask for arms, but their attempt to help came too late. The Communist Party leadership, which learned from the radio that they were supposedly making a coup, took one look around, judged the situation hopeless, and stated that it was all a "provocation" with which they had nothing to do. The radical officers leader, Otelo de Carvalho, simply stated "Count me out" and went home. On the next day many units of the Portuguese army and air force were dissolved. Thousands of soldiers and airmen were discharged. Hundreds of soldiers, NCOs, and officers were arrested and imprisoned. SUV ceased to exist. The Portuguese revolution was now definitely over.

Could It Have Been Otherwise?

It is easy to recount facts but far more difficult to venture into speculation about what might have been. Could the SUV movement have preserved power for the revolution? What would have happened if, after the March 11 defeat of the right when the revolution was riding high, the left had supported and encouraged not only progressive officers but also an independent soldiers' movement? Would things have turned out differently?

Prior to the revolution of the carnations no independent soldier organizations existed, and it would have been extremely difficult to build an effective soldiers' movement. But after the captains made their revolution, the soldiers began to stir. Could the revolutionary forces have changed the course of events if they had helped soldiers build their groups? Or was the line of the Communist Party that ordinary soldiers should not develop independent organizations the only practical position? Perhaps strong and independent soldier organization in the months prior to August 1975 would have strengthened the leftist officers within the MFA. It is even possible to speculate that a broad-based soldiers' movement might have reduced the conflicts between communists and radicals that in practice proved so damaging to the Portuguese revolution.

Practically speaking, the nineteen-year-old draftees of SUV probably never had a chance. They had little hope of creating a peoples army, or of converting an army of revolution into an army of revolutionaries. But for a few short months in the second half of 1975 their star burned brightly, as they held back the forces of reaction and preserved the spirit of the carnations. The SUV is now gone, but the example and lessons of their experience will live on.

15

Chile

In 1975 the soldiers of Portugal often compared their situation with that of Chile two years earlier. They were determined that the Portuguese revolution would not go the way of Chile. Their motto was: "Portugal will not become the Chile of Europe." For soldier organizers everywhere the bitter events in Chile in 1973 serve as a constant reminder of how the army should not be used and why the military must be held democratically accountable.

Allende and the Military

Many in the United States, Europe, and throughout the world were shocked at the ease with which General Augusto Pinochet defeated the Popular Unity government of Salvador Allende in September 1973. The Chilean armed forces brutally overthrew the elected government, killing thousands of Chilean citizens. A fascist dictatorship under Pinochet was installed with the blessings and assistance of the United States. During the putsch, Chile's army privates followed their officers' orders. Despite considerable support for the Popular Unity government (which had increased its plurality in the popular vote from 36 percent in 1970 to 44 percent in March 1973), and despite the improved living standards that had been achieved for the poor and working classes, the armed forces performed obediently and without dissent in smashing Chilean democracy. Allende seemed totally unable to control the military and prevent the fascist coup.[1]

Allende's failure was not out of blindness to the dangers of a coup. Obviously many on the Chilean left knew there was a risk that the armed forces might rebel against the elected government. Chileans familiar with their own history knew that in this "Switzerland of South America" there had been a previous army coup, in 1924, followed by seven years of military dictatorship. The left was well aware of this danger and knew that parts of the armed forces, aided and abetted by the CIA, might putsch against the Popular Unity government. Unfortunately the different factions of the Popular Unity coalition could not agree on their analysis of the problem and how to counter it.

The Communist Party and some socialists, including Allende himself, believed that a coup could be prevented, or if it did occur defeated, by keeping a maximum number of generals loyal to the government. Allende wanted to split the military vertically. He sought to isolate the disloyal generals at the top and hoped that a majority of the other military chiefs and the rest of the armed forces would support the constitution. This analysis assumed that the opinions and actions of the generals were all that counted. The lower-ranking officers and NCOs, and certainly the rank-and-file soldiers, would simply follow orders and do as they were told.

This concept of trying to split the military vertically and retaining the loyalty of the top generals can be depicted as follows:

Figure 15.1

Loyalist Generals	Insurgent (Rightist) Generals

(troops simply follow orders)

Not everyone in the Popular Unity coalition shared the communist/ socialist strategy for dealing with the military. A large part of the left believed (as it turned out correctly) that the armed forces could not be trusted and that the people should be armed in order to support the government and resist a coup. They argued that arms should be bought, stolen, or manufactured in the factories and that they should be distributed to workers. The Movimento Izquierdista Revolucionario (MIR), Movement of the Revolutionary Left, emphasized the formation of specialized mobile combat groups. The arming of the population was necessary, according to these groups, not only to prevent the feared military coup but also to defend workers against the growing terror of the fascist group "Patria y Libertad." This position was shared by some rank-and-file communists and by many Socialist Party members.

But Allende himself equivocated. At first he opposed the arming of workers. Later he closed his eyes to it. Finally, in the last hours of the Popular Unity government, when the armed forces were bombing and storming the Moneda, the elderly president, a doctor by profession, picked up a gun himself and died in combat.*

---

* According to 1990 reports in the Chilean press, Allende took his own life in the final moments of the bloody assault.

This concept of the left socialists can be depicted as follows:

Figure 15.2

Loyalist Forces:	Rightist Insurgents:
Armed Workers and Peasants, and Civilian Combat Groups	The Armed Forces Fascist Terrorists

There was a third alternative for dealing with the military, but this approach was supported only by the MIR and some far-left elements of the Socialist Party. Their plan was based on a class analysis of the military and the idea of exacerbating the natural divisions between the ranks. This third strategy sought to win the active political support of the soldiers and sailors and to encourage resistance to the generals planning a coup.

This concept of a horizontal split is illustrated below:

Figure 15.3

Insurgent (Rightist): Generals/Admirals/Officers
Loyalist: NCOs/Soldiers/Sailors/Airmen

Unfortunately, the Allende government remained wedded to the strategy of winning the trust and support of the generals. As a result they refused to back their supporters within the lower ranks. Allende and his communist supporters felt that organizations for democracy in the lower ranks would antagonize the "constitutionalist" officers. To the bitter end they held on to the illusory hope that the generals could be trusted.

A Lost Opportunity?

Was an attempt at the third alternative, resistance within the ranks, realistic? We can never be sure. Certainly there is little evidence that rank-and-file Chilean soldiers would have been receptive to a message from the left. As we have observed throughout this book, leftist movements among enlisted soldiers in recent years usually occur only in highly capitalized nations. In the developing nations, Chile included, resistance movements within the lower ranks have been absent. Only in Portugal did an autonomous soldiers' movement emerge in a country below the threshold. But this happened only after a turbulent year during which revolutionary officers politicized the entire country, including rank-and-file soldiers.

Nothing of this sort occurred in Chile, however. There was no progressive movement of junior officers equivalent to the MFA. No antiauthoritarian example was given to the Chilean soldiers by their officers. The more progressive generals who supported the constitution and the government, such as generals Carlos Prats and Rene Schneider, accepted and reinforced the military hierarchy and the chain of command. These officers gave no impetus to an independent soldiers' movement.

As for the rightist generals and admirals who were to lead the coup in 1973, they did everything in their power to take advantage of the situation and crush all opposition, both in the barracks and in civilian society. For example, when Chile's workers tried to manufacture and store weapons in factories, the generals instituted a series of brutal searches. The searches were carried out only against government supporters; no attempt was made to find and confiscate arms in the hands of subversive right-wing groups, such as Patria y Libertad. Apart from disarming the workers, these raids had other effects: When soldiers shot and killed workers during these searches, it became very hard to establish links between the left and rank-and-file troops. Many soldiers, aware of the hatred they aroused, then became even more alienated and driven to further excesses. Those soldiers who tried to oppose such actions were identified by military intelligence as "troublemakers" and discharged. They received no support from the outside, and they were completely isolated within the ranks.

Unlike their counterparts in Portugal two years later, rank-and-file soldiers in Chile received no democratic rights during the Popular Unity government period. Allende and his ministers maintained the tradition of draconian discipline and absolute obedience within the ranks that had been carried over from earlier times. Little was done by the socialist government to improve the status of the low-ranking soldiers for fear that this would antagonize the generals.

Nonetheless, it is possible that independent attempts to provide democratic rights and political education for rank-and-file soldiers might have changed the balance of power within the Chilean army. If a concerted campaign had been waged to win the loyalty of lower-ranking soldiers and NCOs, the soldiers might have been less willing to overthrow the elected government. A more democratic army might have been more difficult for the generals to control. It is a sad commentary that only small groups like the MIR even attempted to reach the soldiers.

In September 1971, for example, the MIR published a program on the armed forces in its weekly paper, *El Rebelde*. It read:

We demand the immediate democratization of the armed forces and police:
• the right to vote
• an end to internal discrimination
• one salary scale for officers and men
• integration of professional schools belonging to the different branches
• the right for the ranks to meet freely and discuss their problems
• the right to read and have copies of all kinds of magazines within the barracks
• a just wage
• an eight-hour day, in practice, with compensation for overtime
• the right to participate in mass organizations, like all workers
• the right for all soldiers and policemen not to be used as a force of repression against the working class
• the right to disobey officers calling for a coup
• the right to join with the people in their struggle against the capitalist class.[2]

Obviously the MIR program was not merely democratic but revolutionary in nature. Nonetheless, if the Popular Unity government had introduced even a few minimal reforms, particularly a "just wage," Chile's rank-and-file soldiers might well have begun to feel less isolated from their government. A program of reform and initial democratic rights might have started Chile's soldiers on the road to organization and to increased loyalty and support for the government.

Not only did the government reject the MIR program, it also removed that issue of *El Rebelde* from the newsstands and brought legal charges against its author, Andres Pascal Allende, who happened to be a nephew of the president. Although the charges against the writer were quietly dropped a few weeks later, the point had been made: no "political interference" [sic!] would be tolerated in the armed forces. The army was to remain firmly under the control of its officers.

The MIR thereafter downgraded its attempts to work with soldiers. The fact of the matter is that this largely student and middle-class-based organization had little or no direct contact with the peasant-based enlisted ranks. For the MIR and other leftist groups, rank-and-file soldiers were a separate group, not part of themselves. The student revolutionaries were largely of middle-class, urban backgrounds, while the rank-and-file soldiers came from the rural peasantry and the poor and working classes. Members of MIR had little or no personal contact with rank-and-file soldiers, and there was no concerted effort to encourage activists to join the army and organize from within. A few student leftists might have ended up as junior officers, but very few activists intentionally joined the military or allowed themselves to be drafted. Had leftists worked inside the army and demanded elementary rights such as better pay and access to reading material, the fate of the Popular Unity government might have been different.

Mutiny in Valparaiso: Coup or Countercoup?

While the Popular Unity government may have missed an opportunity in 1971 in not supporting democratic rights for rank-and-file soldiers, two years later it virtually sealed its destruction when it betrayed its supporters in the navy. In August 1973 naval petty officers and sailors attempted to seize their ships as a way of thwarting the then-imminent putsch by the generals and admirals. The Valparaiso uprising was quickly crushed and was followed a month later by the coup that eliminated the Popular Unity government.

As noted above, the Popular Unity government increased its popular support in the congressional elections of March 1973. Contrary to the hopes and expectations of the Chilean right, which had been waging a bitter campaign against the Allende coalition (heavily funded and assisted by the CIA), the Popular Unity coalition was gaining in popularity. After these elections the Chilean right abandoned attempts to win through the democratic process and actively prepared the option of a military putsch. The Allende government, however, continued to place its hopes in the generals, still believing that an effective majority of the military leadership would respect the constitution.

To some extent Allende's faith in the loyalty of the military seemed confirmed by the Tancazo incident, a first attempt at a military coup on June 29, 1973. Officers commanding the Second Armored Regiment sent their tanks and armored cars against the Moneda (the Chilean White House) and the Ministry of Defense. After some initial successes, the revolt broke down when other units failed to support the rebels and when loyalist general Carlos Prats approached the insurgent tanks and successfully convinced the soldiers to surrender. The colonel commanding the putsch attempt had jumped the gun. He did not know that his superiors and the CIA were already preparing for a more extensive, ultimately successful attack on the government a few weeks later.

Although the Tancazo coup attempt had failed, the political atmosphere within Chile became increasingly tense. The Nixon Administration's wide-ranging international campaign to strangle the Chilean economy was having a serious impact internally, and the CIA-supported domestic opposition became ever-more brazen. A long truckers' strike disrupted food supplies, and middle-class housewives banged empty pots against Allende in the streets of Santiago. Rumors of coup preparations by the armed forces circulated widely.

In the midst of this highly charged atmosphere a group of petty officers and sailors in Valparaiso and the main naval base at Talcahuano learned from internal documents passing through their hands that their commanders, the top admirals of the navy, were preparing a major coup attempt in September.[3] Apparently this group of sailors included a number of supporters of the Popular Unity government and the left. This progressive block was concentrated among petty officers, primarily career enlisted men working in skilled technical positions. It was here, among the middle ranks of the military in the technical branches of the navy, that the Chilean left enjoyed a modest but genuine base of support.

Unfortunately the sailors in Valparaiso were completely isolated from the Allende government and the established left. The sailors tried by all means to alert the Popular Unity forces, but only the small MIR and the left wing of the Socialist Party paid any attention to their warnings. They had previously counted on the trust and help of president Allende's naval aide, Captain Arturo Araya Peters, but the captain had been shot and killed on the balcony of his home on July 27. (It was suspected that this suspiciously-timed murder had been carried out by the fascist Patria y Libertad, working as a hit squad for the generals and the CIA.) When the Valparaiso sailors discovered documents confirming preparations for the coup attempt, they knew that the hour of judgment was approaching. Unheeded by the government and lacking external support from the civilian left, the sailors decided they had no choice but to take matters into their own hands.

What happened next in Valparaiso is still unclear even seventeen years later. The official story is that the left attempted a coup. In fact, however, the sailors were acting to prevent a coup by their superiors. According to a petty officer who participated in these events and was interviewed by the authors, the sailors and petty officers decided to take over the principal warships at the base as a way of preventing their use in the coming putsch.[4] The mutiny action was initially successful and largely nonviolent, but the action subsequently collapsed when naval officers, backed by the Allende government, brought force against the rebels.

News reports at the time and the subsequent official accounts confirm that a naval revolt took place but tend to confuse what actually happened. For example, Marvin Howe, the *New York Times* correspondent in Chile, wrote laconically in the August 8 issue:

The office of the commander of the navy confirmed reports of the discovery of a subversive movement in two units of the navy. The navy statement said that investigations had shown that the movement was backed by extremists from outside the navy but did not say they were of the left or right.[5]

That was all. Neither the *New York Times* nor the naval command found it necessary to clarify whether the "subversives" were officers planning to overthrow the leftist government, or, as our sources suggest, leftist sailors attempting to prevent a putsch.

In his book, *The Last Two Years of Salvador Allende,* then-U.S. ambassador to Chile Nathaniel Davis also recalled the Valparaiso incident:

On August 7 the office of the commander in chief of the navy announced the discovery of a mutinous plot that was supposed to have been executed on the 11th in Valparaiso and Talcahuano, the naval base outside Concepcion. Twenty-three sailors were arrested . . . in Valparaiso it was reported, small cells of sailors on board the cruiser Almirante Latorre and the destroyer Blanco Encalada were conspiring to murder their officers and to bombard marine and navy barracks near the Naval Academy.[6]

General Carlos Prats also commented on the incident in his diary. Prats noted that two left-wing members of parliament had been implicated in the sailors' action, but he believed, incredibly, that the incident had been trumped up by "anti-UP (Popular Unity) people, or perhaps naval intelligence." Prats gloomily noted that "the politicians' folly permitted coup-minded admirals to gauge loyalties and political orientation of non-commissioned officers" in the navy.[7] That the sailors had been correct, that an antigovernment coup was being prepared, never seems to have entered his mind. That the rank-and-file sailors had heroically risked their lives to defend the government and constitution was never mentioned.

Many of the sailors involved (according to the petty officer we interview there were hundreds, not just twenty-three) were imprisoned and tortured. President Allende, their commander-in-chief, gave them no support. The military chiefs who were at that moment planning the coup were allowed a free hand inside the military. Allende made a public statement condemning what he called a seditious movement by the ultraleft and vowing that political infiltration in the armed forces would be stopped.[8] It was a pathetic spectacle: The socialist president decrying left "infiltration" in the military while continuing to appease the fascist generals plotting his demise. Allende went so far as to accept the resignation of his leading constitutionalist supporter in the military, General Prats. On August 24 the president appointed Augusto Pinochet as the new commander-in-chief. Three weeks later that same Pinochet led the coup that killed Allende and Chilean democracy.

The September 11 coup was a dark moment in history and a grim reminder of the importance of ensuring democratic control of the military. The Chilean experience was a graphic illustration that the "ultimate resort" of armed force remains the underlying foundation of state power. Without a successful formula for maintaining control of the armed forces, the Popular Unity government succumbed to fascism.

Chile is also a powerful symbol for the soldiers' movement. It is the ultimate example of what can go wrong and why the movement for a democratic military is so vitally important. For soldier activists in Italy, Spain, and throughout the world, the rallying cry is, "Chile will never happen here."

The experience of Chile also contains an important clue to understanding resistance in the armed forces in developing nations. In nations below the capital accumulation threshold, effective resistance is unlikely to be found among conscripts and lower-ranking soldiers. Nor are we likely to find many generals and admirals with leftist leanings. As we noted in Chapter 6, when the tanks rolled in Santiago on September 11, only five of Chile's twenty-one top commanders remained loyal to the government. The one place where the support for the Popular Unity government was evidenced was in the middle ranks of the navy. Only within the technical branches of the navy, among enlisted petty officers, was there overt and organized support for the Popular Unity government. It is particularly interesting to note that these developments surfaced in the skilled, technical branches of the navy. As we shall see, a similar development occurred in Iran a few years later, where air force cadets and junior officers sparked the final revolt that led to the overthrow of the Shah.

Iran: The Airmen's Revolt

From 1953 to 1977 the Iranian regime of Shah Reza Pahlavi seemed rock solid, the foundation of United States influence in the important Persian Gulf region. A large army and air force, backed by thousands of U.S. advisers and an enormous secret police, appeared to guarantee the stability of the dictatorship against all external and internal enemies. In 1979, however, after eighteen months of upheaval, the entire edifice crumbled into dust, shattered by an unexpected mass revolt. Millions of ordinary people, inspired by religious fervor, stood up to the army's guns and bullets.

What began in 1978 with demonstrations in the holy city of Qum soon spread to mass rebellion throughout the country, including in the capital city of Tehran. As the size and intensity of the demonstrations steadily grew, so did the determination of the participants. The increasing possibility that they might be killed by the police and the army did not deter them. They were, according to some, fanatical. But they were also unarmed, and for months they were unable to break the power of the state.

Even after the Shah left the country and the exiled Ayatollah Khomeini returned to Tehran, the Iranian army, backed by the United States, continued killing demonstrators. Despite the popular upheaval the army had not cracked. The decisive turning point in the revolution finally came when revolt broke out within parts of the air force. The collapse of the Shah came when a small but significant sector of the military, skilled air force NCOs and officer cadets, passed over to the side of the revolution.

The Airmen Rise Up

Although the power of the regime was slipping in early 1979, state power and the support of the military still remained firmly in the hands of the Shah's prime minister Gama Bakhtiar.[1] Within the armed forces the situation seemed calm. The highly paid and well-purged ranks of the upper officer corps remained solidly on the side of the government. The rank-and-file draftees continued to follow orders. Although there were dramatic, staged presentations of deserted soldiers to the Ayatollah, these were more on an individual rather than mass basis. There is no evidence of groups of uniformed soldiers going over to the side of the people during the many bloody street battles that occurred, nor of any effective conscript organization within the barracks.[2]

The situation was quite different among the junior ranks of the air force, however, particularly the technicians responsible for the maintenance and repair of Iran's modern aircraft. This group included some civilian technicians who lived on base and were subject to military discipline. Those on active duty were equivalent in rank to warrant officers and senior technical sergeants. These technicians were in close contact with air force draftees who performed support work and served as air force police. Here resistance was widespread, cohesive and, as it turned out, decisive.

By the latter part of 1978 it was clear that a major revolt was brewing, although government censors tried to keep it secret. A dramatic series of events in December brought the rebellion into the open. At the Lavizam Air Force base, east of Tehran, three uniformed men went into the officers' mess, weapons in hand, and demanded that the officers, members of the Shah's elite Imperial Guard, "praise Khomeini." When the officers refused, the three opened fire on the group, killing twelve and wounding twenty before being killed themselves.[3] Embarrassed government spokesmen insisted that these "terrorists" were not airmen but civilians who had stolen uniforms. This interpretation was difficult to sustain in another incident during the same month. Air cavalry commander Major General Manoucher Khosrodad was shot out of the air in his own helicopter by his men at the Bagh-e-Shah barracks in southwest Tehran. Although the general survived, the attack shook up the command.[4] Officer-pilots were also shaken in Tabriz, after they found that air force enlisted men had tampered with the control mechanisms of their F-4 and F-5 jet fighters. The air force claimed that the sabotage was discovered before there were any "accidents."[5]

By early February it was no longer possible to hide the fact that scores of air force technicians had been arrested for organizing and demonstrating on the air bases. Although some had been quietly freed, a sit-in by relatives of detained NCOs at the Justice Ministry testified to the continuing resistance movement.[6]

The Explosion

To maintain discipline and prevent further demonstrations by the airmen, the government now sent units of the elite Imperial Guards to the air bases. On the evening of February 9, 1979, NCOs at Tehran's Farahabad Air Force barracks, apparently celebrating the release of some airmen earlier arrested, were ordered out of their barracks by the guards and simply shot down. Estimates of the death toll among the unarmed airmen range from twenty to seventy.[7]

On the same evening, at Doshan Tapeh Air Base, also in Tehran, NCOs were watching a television program showing the Ayatollah's return to Iran. They responded to the program with pro-Khomeini chants, whereupon the small unit of Imperial Guards stationed at the base called for reinforcements. When additional guards, apparently from the crack Gavidan regiments, arrived with tanks and machine guns, the technicians "became unruly."[8] The guard's colonel ordered an air force sentry to fire at the technicians. When the sentry refused, he was shot on the spot. Thereupon the technicians, now joined by other air force personnel, including cadets and junior officers, began to defend themselves with bricks and building blocks. Under fire from the guards and military police, the airmen rushed the armory, killed the sentry, armed themselves, and began to shoot back.

For the first time the Shah's "elite" guards faced an armed opposition. Although they called in reinforcements, including helicopters, they were unable to recapture the air base. Thousands of civilians rushed to support the rebels, and the airmen now began to distribute arms to the population. After heavy fighting, the Imperial Guard, one of their helicopters hit by antiaircraft fire, withdrew. The rebellion then took on a new and decisive stage, leading to a short-lived civil war and the final victory.[9] On February 12, 1979, with rebellion having reached even to the ranks of the armed forces, the army command declared its "neutrality," and the Shah's regime collapsed.[10]

Was It Decisive?

Would the Iranian dictatorship have been overthrown in any case, or did the airmen's revolt decide the issue? It is certainly possible that the continuous willingness of the Iranian population to face the army's guns eventually would have eroded the military's power to maintain the system. In that case the airmen's revolt was but one more straw, and just by chance the one that broke the camel's back. But some of Iran's generals believed that they could reestablish order by a military coup, by imposing a really serious repression. In 1965 this model had "worked" in Indonesia, where the armed forces and police unleashed a reign of terror that left more than a half-million people dead. Indonesia is still ruled by the military, so why not at least try this also in Iran? To the extent that they made such a coup impossible and inflicted defeat on the Imperial Guard, the airmen made history.

Unexpected Rebels

Why did the air force technicians rebel and help bring down the established government? The answer lies in the background of the revolution and Iranian society.

Some have argued that the Shah for all his faults was relatively progressive, while the Islamic revolution led by the ayatollahs was a return to an irrational, reactionary past. The Shah and his Washington allies said they were carrying out a revolution from above, dragging a reluctant Iran into the modern world. The fight was between modernism and "old-time" fundamentalism.

A far more important and fundamental reality, however, was that the Shah had always been linked to foreign imperialism. In 1941 he had been installed on the throne by the British, who had forced his father, considered pro-German, to abdicate. For ten years the Shah served England and the Anglo-Iranian oil company. In 1953 he opposed the Mossadegh government, a first attempt by the Iranian bourgeoisie to gain control of their country's oil. After 1953, when a CIA-organized coup overthrew Mossadegh, the Shah switched his allegiance to the United States.

The Shah and his regime did not represent national interests, not even of the bourgeoisie, but rather foreign interests, especially those of U.S. capitalism. This arrangement worked for some time, but inevitable contradictions emerged. Foreign capital is not interested in domestic change or revolution. It does not want nationalism to get out of hand. Its aim is to increase exports and imports. But these imports undermine domestic handicraft industries and antagonize the national bourgeoisie, which wants to increase domestic production. The more imports grow, the greater the destruction of the peasant economy, the stronger the pressure on the national bourgeoisie.

Eventually a broad revolutionary coalition emerged. It was patriotic, antiimperialist, and rabidly antiforeign. Workers and students were joined by the national bourgeoisie, who wanted to end foreign control of wealth, and by the mullahs, who were the religious leaders of the peasantry. The revolution took on an Islamic and religious character in part because British and U.S. interests had devalued the native religion and looked down on the Iranian mullahs as backward fanatics. The Shah, America's stooge, had exiled the Ayatollah Khomeini, thus making him a symbol of resistance. Nonreligious rationalism or other liberal ideologies were at a disadvantage, since they were associated with the hated foreign imperialists. Revolutionary anti-imperialism thus mixed with domestic reaction.

The air force NCOs were at the heart of these contradictions, and reflected the impulses of the revolution well. They were increasingly resentful of the foreign influence blocking their progress. Although those highly skilled technicians may not have been fanatically devout followers of the mullahs, they saw the long-exiled Khomeini as a leader of the antiforeign movement and supported his return to Iran. The particular development of the revolt in the air force grew in part from the special importance placed on the Iranian air force by the Shah and his U.S. sponsors. As the air force grew and increased demands were placed on it, deep contradictions emerged.

Paid for by an appreciable portion of Iran's share in its oil wealth, the Iranian air force was destined to play a preeminent role in the Persian Gulf. It was supposed to consolidate U.S. interests in the region, and had already actively participated in suppressing left-wing guerrillas in Dhopar/Oman. But a modern air force needs not only planes, but also highly trained technicians who can service these aircraft and their increasingly sophisticated weapons systems. Here was a fatal flaw for the Shah. Initially many air force technicians were foreign, Americans from the Military Assistance Groups. As the size of the air force and the demand for specialists increased, it became necessary to recruit and train more "natives" for the job. By necessity these recruits came from more educated, urban sectors of society. Illiterate peasants were of no use to the air force. The armed forces needed more upwardly mobile middle-class youth to serve as their technicians.

Inevitably the interests of this rising technical class began to clash with those of the foreigners, in this case Americans. As the specialists gained technical skill and experience, they became more equal with their instructors and less dependent. The relationship became antagonistic when the native technicians perceived that Americans were blocking opportunities for advancement and promotion. When the trainees were sent abroad for instruction, usually to the United States, they often learned more than their commanders bargained for. The experience had an "eye-opening effect" on many. The Iranians saw the "freer" life style of the Americans and their frequent disrespect for hierarchy. They also became increasingly aware of their new-found power vis-a-vis their superiors, the higher-ranking officers. This process was described for the authors by a U.S. sergeant who worked as a helicopter technical instructor for the Military Advisory Group in Tehran before the revolution. "Once they knew only they could fix the birds, they stopped kissing the ground the officers walked on."[11]

The army draftees by contrast remained in the barracks and followed orders. Although they were drawn from the same strata of society as the demonstrating crowds and were subject to the same religious and political influences, the Iranian conscripts continued firing on their brothers and sisters throughout the revolution. There were individual cases of desertion, but no instances of organized rebellion. The army stopped fighting only when its generals, the Supreme Council, decided to abandon the Bakhtiar government and announced army neutrality.

Why did the peasant-based army continue to fight against the people, while more advantaged airmen supported the revolution and gave it a decisive boost? The essential factors seem to have been social class and the relative development of society. For Iranian privates the army still represented "three square meals and a cot." Although their (military) standard of living might seem atrocious to soldiers from highly capitalized countries, many peasant draftees found it an improvement on their previous poverty-stricken life. If the draftee was ill-paid, at least he was now fed. Also, the peasant's traditional patriarchal lifestyle made them more ready to accept authority, the father being replaced by the officer.

Air force technicians, on the other hand, were more middle class. As noted earlier, they came from more-educated, usually urban families. They were in a prestigious profession where there were many more applicants than openings. They were often the brightest youths, those most open to critical thinking. From the beginning they were more questioning of authority than the kid who stayed home in the slums or on the farm or who went into the army as a private. Where army privates followed orders to the bitter end, the consciousness and class interests of the air force NCOs led them to revolt.

Iran shows that in below-the-threshold countries, where the mass of the rank-and-file is not yet ready to organize independently, a technical core, influenced by nationalism and by contact with more highly capitalized societies, can develop effective forms of resistance. And sometimes, under quite unexpected conditions, they can turn an instrument of repression into one of revolt.

17

The Philippines: Another Portugal?

The "Official Story"

By late 1985 the regime of Ferdinand Marcos, long a favorite ally of Washington, was badly discredited by years of corruption and the botched assassination of opposition leader Beningno Aquino in August 1983. Under pressure from the United States to "clean up his act," Marcos surprisingly and suddenly calls for presidential elections in February 1986. On December 2, Corazon Aquino, wife of the slain leader, announces her intention to run for the presidency. The Catholic Church and middle classes make it clear they are dropping their erstwhile hero, Marcos. He has simply stolen "too much." They organize NAMFREL, an election watchdog agency that reduces the customary fraud and gets out the anti-Marcos vote. The left considers the elections a sham and ignores them (which turns out to be a mistake).

Polls and meetings show that the opposition candidate, "Cory," has a chance. Marcos and his cronies begin to run scared. Despite the murder of at least ninety-three people by government thugs, on February 7 Aquino gets a majority. Marcos, as expected, ignores the result and is confirmed in office by his National Assembly. Initially he is supported by his friend in Washington, Ronald Reagan. Aquino refuses to accept the steal, though, and on February 18 the Catholic bishops condemn the Marcos fraud. Thereupon Defense Minister Juan Ponce Enrile, suddenly shocked by such blatant violation of democratic principles, calls on the people and the army to recognize Cory Aquino as the elected president. Marcos sends troops against Enrile's Defense Ministry headquarters, but in a dramatic display of "people power" a million Filipinos surround the area and plead with the soldiers to desist. Under the influence of the Reformed Armed Forces Movement, RAM, the soldiers refuse to shoot the civilians. Within three days the armed forces abandon the dictator and offer their support to Aquino. Marcos, belatedly abandoned by Washington, flees to Hawaii with his stolen funds and family (and some of his wife's 2,000 pairs of shoes). Aquino becomes president.[1]

The officers of the Reformed Armed Forces Movement, the RAM, gave decisive support to the restoration of democracy in the Philippines. Does this mean that the RAM can be equated to its Portuguese predecessor, the Armed Force Movement, MFA? Does this mean that RAM will protect Filipino democracy from attempts to reintroduce dictatorship? Not necessarily.

The Real Story

The official version is true as far as it goes, but it is also incomplete. In fact, long before Aquino decided to run against Marcos, the founders of the RAM had been plotting a coup against the Marcoses, above all against Imelda, the president's wife. Marcos had made it clear that he expected Imelda to take over the presidency when he died or became too feeble to govern. This interfered with the ambitions of Juan "Johnny Rambo" Enrile, who wanted the job for himself. Unfortunately, Minister Enrile was deeply identified with the Marcos regime, whose corrupt practices had enabled him to become one of the richest men in the Philippines, and he could hardly expect the opposition to nominate him as their candidate in any foreseeable elections. He knew as well that Marcos would fire him, or worse, were he to openly oppose Imelda.

Meanwhile, around 1983, a group of officers, initially almost all graduates of the Philippine Military Academy Class of 1971, began to meet for informal gripe sessions. They claimed to be shocked by the corruption endemic in the army, in the government, and in the country. Soon they formed a clandestine group and named it the Reformed Armed Forces Movement, RAM. As students of military history, the officers were well aware of the Portuguese MFA and of its historic role. By March 1985 the RAM was strong enough to "go public." As the Philippine Military Academy alumni paraded before the reviewing stand, the marching officers unfurled their banners: "Unity Through Reform." Marcos and his armed forces chief Fabian Ver were not amused.[2]

The RAM was never a revolutionary movement. Enrile had been involved for months, if not from the start. The de facto leader of RAM was Colonel Gregorio Honasan, a close friend of the minister. (Honasan later became the leader of major revolts against the new Aquino government.) The entire core of the leadership group of RAM were members of Enrile's personal staff at Defense Ministry headquarters. RAM had become Enrile's tool, although most of the 2,000 officers who eventually joined were not told.

During 1985 the RAM leaders began plotting a reformist coup that would "restore democracy", that is, replace Marcos with Enrile. By September 1985 plans for a New Year's Eve coup had been finalized and were proceeding apace. The plotters intended to capture the presidential palace, Malacanang, the Philippine White House, and arrest the Marcoses. Unfortunately for Enrile the plot had to be postponed in November, when Marcos suddenly called for an election. A preelectoral putsch could hardly be for democracy. Perhaps Marcos had smelled the coup coming and pulled the rug out from under it.

The elections came and went, but Marcos was still president. A new putsch was planned, this time for February 23d. As before, the target was the palace. At this point the plotters made a mistake. They told the CIA of their plans, since after all the United States was "for democracy." CIA station chief Norbett Garrett foiled their efforts, though, and informed Marcos and Ver. When Ver brought loyal troops into the palace, the colonels saw that their plot was known, and they called off the attack. To continue would have been suicide.

Knowing that he would soon be arrested or shot, his plans having failed, Enrile made a bold move. He fled forward. He went to the Ministry of Defense headquarters and called for a revolt, no longer for himself, but for democracy, for Cory Aquino as president. Aquino was suspicious but played along. By doing so she won the game and the presidency, and Enrile wound up second.[3]

The RAM had been Enrile's tool but it was never effectively used. The planned coup, intended to bring Enrile into power, never happened. Instead the RAM officers sided with "people power" and helped Aquino become president. The RAM had served a progressive role in getting Cory Aquino into office, although in subsequent years some of the same officers joined Colonel Honasan's attempts to overthrow her.

Similarity, or Contrast?

At first sight there seem to be many similarities between the RAM of the Philippines in 1986 and the MFA of Portugal in 1974. In both countries reform-minded officers sided with the people and helped bring down corrupt dictatorships. Upon closer examination, though, we see more contrasts than similarities. In the Portuguese MFA the reality of power and decision making lay with the middle-ranking officers, captains and majors, not the generals. The higher officers, such as Spinola, who wanted only a cosmetic change, were being used. In the Philippines it was the other way around, at least in part. The junior officers who believed they were conspiring for democracy were being manipulated by Juan Enrile. The RAM was not intended as an instrument for installing democracy or making far-reaching changes, since such reform would have swept away not only Marcos but Enrile as well.

The primary thrust for the overthrow of Marcos and the installation of Cory Aquino came from the people themselves, primarily the church and the middle classes. The officers of RAM played a supporting role, not a leading role as had been the case with the members of the Portuguese MFA.

Another major difference is in the role of ordinary soldiers. As noted earlier, the Portuguese captains eventually were obliged to call upon the privates to support them in their struggle. In 1975 politicized Portuguese soldiers formed an independent movement, SUV, Soldiers United Will Win, and continued the Revolution of the Carnations for several crucial months. In the Philippines, by contrast, there is no evidence of any independent resistance or political action from rank-and-file soldiers. As in other below-the-threshold countries, Filipino privates continue to carry out orders--and if need be still shoot and torture their own people--without organized dissent.

Based on the relatively low level of economic development in the Philippines (the country is ranked ninety-first on the chart of GNP/capita), we should not expect to see any development of independent left resistance among low-ranking Filipino soldiers. As we have noted repeatedly, independent soldier and GI resistance movements usually occur only in countries above a certain threshold of capital accumulation.

ECCO and the Continuing Soldiers' Movement in Europe

In the soldier movements of many highly capitalized countries a similar pattern has emerged: An initial period of mass protest is followed by a decline in activity. Repression and reform greet the new soldier movements, which then go into decline. Resistance and the organized movement may continue, but at a lower level.

In many Western countries the initial militant stage of the movement came in the early 1970s. These peaks usually did not correspond to the high points of the "youth revolt," but followed them by some years. May 1968 was the high-water mark of the French student and worker revolt, but the soldiers' resistance developed only in 1974. After a stormy upswing over one or two years the soldiers' movement usually went into decline. The political establishments, both left and right, regretfully or happily buried the soldier's movement and saw it as dead, departed with the youth revolt of the 1960s. But they were too quick. Soldier committees, GI newspapers, and protest movements continued in nearly all highly capitalized countries into the 1980s.

Perhaps the best sign of this continuation of the soldiers' movement is the birth and growth of ECCO, the European Conference of Conscripts' Organizations. As noted in Chapter 8, ECCO was founded in 1979 at a conference in Malmö, Sweden, at a time when many thought the soldiers' movement already dead. ECCO has continued to meet every year since and has remained active into the 1990s. A living embodiment of the continuing soldiers' movement, ECCO has become an effective vehicle for communication among the conscripts of Europe. Throughout the 1980s ECCO brought together low-ranking soldiers from more than a dozen different countries. Then in 1989 new conscript-participants arrived from the Soviet Union and Hungary. At the 11th ECCO conference in Helsinki, nineteen-year old conscripts Armen Handkaryan of the Soviet Union and Krizstian

Winckler of Hungary came to share information about conditions in their changing armies and to learn about the soldier movements of the West. United by their common fate at the bottom of the military hierarchy, the soldiers of ECCO are forging programs for greater democracy in the ranks and peace in the world.

After the first conferences in Malmö and Putten, Holland, ECCO conferences were held each year in Paris (1981); Copenhagen (1982); Helsinki (1983); Athens (1984); Malmö (1985); Vienna in (1986); Dworp, Belgium (1987);Helvoirt,Netherlands (1988);Helsinki (1989);and Madrid (1990). At the Paris meeting, an official program and statement of purpose were established. A steering committee is elected each year, consisting of conscript or recent veteran representatives from different countries. The secretariat has been at the VVDM office in Utrecht, Holland. A special ECCO newsletter, *Newssheet*, is published several times a year.[1]

ECCO has received considerable political and media attention. It has gained official recognition and support for travel expenses from the European Youth Foundation, which is affiliated with the European Economic Community, EEC. The efforts of ECCO, along with those of Euromil (an international organization of officers and professionals) were partly responsible for a remarkable April 1984 decision by the European Parliament. It urged that member countries grant soldiers the right to organize and form associations. (The recommendation has of course been ignored by most members.)

The proceedings and final declarations of the ECCO conferences show a consistent focus on improving the conditions of service, democratizing the military, and ensuring international peace. The official ECCO program urges a reduction in length of service, fixed working hours, compensation for overtime, improvements in barracks living standards, and safer working conditions. The soldiers also demand complete freedom to form unions and publish newspapers. At the ECCO conference in Helsinki in 1983, for example, a resolution was passed opposing command or Ministry of Defense control of soldier newspapers and urging complete freedom in the writing and distribution of information. ECCO also addresses the everyday problems of barracks life. At the sixth and seventh ECCO congresses, in Athens and Malmö, the conscripts emphasized the problem of military medical care. They underlined the necessity for civilianizing health care inside the armed forces. As soldiers on sick call have long known, military medicine is to medicine as military music is to music. It serves, in the first place, the interests of the command, not the patient. ECCO wants to make health care in the armies totally independent of the command.

At their congresses, the ECCO activists also express support for conscription. As we noted earlier (Chapter 5), soldier organizers and peace activists in Europe usually support the draft and strongly oppose the professionalization of the army. Conscription is seen as an important guarantee of a democratic army.

As the cold war heated up in the early 1980s, the declarations of ECCO became increasingly focused on peace issues, especially opposition to nuclear armaments. At both the Copenhagen congress in 1982 and the Helsinki meeting in 1983, strong statements were issued condemning the nuclear arms race and supporting the peace movement. At the Denmark congress the conscripts officially supported the establishment of nuclear-free zones in Scandinavia and Central Europe. As Torbin Kristensen, the Danish representative to the ECCO Board, said in Copenhagen: "We conscripts have a very obvious interest--in fact a life-and-death interest--in escaping war, especially an all-out atomic war."[2]

Anglophones and Professionals

In practice the lingua franca, the common language, of the European conscripts' organization is English. It is an understandable, though sometimes original English, often quite distant from that of the Windsor Queen. There was no formal decision to use English at conferences, in correspondence, and in the ECCO *Newssheet*, but it became the neutral ground uniting Scandinavians, French, Dutch, Flemish, Germans, Spaniards, and Greeks.

It is ironic that English is the official language, since there are no native English-speaking conscripts in Europe and none have participated in ECCO. The British, U.S., and Canadian troops stationed in continental Europe, as well as Irish soldiers, are all volunteers. The ECCO draftees decided early on at their first congress in Malmö that they did not want nonconscripts in their meetings. At that time, one of the authors, then attending the meeting as an observer, pointed out that U.S. soldiers in Europe were often "economic draftees" and that the GIs had considerable interest in forming a soldiers' union. The European privates were unconvinced. They could understand intellectually, but not in their guts. For them "volunteer" meant "professional," and in most of their armies "professional" meant "lifer." They had no intention of opening their organization to officers. They did not want another German Bundeswehr Verband (see Chapter 9). They were still too unsure of themselves to meet as equals with the volunteer soldiers.

In recent years, though, the fear of professional soldiers has diminished. In fact, at the 1986 congress in Vienna, one of the main themes was establishing better relationships between conscripts and professionals. The conference decided to endorse cooperation with professional groups. As the *Newssheet* reported (July/August 1986): "Everyone agreed more or less on the idea of working together in certain areas where there are specific

interests." Whereas in 1979 the ECCO draftees had lumped all professionals together, as if they were officers, by 1986 they recognized: "In a number
of European armies there is a growing number of so-called 'time soldiers,'
who live in a situation which in many cases can be compared with the
situation of conscripts." This was the objective basis for urging cooperation
with professional associations. Said the conference report: "In some
countries this cooperation is already reality."[3]

Despite these advances in understanding, though, ECCO has not yet
established ties with the all-volunteer soldiers of the British Army of the
Rhine, the U.S. 7th Army, or the smaller Canadian contingent in Europe.
The problems of the English-speaking volunteers are still remote from the
European draftees. The fact that in "the world's greatest democracy"
American soldiers have been legally forbidden since 1977 from forming or
even joining unions has not even been considered. It is almost as if the
American, British, and other volunteers speak a foreign language.

The Struggle Continues--Reports from the ECCO Countries

At the ECCO conferences of the 1980s reports have come in of continuing soldier organizing in Germany, Scandinavia, France, and Italy, as well
as new developments in Austria, Belgium, and Greece. The following are
brief accounts of these developments in each country.[4]

Austria. After an abortive start in the mid-1970s, a more permanent
soldiers' movement has emerged in Austria in the 1980s. A union-like
organization, Vereinigung Demokratischer Soldaten Oesterreichs (VDSOe),
the Association of Democratic Austrian Soldiers, has become an important
voice for democracy and peace. The association was founded in 1980 by
conscripts at a barracks in Vienna, with assistance from the youth organizations of the major trade unions and political parties. The first evidence of
this new movement was the appearance of the paper, *Blindgaenger (The Dud)*
in 1980. The paper publicized the poor conditions of life in the barracks. The
initial group of soldiers who published this paper were harassed and
dispersed to barracks around the country, but the movement continued and
grew. VDSOe was founded soon afterwards, with the support of the youth
organizations, and the association spread to soldiers in other barracks.

The program and activities of VDSOe are very comparable to those of
the Dutch VVDM. The group works primarily for improved conditions and
greater democracy in the ranks but also seeks to work with the labor
movement and the peace movement in improving the conditions of society.

In the mid-1980s VDSOe made a special effort to assure soldier participation in peace activities and commemorations in Austria of the resistance
to fascism prior to World War II. For example, in 1984 during the fiftieth

anniversary commemorations of the bloody antifascist struggles in Vienna and other Austrian cities, VDSOe initiated discussions about the need for democratization of the army. They distributed 15,000 copies of a special pamphlet on the subject at the gates of barracks. Also, during the massive peace demonstration in Austria in October 1983, VDSOe organized a contingent of conscripts to participate in the march and arranged for a soldier to appear as a speaker.

VDSOe has not been short-lived. The Austrian conscripts have maintained and strengthened their organization. In 1986 VDSOe successfully hosted the eighth ECCO conference, at Vienna's Frederick Engels Square. The organizing efforts of VDSOe also helped force a reform in Austria's outdated military code of justice. The new code, which entered into force in January 1986, greatly decreased the punitive powers of the command. However, the reform also contained several negative changes, and the association is continuing its campaign against these provisions and for greater democratization within the ranks.

Belgium. In the 1980s a new group formed in Belgium, Soldaten Actie (SOLAC), Soldiers' Action, to replace a previous union organization, the Belgian VVDM. The VVDM group had been created fifteen years earlier among Flemish-speaking conscripts. Named after its Dutch counterpart, it attempted to emulate VVDM's influence and power.[5] However, the Belgian group never approached the scale or success of the Dutch union, and it eventually faded altogether.

SOLAC arrived on the scene in the mid-1980s to fill this vacuum, and it immediately launched major organizing programs. In addition to demanding higher wages, SOLAC organized opposition to the proposed plan of the Ministry of Defense for an increase in the length of draftee service. In recent years as the "manpower pool" of draft-aged youth has declined in Belgium and other European countries, military officials have faced a dilemma. To maintain military commitments with fewer people they must ask draftees to remain in the ranks longer, in the case of Belgium for two months longer. Not all soldiers are happy with this, of course, and soldier organizers have found a ready audience.

SOLAC has connected this campaign to larger military policy issues. If declining birth rates are a problem, the answer is not to increase the length of service but to decrease the military commitments. If the government wants to diminish military expenditures, it should do so by reducing weapons purchases rather than by cutting soldier pay.

Greece. The Greek soldier committees operate in conditions of repression and illegality, but just as with earlier "illegal" groups in Spain, France, and Italy, they have been able to obtain official "tolerance." Three distinct groups have been formed by conscripts and recent veterans: 1) the Committee for Soldier Rights (CSR), closely affiliated with the Democratic Union of

Soldiers; 2) the Committee for the Army (CFA) with coordinating centers in Athens and northern Salonica; and 3) the Committee for Democracy in the Army. The different committees are associated with different political tendencies in civilian life and have close relationships with various student and youth organizations. While CFA and CSR often work together within the barracks, political divisions have hampered cooperation between the civilian support groups.

The Greek soldiers' movement has its work cut out for it, since conditions in its army are among the worst in Europe. Military service is longer here than elsewhere in Europe (twenty-two months for the army), pay is abysmal (approximately $5 per month), living conditions are very poor, and any form of independent organization or freedom of expression is forbidden. Soldiers who speak out or challenge authority are punished. The reaction of the socialist Papandreou government to their demands was disappointing to the soldiers. A new military discipline regulation was issued, with some slight changes in the penal system. Soldiers are now allowed to wear civilian clothes outside the barracks. But the overall condition of the conscripts remains abysmal, and the soldiers' movement continues.

Germany. Organized protest has continued at a modest level in the Bundeswehr, with a number of soldier committees and working groups still active in barracks around the country. A particularly interesting development occurred in the Hamburg region in the early 1980s. The local youth section of the German Labor Federation, DGB, initiated a novel experiment in soldier organizing. In 1981 the DGB national congress approved a pilot project among conscripts in the northern part of the country. An independent newspaper was founded, *Zugleich*, written "by conscripts and for conscripts." Small groups were formed in many of the barracks of the region, and weekly meetings were held at DGB offices. In 1982 the experiment was extended. DGB seemed pleased with the project, and ready at last to begin real soldier organizing.

The efforts of the working groups inevitably came into conflict with the military command, though, and pressures soon mounted for DGB to abandon its effort. Even though the demands of the soldier groups were moderate—more pay, free transportation home, overtime compensation, improved barracks conditions—military commanders wanted the organizing stopped. The Ministry of Defense pressured DGB to end its project. Soon the publication of *Zugleich* was suspended, and in 1983 DGB cut off its support for the working groups entirely. A few of the groups managed to survive without the labor federation, but the lack of outside help ended many.

Elsewhere in Germany a number of independent soldier groups continued to operate. The old ADS groups continued to exist, although their close affiliation with the pro-Moscow Communist Party remained an impediment. Thanks to a core of dedicated activists, though, the ADS groups have maintained continuous activity, where other more spontaneous soldier groups have waxed and waned.

Apart from the ADS groups there have been a number of independent "Soldiers Against Nukes" committees in West Germany. Some of these groups have declared "nuclear-free companies" and have organized soldiers to appear in peace rallies. Since the nuclear accident at Chernobyl the interest of soldiers in the antinuclear movement has increased. The communist groups are also involved, since they are no longer able to distinguish between "capitalist" atomic energy and its "socialist" variant to the East. The soldiers and their civilian allies were particularly concerned about the proposed nuclear reprocessing plant at Wackersdorf, which was initially planned to produce weapons-grade plutonium, but which later had to be abandoned due to popular resistance and financial and technical problems.

Scandinavia. In the Nordic countries the antinuclear focus of the soldiers' movement is also strong, especially in Finland and Denmark. This was greatly aided by the radioactive and psychological fallout of Chernobyl.

The most important question for the soldiers' movement, though, is its relation to the government's "spokesman" systems. The strivings of the elected soldier representatives for greater autonomy constantly clash with the command's desire to have company unions. In Sweden the draftees set up a separate fund and started on the road toward unionism in the 1970s. As elsewhere, this development occurred some years after the high point of the youth rebellion and ran counter to a general conservative trend. In 1980 the Svergis Centerala Vaernplikts Rad (SCVR), the national assembly of Sweden's 55,000 conscripts, set up a committee to plan for the creation of an independent union. This group decided that there should be a minimum threshold before such a union could be created. That level was set at approximately 7,000 conscripts. A great deal of work was done to sign up members, but the threshold level could not be reached. As more conservative representatives increased their hold on the central board, the assembly decided to abandon the union drive. Since the early 1980s, Swedish conscripts have contented themselves to work within the "spokesman" system. The emphasis towards building an independent union has shifted to Denmark.

In Denmark, the two conscript organizations, LTU (representing the 1,800 members of the Civilian Defense Corps) and FU (representing the 10,000 conscripts) decided to build a trade organization for conscripts. They saw such an organization as closely connected to the existing "spokesman" system. The two groups have worked together to organize a campaign for better wages and have succeeded in keeping their pay levels the highest in Europe.

In Finland, where the 12,000-member VML conscript organization is less controlled by the government than in Norway, Denmark, and Sweden, the soldiers also remain active in fighting for better conditions.

All of the Scandinavian conscript groups continue to participate in ECCO and regularly attend the annual congresses, with the exception of the TMO (tillitsman) group in Norway. There the government retains tight control over the soldiers and does not allow them to participate officially. When they attend, the Norwegian conscripts are confined to the role of observers.

France. In France the soldiers' movement also continues, although at a low level. The IDS, supported by the PSU (United Socialist Party), remains active and continues to publish the national newspaper, *Le Soldat.* Leafleting of conscripts continues on weekend evenings in the major railway stations of Paris and other cities. A number of independent groups are still active in local barracks, but their efforts are quite isolated and low-key. Some of the major GI newspapers of previous years, especially *Spirate Rouge* and *Crosse en l'Air,* have not been seen for some time.

As elsewhere in Europe, the French soldiers' movement is participating in the antinuclear peace movement. For IDS, this has meant cooperation with the Committee Against Nuclear Weapons in Europe, CODENE, as opposed to the other large peace movement in France, Le Mouvement de la Paix, which is strongly influenced by the Communist Party and the CGT. The former group, CODENE, has taken a comprehensive position of opposing not only NATO missiles but also Soviet and French nuclear forces. The Mouvement de la Paix, on the other hand, often criticized NATO but was usually silent about Soviet weapons and the French "Force de Frappe." IDS circulated the appeal of the ECCO fifth conference, which included a strong demand for nuclear disarmament, as a petition in the barracks.

Other groups also remain active in the French army. The trotskyist LCR still works with several barracks groups. They have initiated a new campaign of the "one hundred conscripts" (a throwback to the old Appeal of the One Hundred?) demanding a reduction in the length of conscript service. Each year at the annual May Day labor demonstrations, small groups of soldiers continue to appear and march with the union delegations. While there has been no attempt to renew the open drive for a soldiers' union, individual conscripts and soldier committees maintain close relations with union locals in their region.

Italy. Information about developments in the Italian army is scanty. Many of the leftist groups, such as Lotta Continua and Avanguardia Operaia, that initially supported the Italian soldier committees and gave them a voice to the outside world, have gone. News of soldier activities fails to reach even Italian ears, much less ECCO groups abroad. The ECCO organizers have heard almost nothing from Italian conscripts.

Among the sergeants or non-commissioned officers, it is a different story. As we found earlier in our encounter with Marcello Bettin, a strong union-like movement has emerged among the technicians. The demonstrations and protest movements that occurred in the 1970s have continued. In 1982 a group of sergeants held a demonstration for improved conditions, for which they were punished. The sergeants also organized mess-hall boycotts. In June 1983, thirteen NCOs were arrested in Cagliari. The Italian sergeants are continuing their fight for greater rights and democracy within the military.

Why the Decline?

In the United States, Holland, Spain, Italy, France, and other countries, the soldiers' movement experienced a sharp decline in the late 1970s. When asked to explain, soldiers in each country pointed to local factors. In the United States it was the volunteer army; in Italy, the rise of the Communist Party; in France, the repression after Besançon. But these specific developments could not explain a generalized phenomenon that affected nearly every army. Larger social and political trends must have been at work.

The decline in soldier activism came at a time of general slowdown in the rate of capital accumulation within the industrialized world. Economic recessions appeared with unusual severity and frequency in the major capitalist countries. Employment and economic opportunities dwindled. For certain classes of workers the standard of living leveled off or even declined.

The result was a narrowing of economic and social horizons, especially among the rural populations and working classes most likely to serve in the army. This produced a slight but perhaps significant alteration of social outlook. For many blue-collar and working-class youth, previous expectations of affluence and upward social mobility gave way to a greater sense of economic insecurity. The confidence and sense of hope that helped propel previous protest movements faded. The inclination to protest working conditions or demand more rights weakened. Within the army, volunteers and contract soldiers sought to keep their army "job" to avoid the unemployment line. All of this contributed to a lessening of the resistance impulse, both within the army and in society in general.

Ironically, the decline of soldier resistance also resulted from the movement's success in reforming the conditions of service. In every country the rise of soldier activism has led to fundamental improvements and reforms within the ranks. The general condition of the soldier in 1985 is far superior to what it was in 1965. Military discipline, service conditions, pay levels--all have changed significantly to the advantage of low-ranking soldiers.

These reforms were not simply given by benevolent leaders but were won through struggle. The changes are not due to the magnanimity of the generals and politicians but to the great political campaigns of the soldiers during the 1970s. These victories are a double-edged sword, however. They show the importance of the movement and confirm that gains can be achieved through struggle. They also make military life more tolerable, though, and thus ameliorate some of the conditions that lead to resistance in the first place. This phenomenon has occurred not just in the French and Italian armies but in all the armed forces we have studied. As the Dutch soldiers complain: "When we've won so many victories, what do we fight for next?"

Looked at as a whole, the victories of the soldiers' movement of the last twenty years have significantly altered the terms of service. Nearly everywhere soldiers are less subservient now than in the past. The old model of unthinking soldiers blindly following orders has gone forever. The soldiers now want a say over the conditions of service, and they demand the right to be heard.

Most of the reforms of recent years have tended to narrow the gap between military and civilian life. Financial gains have been widespread (a tripling of pay in France; a twelvefold increase in Holland), and soldiers thus have a greater opportunity to travel and participate in society. Physical punishment is largely gone, and many of the worst abuses of military discipline have been eliminated. Hair-length and uniform-wearing requirements have been relaxed, allowing the soldier to feel and dress more like a civilian. In all countries fewer soldiers now wear uniforms home on leave. Overnight passes, weekend leave, and travel home all have become more frequent. The amount of personal time when the soldier is free of command control has increased.

Some of the reforms introduced by military authorities were specifically designed to co-opt soldier activism and have had the effect of defusing the organized movement. This is especially so with soldier representation councils, the so-called "spokesman" system pioneered in Scandinavia. The soldiers are given all the trappings of union democracy, including delegate elections, national conferences, and consultations with the government, but without the substance. The spokesman groups are not financially or politically independent and have no power to enforce their demands. In fact the representation councils help to channel soldier grievances into controllable outlets and enable the command to limit more independent stirrings within the barracks.

It would be wrong to conclude from all of this, however, that the soldiers' movement is over, that the soldiers struggled and won some rights but have now gone back to their previously quiet ways. The underlying potential for resistance remains strong in all of these countries, and still occasionally boils to the surface. Should any of these armies be used for internal repression or unpopular wars abroad, the soldiers' resistance movement could come surging forward again.

Postscript: A Further Update

Perhaps all authors of books such as *Left Face*, that attempt not only to analyze the past and present but to predict the future, must wish that the world would stand still for a moment. Events move so fast that they may overtake, or discredit, or perhaps even confirm a work before it is published. In the present instance, we note a number of events in the latter part of 1990, as we prepare the manuscript for publication, that tend to confirm the analyses of the preceding chapters, and that corroborate our threshold concept.

In Eastern Europe the growth of officer and soldier movements has been quite rapid. In the Soviet Union the military union Shield has established contact with conscript groups and military unions in Western Europe. According to Vitaly Urazhtsev, president and founder of Shield, the organization had its origins in clandestine junior officer groups that first formed in the Soviet army in 1982. This was three years before Mikhail Gorbachev came to power and changed the face of Soviet life through the policies of glasnost and perestroika. These military resistance efforts thus antedate the official changes in the party line and cannot be attributed to them. They were part of the general evolution of an increasingly highly capitalized Soviet society.

Developments in the Soviet Union seem to confirm our observation that the rank at which resistance occurs tends to be inversely proportional to the degree of capital accumulation. In the highly developed Baltic republics resistance is concentrated among conscripts, while in less developed Russia and the other republics it exists among lower-level officers as well as soldiers.

In East Germany prior to unification a strong rank and file movement emerged among draftees. In Hungary soldiers have participated in the meetings of ECCO and there are signs of growing organization within the ranks. In 1990 conscripts from Czechoslovakia participated in ECCO for the first time and reported on the existence of a "Union of Youth in Uniform", the SVM. In Romania, a country just below the capital accumulation threshold, middle-level officers played a leading role in the revolutionary uprising that toppled the Ceausescu dictatorship.

In Yugoslavia we find a north-south differential similar to that in the

Soviet Union. In the northern, more highly capitalized republics of Slovenia and Croatia, rank and file soldiers and low-ranking NCOs have played a considerable role in loosening the grip of the bureaucratic dictatorship. In the less capitalized south, Serbian generals have sought to maintain an authoritarian grip on backwards Kosovo and stifle reform in other republics.

Trouble in the Gulf

The Persian Gulf crisis has raised critical challenges for the armed forces of the United States, France, Australia, and a number of the other nations involved. Although as of this writing no shots have been fired, incidents of soldier antiwar opposition have already surfaced. In the United States dozens of soldiers and reservists have publicly refused to go to Saudi Arabia in the first three months of the deployment. The most famous case was that of marine corporal Jeff Patterson, stationed in Hawaii, who refused to board a plane to Saudi Arabia in August 1990. Patterson's press statement at the time of his refusal shows a highly evolved political understanding of the Persian Gulf crisis:

Although the U.S. is facing off against a truly despicable man in Saddam Hussein, the reality is that U.S. foreign policy created this monster. It was the U.S. who tacitly endorsed the Iraqi invasion of Iran ten years ago. It was the U.S. and West Germany who sold Hussein chemical weapons throughout the war. It was the U.S. who remained silent when Hussein used these weapons on his own populations. . . . I cannot and will not be a pawn in America's power plays for profits and oil in the Middle East.

Although Patterson refused a direct order and made frequent antiwar statements to the press, the marine corps dropped all legal charges in December 1990 and granted him an administrative discharge. This unusually lenient treatment no doubt reflected the military's fear that the example of his refusal might spread to others. Better to get the case (and the attendant publicity) over with quickly than to "make an example" of the young marine. This was especially necessary in the case of Patterson because of his strong political opposition to U.S. policy and his frequent appearances at "no blood for oil" antiwar rallies.

One of the first incidents of group protest came in November 1990 when six members of Fox Company in a marine corps reserve unit in the Bronx, New York, refused call up orders. According to a December 5, 1990 report on the incident in *The Guardian* (New York), the refusal by the Bronx reservists was another in a growing number of acts of resistance by soldiers and reservists mobilized for the Middle East crisis.

Because of the military's extremely tight control of news coverage in the Persian Gulf (beginning with the Grenada invasion, reporters were no longer allowed to travel or report freely on U.S. military operations), it has been difficult to determine how much resistance has developed among U.S. troops. Even within the restrictions imposed by the military, however, evidence of discontent within the ranks has occasionally slipped through. In an October 17, 1990 dispatch from Saudi Arabia in the *New York Times* a disgusted GI exclaimed, "Tell George Bush to get off the golf course and out of his fishing boat . . . and drink hot water with us." Another angry private exclaimed, "I had to come out here to find out what the army really thinks I'm worth--nothing . . . Why is it that when the U.S. economy gets bad we always go to war?"

Enlisted opposition to the Persian Gulf deployment has not been confined to U.S. forces. In France two conscripts were arrested for demonstrating against war in the Gulf, according to reports from ECCO. In Australia seaman Terry Jones jumped ship from HMAS *Adelaide* in Perth in August 1990 and refused to participate in military operations in the Gulf. As Jones explained to the press:

I am not a coward and I would be prepared to die for my country, but I am taking a political stand because this is not our war, we are just following the Americans. . . . Who gave the Americans and the British the right to impose their ways of life on others and to get Australians to die for it?

As was the case with Jeff Patterson, Terry Jones received very light punishment for his refusal. In October 1990 he was found "guilty" of four days AWOL (absent without leave) and was sentenced to a reduction of one rank, forfeiture of four days pay and a suspended sentence of twenty-one days restriction. Considering that he could have received a year in prison and a dishonorable discharge, Jones and his family and friends were quite pleased with the "non-sentence" and considered it a victory.

So far these examples of opposition within the lower ranks have appeared only in the armies of industrialized nations, such as the United States, Australia, and France. No GI resistance has been observed in the armies of the less-capitalized nations participating in the Persian Gulf deployment, such as Egypt, Syria, Saudi Arabia, and Morocco. This might be considered surprising in light of the pressures of Moslem solidarity and widespread opposition within the Arab world to the policies of the "infidel" West. As we have observed throughout the book, however, enlisted resistance rarely appears in the armies of nations below a certain threshold of capital accumulation. Perhaps opposition tendencies will arise in the officer corps of these armies, but conscripts and low ranking soldiers are likely to "follow orders," even if this means killing their Arab brothers.

During the Vietnam War it took more than a year of heavy combat before the first case of soldiers publicly refusing to go to Indochina, the "Ft. Hood 3," was reported. Only in 1968, when war had raged for three years and U.S. casualties already totaled 30,000, did an organized antiwar movement emerge. In the case of the Persian Gulf crisis, opposition has surfaced before the outbreak of war and has quickly become a worrisome problem for the military command. GI resistance in the United States and other industrialized countries has started out rapidly and at a far higher level than at the beginning of past wars, including not only Korea but also Vietnam. As we have observed, in the post-T armies of nations above a certain capital accumulation threshold, the behavior of low-ranking soldiers has changed, creating a greater readiness to question authority. Even though organized dissent has declined in most armies from the peak levels of the 1970s, GI resistance remains an important factor that could have a significant impact on the prospects for peace.

Why?

How do we explain the rise of soldier unions and protest movements in the army? Why is it that, at approximately the same point in history, in more than a dozen highly capitalized countries, soldiers began to form committees, publish newspapers, and take collective action? What happened in society or the army to bring about this change?

Outside Agitators

Some dismiss GI resistance as solely the product of outside agitators. Everything has been instigated by communists trying to subvert the army. This is the view of French General Bigeard and of the American Senator / General Strom Thurmond. It is also the view of many in the U.S. Congress. For example, the 1972 House Committee on Internal Security report on the GI movement was entitled "Investigation of Attempts to Subvert the United States Armed Forces." The report searched at length for connections between GI committees and outside leftist groups (there were very few) while ignoring the many independent soldier committees and such forms of spontaneous resistance as desertion.[1]

This conspiratorial view of the soldiers movement is not confirmed by the facts. No amount of organized agitation or solicitation would have the slightest chance of success without a prior reservoir of unrest and discontent among the troops. Outside political groups will be unable to arouse soldiers unless the basic soil within the barracks is fertile. An American soldier organizer in Baumholder, Germany, Sp/5 Jim Goodman once described it this way: "Resistance is like the air and gas mixture inside a cylinder. An activist may provide a spark, but if there is no gas nothing will happen."

The myth that external "communists" foster soldier revolt is particularly ludicrous when one recalls the policies of the communist parties in Europe. (The U.S. Communist Party has not played a role in the GI movement and could hardly do so even if it wanted.) The established parties of France, Italy, Spain, and Portugal have not supported modern soldier resistance and have often done their best to discredit it.

Not only do these established communist parties reject enlisted resistance in their own armies, they also fear such tendencies in other nations, even when they actively oppose the war that the soldiers are resisting. A good example is the 1967 experience of private Richard Perrin, then a nineteen-year-old U.S. volunteer soldier, who deserted from the 64th Armored in Kitzingen, West Germany. After fleeing to France, Perrin found himself lost and broke, and after great hesitation and fear ("I really thought they might put me in a crate and ship me to Moscow") he finally walked into the Paris office of *L'Humanité*, the communist newspaper. Expecting open arms he explained "I am an antiwar deserter from the U.S. army." Within thirty seconds he was back on the sidewalk, thrown out.

Nor were the communist governments of the East happy about resistance in their opponents' armies. One would expect that the leaders of the Warsaw Pact would have been pleased to mention that their potential military adversaries faced resistance from within. But if unrest in the NATO armies played into the hands of the Soviets, they showed little sign of being grateful. The idea of collective action by soldiers was equally frightening in the East.

The Media

Some explain soldier resistance as a product of the media. Social observers like Marshall McLuhan and Zbigniew Brzezinski have claimed that television and the electronic media alter consciousness and change social values. According to this view, young people are more restless today because the constant bombardment of media information they receive alters their behavior and makes them more skeptical of authority.[2]

We believe there is something to this argument. We need not accept all of McLuhan or Brzezinski to see that the explosion of information in today's society is important to the armed forces. Commanders no longer have a monopoly of information; they cannot control what their troops are hearing. Soldiers cannot be easily persuaded that a particular mission is one thing if they see on television that it is quite another. Even the most persistent "command information" programs will not prevent soldiers from obtaining most of their knowledge outside of the military. Traditional efforts to isolate and indoctrinate soldiers are thus less effective in highly capitalized countries.

An interesting example of the powerful impact that the diffusion of media can have on an army is the experience of the French army in Algeria in 1961. In April of that year four generals led a putsch to take command of the large French force in Algeria and attempted to overthrow the government of General de Gaulle, an operation similar to the one in May 1958 that installed de Gaulle and his Fifth Republic. The four generals made a concerted attempt to confiscate transistor radios to block communications with France proper, but they were unsuccessful. In almost every barracks soldiers heard the appeal of their commander-in-chief, de Gaulle, and were moved by his impassioned plea to refuse obedience to the "felon" generals. De Gaulle's appeal worked, and French soldiers responded with a mass wave of noncooperation and resistance--a grand tribute to the Good Soldier Schweik. The putsch broke down within four days not because greater military force was brought against it, but simply through total disorganization and resistance from within. The media, in this case transistor radios in the hands of soldiers, clearly had a potent effect.

Obviously the expansion of media is a factor in bolstering soldier resistance. Knowledge is power, and the weakening of command control over information dilutes military authority. However, the influence of the media is not in itself a sufficient explanation of the causes of resistance in the army. Nor can the diffusion of information about soldier struggles in one army create resistance in another. Resistance cannot be implanted from the outside if conditions within are not right for its development. Soldiers resist because of conditions in their own army, not because of the example of foreign soldiers. They accept foreign information only to the extent that it corresponds to their own reality.

The Mission

What about the mission? Surely the changing role and purpose of the army in today's society must have some effect on the rise of protest movements. Some observers contend that soldiers are more skeptical now because of the development of nuclear weapons and the futility of the official mission. Few young people in the West really believe the Russians are coming; they doubted even before the era of Gorbachev and are completely dubious now. Even if there were a major war, most assume it would quickly "go nuclear" and that the position of the soldier would be absurd. Nuclear weapons leave soldiers with no purpose other than being the first incinerated.

While the purpose of the army (or the lack thereof) may be a factor in soldier restiveness, it is not in itself a sufficient explanation for the changes in enlisted behavior we have observed. The lack of a compelling mission does not explain why soldier attitudes have changed at this particular time in history. Why is it that soldiers of the late 1950s, facing a more or less similar military mission (equally dubious), did not publish underground newspapers or form unions? Nuclear weapons were already a dominant factor and the importance of the ordinary soldier was equally suspect.

Consider the Italian army. Its mission is little changed from what it was in 1960. Its nebulous function within NATO, the fact that the "Russian menace" was never taken seriously--these conditions have not changed. Yet in 1960 no soldier resistance existed, while in the 1970s Italian soldiers were among the most politically active in Europe. Soldier behavior changed substantially, but the military mission remained the same.

The purposelessness of the mass army cannot fully account for the emergence of GI resistance. We must look deeper for an explanation of resistance in the army. In our opinion the underlying causes lie within the changing social conditions of modern industrial society.

No Satisfaction

Veterans of army service from earlier generations are often puzzled at the rebelliousness of modern soldiers. They find it curious that the rank-and-file today object to conditions that they would have considered idyllic. "What's going on?" the older generation asks. "Why aren't today's soldiers more grateful?" The pay is better, discipline is less harsh and conditions are more relaxed. What's the problem?

The soldiers themselves are not impressed. It may be true that conditions in the army are better now than they were generations ago, but this is irrelevant to today's enlistee. He or she is not comparing army life with what it was forty years ago. The key contrast is between barracks life today and civilian life a year or two earlier. It is here, we believe, where the explanations of soldier resistance are to be found.

The steady improvement in the mass standard of living that has occurred in certain nations in recent decades has brought with it a change in life experience and consciousness. The material conditions of life for the vast majority of the population have progressed to a point where the restrictions of military life become less acceptable. Young people today have experienced a greater degree of personal independence and affluence and are more educated than earlier generations. They have new expectations and needs that the military cannot meet. The quality of life is better on the outside than on the inside.

A Silent Revolution

A number of academic studies confirm that social values and behavior among youth have changed within the highly capitalized nations. One of the first was the University of Michigan study, *Silent Revolution*, examining public attitudes in Western Europe and the United States.[3] Written by sociologist Ronald Inglehart, *Silent Revolution* draws upon public opinion surveys by leading research firms in Europe and America conducted as a time series over eight years. The Michigan study finds a fundamental change in social values among young people, away from an emphasis on security and material needs (what the authors term *materialism*) toward greater interest in the quality of life and self-fulfillment (defined as *post-materialism*). Young people were found to have considerable dissatisfaction with material goals and hierarchical authority. All of the ten countries studied show the same basic pattern: Younger age groups have a much greater tendency than their elders to value qualitative goals such as greater freedom over materialist goals such as more economic security. On the job they are more interested in a feeling of accomplishment than a good salary.

From humble origins in the 1970s, the theory of postmaterialism has gradually become an accepted part of contemporary social analysis. Recent studies have shown that postmaterialist values are also prevalent among participants in the peace movement and the ecology movements of the 1980s.[4]

The postmaterialist values identified by Inglehart and his colleagues are found most frequently among young people with prolonged schooling (particularly those with some college experience). The important factor, though, is not the content of the educational process itself, but the fact that these youth tend to be relatively well-off economically. It is not schooling per se that determines value structures, according to the sociologists, but the experience of maturing in a relatively affluent family. The main variable in explaining postmaterialist values is thus socioeconomic status, particularly during childhood and early adolescence. Inglehart concludes that the value changes of recent years are due to "changing formative experiences in different historical periods," to the rise of relative affluence on a mass scale within the highly capitalized nations.

This does not mean that all young people are well off, or that the average recruit in the French or U.S. army comes from a two-car home with a swimming pool. It does mean, however, that today's young soldiers have rarely known the kind of material scarcity and hardship that was the common lot of their predecessors in earlier history, and that is still the majority experience for soldiers in such nations as Mexico and Egypt. The experience of youth is easier and freer now than it was generations ago, and this brings with it changing values and behavior.

Down on the Farm

These altered values and behavior are related to underlying changes in the structure of society and the work force. One of the most important of these changes has been the sharp drop in the proportion of people who work on farms and live in rural areas. A very small and still decreasing percentage of the population now provides the basic agricultural goods upon which the rest of society depends. As this process has spread within the highly capitalized nations, the class makeup of the army has altered.

In earlier times, armies traditionally drew a disproportionate share of their enlisted recruits from the peasantry and the rural population, precisely those sectors where relative poverty and a lack of opportunity made military service seem attractive. This tradition within the U.S. military is exemplified in the marching song we learned as recruits:

> You're in the army now,
> You're not behind a plow...

Things have changed, however. In the United States, the proportion of farmers within the total population has declined to less than 5 percent, while among soldiers the proportion is less than 10 percent. The share of soldiers from agricultural areas may still be disproportionately high, but the farming population is extremely small and no longer has significant ifluence within the ranks of the military. In Egypt or Iran, peasant and farm boys still make up a major part of the army, but in France or the United States this is a thing of the past.

Workers Too

The majority of soldiers today in the highly capitalized nations are drawn from the working class. As the standard of living has increased generally, the experience of relative affluence has spread even to the sons and daughters of workers. The rise of postmaterialist values and antiautoritarianian attitudes is not confined solely to the white-collar and professional classes but extends to blue-collar working class groups as well. This is confirmed in an important study by Harold Sheppard and Neal Herrick of attitudes among workers in the United States entitled, *Where Have All the Robots Gone?*[5]

The Sheppard and Herrick study focuses primarily on worker attitudes toward authority. Workers were interviewed on their attitudes toward such concepts as absolute obedience and strong leaders and on the relative importance of high wages and meaningful work. The results showed a strong antipathy toward authoritarianism: less preference for strict leadership and more of a willingness to accept change. Young workers (those under thirty years of age) were found to be twice as antiauthoritarian as their elders. The authors observed: "More than half of the under-thirty workers in our sample must be considered extremely non-authoritarian."

This antiauthoritarianism does not arise solely because of factory life, according to the authors, but is part of the worker's personality before he or she enters the labor force, part of their social character. Borrowing concepts from Erich Fromm, Sheppard and Herrick argue that the changes they identify reflect a new personality type emerging within highly industrialized society. Like Inglehart and his colleagues, they trace these new values and attitudes to the very nature of modern society, particularly the decline of material insecurity during early life. They consider this a fundamental change in social consciousness.

A New Stage of Life

Throughout history many observers have noted the rebelliousness of youth. The Greek philosopher Aristotle wrote 2300 years ago that youth have "exalted notions because they have not yet been humbled by life or learned its necessary limitations." Aristotle's point was correct as far as it went. Youth rebelliousness may indeed be constant, but in recent decades the context in which it takes place has changed dramatically. Contemporary society has lengthened the duration of "youth" and eased life's humbling "limitations." Youth, as Aristotle knew it, was extremely brief and confined to members of the privileged classes. Today the phenomenon of youth lasts longer and has been extended to most of the population. These quantitative changes have created a qualitative transformation.

In modern industrial society adolescence has become a new stage of life, a time between childhood and adulthood when individuality can develop. Children mature physically and mentally at an earlier age, and their entry into the work force is delayed by the prolongation of schooling. These two processes, both by-products of high capital accumulation, account for the lengthening of adolescence. This development inevitably affects social consciousness and is a key factor in the transformation of values among modern youth.

The experience of prolonged adolescence for a majority of the population is a new and recent historic development, made possible in the most industrialized nations only in the last few decades. The average person in these countries now spends a substantial number of years insulated from the vicissitudes and pressures of adult life. "You don't know what it means to make a living," parents frequently complain to their children. The statement may reflect some jealousy, but it also pinpoints a key aspect of life within highly capitalized society. Prolonged adolescence and the relative freedoms that accompany it allow for a greater period of exploration and creativity in personality development.

The length of the educational process is also continually increasing. Many young people now study fifteen years or more. The process is extending even to the working class. Many workers and their sons and daughters have attended college. The experience of prolonged education is becoming a majority phenomenon, and is spreading to classes that previously did not have the opportunity.

This process helps to instill a critical consciousness and a greater readiness to question authority. It is not that education necessarily exposes the impressionable student to humanist or liberal values (although this is not an insignificant factor), but rather that the process demands an ability to examine ideas critically and to look at problems from multiple viewpoints. Even the most narrowly technical education requires an appreciation of change and contrasting opinion; one cannot afford to be rigid in an age of rapid technological progress. Advanced education, for all of its functionalist constraints, can be a subversive force that teaches the relativity of knowledge (and therefore of authority) and strengthens an individual's sense of self-worth.

Higher Needs?

In the "old days" it was commonly assumed that resistance to authority occurred where poverty and repression are greatest. The working class would be driven to revolt, it was said, by bitter exploitation and oppression. Yet when Paris was rocked by near-revolution in 1968, the majority of the population enjoyed a very comfortable standard of living. The young people who revolted and rioted during the new left upheaval of the 1960s and 1970s lived a life of unprecedented affluence. This apparent anomaly of popular rebellion during a period of widespread abundance has baffled many, but is was a central theme of the Marxist philosopher, Herbert Marcuse. His thinking sheds important light on the nature of revolt in highly capitalized society.

Just as Marx saw early capitalism producing the seeds of its undoing, so Marcuse saw similar tendencies within the framework of modern industrial society. According to Marcuse, the very material achievements that allow for affluence and prosperity also create the preconditions for social revolt. In *Counter-revolution and Revolt*, Marcuse wrote: "The historic locus of the revolution is that stage of development where the satisfaction of basic needs creates needs which transcend the state capitalist and state socialist society."[6] In *An Essay on Liberation* he described the process this way:

Technical progress has reached a stage in which reality need no longer be defined by the debilitating competition for social survival and advancement. The more these technical capacities outgrow the framework of exploitation. . . the more they propel the drives and aspirations of men to a point at which the necessities of life cease to demand the aggressive performance of "earning a living."[7]

The foundation of Marcuse's theory of liberation is contained in his important work, *Eros and Civilization,* a long philosophical essay on Sigmund Freud and the concept of the "reality principle." As defined in Freud's *Civilization and its Discontents,* the reality principle symbolizes the repression of higher, more aesthetic needs by material scarcity, by the restraints of making a living and satisfying basic wants. In the era of still-widespread scarcity during which he wrote, Freud saw the harsh requirements of work and daily survival imposing rigid limits on the psychic freedom and personal development of the individual. Marcuse, writing in a later age of growing abundance, theorized that an easing of material conditions might allow for the development of a less repressed personality. With the experience of relative affluence, Marcuse argued, psychic repression would be less necessary. The intensity of the "reality principle" would diminish and other more aesthetic impulses could emerge and seek fulfillment. No longer seared by the experience of scarcity and material uncertainty, the individual would be free to explore needs and wants that at an earlier stage of civilization were the domain of only a few.

Marcuse's theories are founded on the idea of a hierarchy of need, the simple but important notion that the satisfaction of wants, psychological and material, proceeds in a sequential order from one level to the next. This concept is elaborated by the great philosopher Abraham Maslow in his important book, *The Psychology of Being.* When primary needs are satisfied--shelter and economic security--new needs arise: the desire for self-fulfillment and creativity. According to this view, the widespread satisfaction of basic material needs in the highly capitalized nations, an end to scarcity for the majority of the population, brings with it new needs and attitudes. The easing of the "reality principle" weakens psychic repression and the need for authority and unchains previously suppressed wants and impulses.

Still There

These philosophical musings help to explain the rise of the soldiers movement and place it in the context of broader social and economic developments. As we have emphasized, resistance inside the army is a deeply rooted phenomenon resulting from fundamental changes in modern society. For the majority of soldiers in the highly capitalized nations entry into the military is a step down in the quality of life. The restrictions and limitations of military discipline are incompatible with the relatively free and affluent life-style prevalent within civilian society. The resulting clash leads to discontent and, occasionally, to resistance.

While there has been some retrenchment in the movement in recent years, the underlying conditions that lead to resistance have not changed. Although recruits may now find themselves compelled by economic necessity to enlist and sometimes remain in the army, this does not mean that they will find barracks life any more acceptable or pleasant than their recent predecessors. Although the army may have been forced to introduce reforms and improve the conditions of service (thanks to the soldiers' movement), this has not changed the fundamental repressiveness of military life.

There is a limit to the concessions and reforms the military can allow. The tasks that rulers and commanders set for their soldiers, foreign wars and/or internal repression, are in the final analysis opposed to the interests of those who serve in the lower ranks. This contradiction means that the ruling elite and their generals must continue to insist on discipline. It also means that conflict will continue, and that today's soldiers must continue to ask that most subversive of questions, "Why?"

Notes

Chapter 1

1. David Cortright, *Soldiers in Revolt: The American Military Today* (New York: Anchor/Doubleday, 1975).

2. *Antimilitarismus Information: Daten-Facten-Entwicklungen* (Berlin) 19, 4 (April 1989): p. 4.

3. Michael J. Crozier, Samuel P. Huntington, and Joji Watanuki, *The Crisis of Democracy* (New York: New York University Press, 1975), p. 28.

4. Data for this table was obtained from Ruth Leger Sivard, *World Military and Social Expenditures* (Washington, D.C.: World Priorities, 1977), pp. 24-29.

5. *Camp News* (Chicago) 3, (July 15, 1972), p. 8.

6. Interview, David Cortright with Meir Amor and Peretz Kidron of Yesh Gvul, Washington, D.C., October 13, 1988.

7. "Weekend Edition," National Public Radio, Washington, D.C., July 16, 1988.

8. *Friends of Yesh Gvul Newsletter* (Berkeley, Calif.), 2 (May 1989).

9. Based on interviews, Max Watts and David Cortright with William Anderson, New York, New York, July 1977.

10. The story is well documented in John Stockwell's *In Search of Enemies* (New York: Norton, 1978).

11. Testimony of William Anderson, United Nations, New York, Council for Namibia, September 1976.

12. *OMKEER* was published by the South African Military Resistance Aid Fund (SAMRAF), Brooklyn, New York.

13. *The Australian*, September 5, 1985, p. 10.

14. *The Resister (London)* 41 (Fall 1985): pp. 6-7.

15. *New York Times*, August 23, 1988, p. 11; November 4, 1986, p. 1.

Chapter 2

1. David Cortright, *Soldiers in Revolt: The American Military Today* (New York: Anchor/Doubleday, 1975). See also Max Watts, *U.S. Army Europe: Von der Desertion zum Widerstand in der Kaserne oder Wie die U-Bahn zur RITA fuhr* (West Berlin: Harald Kater Verlag, 1989); Andy Stapp, *Up Against the Brass* (New York: Simon and Schuster, 1970); Larry G. Waterhouse and Mariann G. Wizard, *Turning the Guns Around* (New York: Delta, 1971); and Shelby Stanton, *The Rise and Fall of an American Army* (Novato, Calif.: Presidio Press, 1985).

2. Howard C. Olson and R. William Rae, *Determination of the Potential for Dissidence in the U.S. Army*, Technical Paper RAC-TP-410 (McLean, Va: Research Analysis Corporation, March 1971); R. William Rae, Stephen B. Forman, and Howard C. Olson, *Future Impact of Dissident Elements Within the Army*, Technical Paper RAC-TP-441 (McLean, Va: Research Analysis Corporation, January 1972).

3. *Future Impact*, p. 25.

4. Ibid., pp. 31-32.

5. Ibid., p. 25.

6. *Determination*, pp. 37-49.

7. *Future Impact*, p.36.

8. Ibid., pp. 72-73.

9. Office of the Assistant Secretary of Defense, Manpower and Reserve Affairs; Defense Manpower Data Center, Arlington, Va. See also Martin Binkin et al., *Where Does the Marine Corps Go From Here?* (Washington, D.C.: The Brookings Institution, 1976), p. 62.

10. Ibid.

11. Defense Manpower Data Center, Arlington, Va.

12. See, for example, Peter Slavin, "The Cruelest Discrimination: Vets With Bad Discharge Papers," *Business and Society Review* 14 (Summer 1975): pp. 25-33.

13. Defense Manpower Data Center, Arlington, Va.

14. Press Release, Center for Servicemen's Rights, San Diego, Calif., August 6, 1975. See also *Sterett Free Press*, "Special Edition on the Walkout," n.d.

15. *GIPA News and Discussion Bulletin* (published by the GI Project Alliance, San Diego, Calif.) 18 (January 1974): p. 22; *GIPA News and Discussion Bulletin* 22 (August 1974): p. 20.

16. *GIPA News and Discussion Bulletin* 24 (November 1974): p. 94.

17. Interview, David Cortright with Chris Coates (attorney for Hammond and the Midway sailors), August 1989. See also *GIPA News and Discussion Bulletin* 20 (July 1974): pp. 43-44.

18. Interview, David Cortright with Chris Coates; *GIPA News and*

Discussion Bulletin 22 (August 1974): pp. 30-33.

19. *Melbourne Herald,* August 5, 1982.

20. *International Herald Tribune,* January 29, 1974, p. 1; *Stars and Stripes* (European edition), January 30, 1974; *Cambridge Evening News,* January 25, 1974.

21. Author Max Watts was present at Funari Barracks and personally witnessed the incident.

22. *Frankfurter Rundschau,* February 2, 1975; *Stars and Stripes* (European edition), March 15, 1975; *Parade* magazine, March 3, 1975.

23. *Los Angeles Times,* December 17, 1974.

24. *Stars and Stripes* (European edition), November 26, 1974, p. 1; *International Herald Tribune,* November 26, 1974.

25. Pruitt quoted in *GIPA News and Discussion Bulletin* 22 (August 1974): pp. 26-27.

26. Based on interviews, Max Watts with Larry Johnson and other soldiers at Kaiserslautern; and Max Watts with Father Cesare Bertulli. See also Max Watts, "Watergate on the Neckar," *Die Tageszeitung* (West Berlin), April 16, 1980; and *Forward* (West Berlin), nos. 14, 15, and 16 (June, July, and September 1973).

27. John Stockwell, *In Search of Enemies* (New York: Dutton, 1978).

28. Interview, Max Watts and David Cortright with William Anderson, New York, New York, July 1977.

29. Max Watts, "Watergate on the Neckar."

30. Based on numerous interviews, Max Watts with Mike McDougal. See also *New York Times,* August 6, 1973; *New York Times,* August 8, 1973; *New York Times,* August 10, 1973; and *Der Spiegel* 32 (August 6, 1973): pp. 52-53.

31. *Stars and Stripes* (European edition), December 15, 1974.

32. "High Times and Hard Drugs in the U.S. Army--Europe," *The Paris Metro* 2, no. 18 (August 31, 1977).

33. Author David Cortright was present at the demonstration and personally witnessed the event.

Chapter 3

1. For a history and description of the American Servicemens' Union, see Andy Stapp, *Up Against the Brass* (New York: Simon and Schuster, 1970).

2. *GIPA News and Discussion Bulletin* 25 (December-January 1975): pp. 28-29; *Up From the Bottom* (San Diego, Calif.), October 1976, pp. 1-5.

3. Interview, David Cortright with Greg Kenefik (AFGE Press Office), Washington, D.C., July 1975. Interview, David Cortright with Clyde Webber and other AFGE officers, Washington, D.C., August 1975.

4. *Wall Street Journal,* June 27, 1975, p. 1.

5. Clyde Webber, Statement before the Defense Manpower Commission, Washington, D.C.

6. Author David Cortright was present throughout the convention and personally witnessed the debate and vote.

7. *Washington Post,* December 9, 1976, p. 1.

8. The article in question was David Cortright, "The Union Wants to Join You," *The Nation,* February 21, 1976, pp. 206-209. See also *The Congressional Record,* vol. 122, no. 30, March 4, 1976.

9. For Information on the 1968 Presidio "mutiny" see Fred Gardner, *Unlawful Concert: An Account of the Presidio Mutiny Case* (New York: Viking Press, 1970).

10. American Federation of Government Employees, Press Release, September, 1977.

11. Ibid.

12. Statement of Ken Blaylock, "Unionization of the Armed Forces," *Hearings Before the Committee on Armed Services, United States Senate,* 95th Cong., 1st sess., on S. 274 and S. 997, p. 297.

13. Ibid.

14. Statement of Admiral James D. Watkins, "Unionization of the Armed Forces," pp. 90-91.

15. T. Roger Manley, Charles W. McNichols, and G. C. Saul Young, Air Force Institute of Technology, "Attitudes of Active Duty U.S Air Force Personnel Toward Unionization," *Armed Forces and Society* 3, no.4 (Summer 1977): pp. 557-74.

16. "Unionization of the Armed Forces", pp. 211-16.

17. Citizen Soldier, New York, New York, Press Release, July, 1977. See also "Unionization of the Armed Forces", p. 115.

18. Statement of Admiral James D. Watkins, "Unionization of the Armed Forces."

19. Quoted in "Unionization of the Armed Forces," p. 118.

20. Enlisted Peoples Organizing Committee, Washington, D.C.

21. Author David Cortright was present at the press conference.

22. Interviews, Max Watts with various Fulda area GIs, Summer 1976.

Chapter 4

1. David Cortright, "Report to AFGE: Military Unions in Europe," Washington, D.C., July 1976.

2. Based on Interviews, David Cortright with officials of TCO-S; David Cortright with officials of the A Officers' Union, Stockholm, May 1976.

3. Interview, David Cortright with Mr. Ibenfeldt, Norges Befalslag,

Oslo, May 1976.

4. Gwyn Harries-Jenkins, "Trade Unions in the Armed Forces," paper presented to the British Inter-University Seminar on Armed Forces and Society, University of Hull, Great Britain, 1976, p. 15.

5. Based on Interviews, David Cortright with Mr. Parr and Tor Berge, YH and BFO, Oslo, May 1976; David Cortright with Mr. Ibenfeldt, Norges Befalslag, Oslo, May 1976.

6. Based on interviews, David Cortright with Captain Fischer, Embassy of Denmark, Washington, D.C., April 1976; David Cortright with Major Calundan, FTF, Copenhagen, May 1976; David Cortright with Jorn Kristensen, Centralorganization for Stampersonnel, Copenhagen, May 1976.

7. Interview, David Cortright with officials of the A Officers' Union, Stockholm, May 1976.

8. Interview, David Cortright with Jorn Kristensen.

9. Interview, David Cortright with officials of VPL/MG, Copenhagen, May 1976.

10. Interview, David Cortright with Jorn Kristensen.

11. Ibid.

Chapter 5

1. *The Report of the President's Commission on an All Volunteer Force* (London: Collier-Macmillan, 1970), p. 33.

2. Ministry of Defence, "Defence: Outline of Future Policy," Cmnd. 124, London, 1957.

3. Jacques Van Doorn, "The Decline of the Mass Army in the West: General Reflections," *Armed Forces and Society* 1, no. 2 (Winter 1975): pp. 147-57.

4. Morris Janowitz and Charles Moskos, Jr., "Five Years of the All-Volunteer Force: 1973-1978," *Armed Forces and Society* 5, no. 2 (Winter 1979): pp. 172-73.

5. William Westmoreland, *New York Times*, August 17, 1973, p. 31.

6. "Department of Defense Appropriations Bill, 1974," *House Report* 93-662, p. 26.

7. Morris Janowitz, "Statement Before the Defense Manpower Commission," Washington, D.C., July 17, 1975.

8. Harold Wool, *The Military Specialist* (Baltimore: The Johns Hopkins University Press, 1968), pp. 99-100.

9. Jerome Johnston and Jerald Bachman, *Young Men and Military Service* (Ann Arbor, Mich.: Institute for Social Research, 1972), pp. 134-35.

10. Office of the Assistant Secretary of Defense, Manpower and Reserve Affairs, *America's Volunteers*, Washington, D.C., 1978.

11. Janowitz and Moskos, "Five Years," p. 193. See also Charles Moskos, "Making the All-Volunteer Force Work: A National Service Approach," *Foreign Affairs* 60, no. 1 (Fall 1981): pp. 18-21.

12. Janowitz and Moskos, "Five Years," p. 194.

13. Ibid.

14. Defense Manpower Data Center, Arlington, Va.

15. Ibid.

16. Moskos, "Making," p. 19.

17. Charles A. Cotton, Rodney K. Crook, and Frank C. Pinch, "Canada's Professional Military: Trends and Perspectives to the 1990s," paper presented to the Inter-University Seminar on Armed Forces and Society Biennial Conference, Chicago, 1977.

18. Ibid., p. 26.

19. Peter J. Dietz and J. F. Stone, "The British All-Volunteer Army," *Armed Forces and Society* 1, no. 2 (Winter 1975): p. 167.

20. Ibid., p. 169. See also "The British Army," *Labor Research* (London) 63, no. 12 (December 1974): pp. 242-43.

21. David Lamb, "Mutinies: 1917-1920," Leeds Community Press, Leeds, Great Britain, n.d.; Andrew Rothstein, *The Soldiers' Strikes of 1919* (London: The Journeyman Press, 1985).

22. See Anthony Carew, *The Lower Deck of the Royal Navy, 1900-39: The Invergordon Mutiny in Perspective* (Manchester: University of Manchester Press, 1981).

23. *The Guardian*, May 31, 1975, p. 11.

24. Christopher Hitchens, "Barrack Room Rumblings," *New Statesman*, March 22, 1974, p. 390.

25. "Bring Our Services into the 20th Century," *ASTMS Journal* (March/April 1978). See also *Guardian*, April 8, 1978.

26. *The Soldiers' Charter* (London: Chartist Publications, 1971).

27. Interview, Max Watts with Warrant Officer II John Barry (ret.), Sydney, February 1984.

28. *Australian Defence Reporter* 1, no. 2 (October 1972): p. 17.

29. *Defence Force Journal* 19 (November/December 1979): p. 50.

Chapter 6

1. Samuel Stouffer et al., *The American Soldier*, Volume 2: *Combat And Its Aftermath* (Princeton, N.J.: Princeton University Press, 1949).

2. Interview, David Cortright and Max Watts with officials of the Italian Communist Party, Rome, May 1975.

3. Jack Woddis, *Armies and Politics* (New York: International Publishers, 1977), p. 297.

Chapter 7

1.   Based on interviews, David Cortright with VVDM and BVD offi-cials, Utrecht and Amsterdam, November 1974, May 1975, June 1976, March 1981, and August 1984; David Cortright with Mr. J. De Waart, Ministry of Defense, Utrecht, June 1975; David Cortright with Col. Brauer, Dutch Embassy, Washington, D.C., March 1976; David Cortright with Mr. Drees, Ministry of Defense, The Hague, May 1976. See also "The VVDM Then and Now," a special edition of *Twintig* on the occasion of the tenth anniversary of VVDM, Utrecht, 1976; Walter J. P. Kok, "The VVDM, 1966-1973: Action and Reaction," paper delivered for the ECPR Workshop on Political Behavior, Dissatisfaction and Protest, Louvain, April 1976. Special thanks to Ben Dankbaar for substantial editing and research support in the writing of this chapter.

2.   Joseph Lelyveld, "Dadaists in Politics," *New York Times Magazine*, October 2, 1966, p. 32+.

3.   Kok, "The VVDM Then and Now."

4.   Ibid.

5.   Ibid.

6.   The authors possess an undated clipping of Vredeling's quote from the popular U.S. Sunday magazine, *Parade*.

Chapter 8

1.   Based on interviews, David Cortright with officials of the tillits-mann organization, Oslo, May 1976; David Cortright with officials of VAG, Stockholm, May 1976; David Cortright with officials of VPL/MG, Copen-hagen, May 1976; Max Watts with officials of the Finnish VML, Malmö, March 1979.

2.   Author Max Watts attended the Malmö Conference.

3.   Author Max Watts attended the Putten Conference.

4.   Malmö conference documents.

5.   Ibid.

Chapter 9

1.   Quoted in *Der Spiegel*, January 2, 1957.

2.   For a full story of the founding of the Bundeswehr, see Eric Walden, *The Goose Step is Verboten* (New York: Free Press of Glencoe, 1964).

3.   Ibid.

4.   *Antimilitarismus Information: Daten-Fakten-Entwicklungen* (Berlin)

19, no. 4 (April 1989): p. a-4, based on *Stichworte zur Sicherheitspolitik*, 2/80, 4/83 and 2/85; Sitzungsberichte der Zentralstelle fur Recht und Schutz der KDV sowie des Zivildienstbeirates; Blumenwitz (Hrgs.): Wehrpflicht und Ersatzdienst, Munchen, 1978; Mullender/Vermeulen: Nicht mehr mit uns!, Koln, 1983.

5.   "Notes for Soldiers" from *Tolstoy's Writings on Civil Disobedience and Non Violence* (New York: Bergman Publishers, 1967), p. 43.

6.   David Cortright, *Soldiers in Revolt: The American Military Today* (New York: Anchor/Doubleday, 1975), p. 5.

7.   Based on interviews, Max Watts with Berndt Plagemann, 1974 and 1975.

8.   Tad Szulc, "Germany Re-Arms," *Penthouse*, March, 1978.

9.   For an informative analysis of labor union organizations in the Bundeswehr, see Bernhard Fleckenstein, "The Military and Labor Union Organizations in Germany," *Aus Politik und Zeitgeschichte*, May 22, 1976.

10.   Interview, David Cortright with Col. Heinz Volland, Bonn, May 1976.

11.   As told to Max Watts by participating soldiers from both Germany and Holland.

12.   See David Cortright and Boykin Reynolds, "Armed Forces' Union Runs Into Many Snags," *Federal Times* (Washington, D.C.), December 24, 1975, p. 13.

13.   Interview, David Cortright and Max Watts with Heinrich Linden, Koblenz, May 1976.

Chapter 10

1.   Interview, Max Watts, discussion between American GIs and Czech student resisters, Paris, Spring 1969.

2.   Serge Schmemann, "In East German Army Ranks, A Headlong Farewell to Arms," *New York Times*, March 9, 1990, p. 1.

3.   Yuri Teplyakov, "The Other Face of War: Talks With Different Afghanistan Vets", *Moscow News*, 38/89, September 17, 1989, p. 2.

4.   Gennady Zhavoronkov, "We Should Tell the Truth About This War," *Moscow News*, 30/89, July 23, 1989, pp. 8-9.

5.   *New Times* (Moscow), February 13, 1990, pp. 2-3.

6.   Richard Pipes, "Soviet Army Coup? Not Likely", *New York Times*, November 20, 1990, p. 15.

7.   *Sydney Morning Herald*, October 23, 1989.

8.   *Moscow News*, 38/89, September 17, 1989, p. 2.

9.   Interview, Patrick LeTrehondat with Vitaly Urazhtsev, translated by Max Watts, Madrid, 1990.

10. *Washington Post*, April 15, 1990, pp. 1 and 28.

11. Richard Denant, "URSS: L'armee Rouge Se Syndique," *Politis*, (Paris) 86 (January 1990): pp. 35-36.

12. *Moscow News*, March 11, 1990, pp. 8-9.

13. *Washington Post*, January 28, 1990, p. 20.

14. Michael Tsypkin, "The Soviet Union: The Conscripts," *Bulletin of Atomic Scientists* 39, no. 5 (May 1983): pp. 28-32.

15. *Washington Post*, January 28, 1990; Michael Tsypkin, "The Soviet Union: The Conscripts."

16. *Washington Post*, April 15, 1990, p. 1.

17. *Pipes*, "Soviet Army", p. 15.

18. Ilana Kass, "In Moscow, the Red Army Blues", *The Christian Science Monitor*, August 21, 1990, p. 19.

19. "All Things Considered," National Public Radio, Washington, D.C., March 22, 1990.

20. *New York Times*, March 26, 1990.

21. "URSS: A Visages Decouverts," *Le Soldat* (Paris), October 1989.

Chapter 11

1.   Based on interviews, David Cortright with representatives of the Comite Anti-Militariste, Amsterdam, November 1974; Max Watts with French soldiers stationed in Speyer, Landau, Neustadt, Karlsruhe, and Kaiserslautern, 1973-1978; David Cortright and Max Watts with representatives of Comite Anti-Militariste, Paris, June 1975; David Cortright and Max Watts with officials of Jeunes Communistes, Paris, June 1975; David Cortright and Max Watts with representatives of the Committee for the Defense of Conscripts, Paris, June 1975; David Cortright with Jean Luc Hennig of *Liberation*, Paris, May 1976; David Cortright with Janet Finkelstein, Centre d'Etudes de Politique Etrangere, Paris, May 1976. Special thanks to attorney Robert Rifkin, who lived in Paris during the time of the events described in this chapter. In 1976 Rifkin wrote an excellent though unpublished first-hand account, "The French Government Cracks Down," from which we draw heavily.

2.   *New York Times*, March 23, 1973, p. 2.

3.   A copy of L'Appel des Cent is in the files of Max Watts, Weichselstrasse 37, D 1000 Berlin 44. See also *Washington Post*, January 8, 1975, p. 17.

4.   See Denis Richard and Elisabeth Carriere, eds., *Le Proces du Draguignan* (Paris: Editions du Rocher, 1975).

5.   Ibid.

6.   *Washington Post*, January 14, 1975, p. 16; *Christian Science Monitor*, January 22, 1975.

7.   *Baltimore Sun*, February 21, 1975, p. 4.

8.   *Les Boeufs Voient Rouge, Arrete Ton Clar, Spirate Rouge* and dozens of other French GI papers are in the files of Max Watts.

9.   *Time*, December 15, 1975, p. 35.

10.   Ibid., p. 36.

11.   Robert Rifkin, "The French Government Cracks Down."

12.   Ibid.; *New York Times*, November 30, 1975.

13.   *Le Monde*, English section in *Guardian*, December 14, 1975.

Chapter 12

1.   Interview, Max Watts with Marcello Bettin and five other Air Force NCOs, Mestre, June 1976.

2.   Interviews, David Cortright with representatives of Lotta Continua, Amsterdam, November 1974; David Cortright and Max Watts with representatives of Avanguardia Operaia, Milan, May 1975; David Cortright and Max Watts with representatives of Lotta Continua, Rome, May 1975; David Cortright and Max Watts with representatives of Partito Radicale, Rome, May 1975; David Cortright and Max Watts with officials of the Italian Communist Party, Rome, May 1975.

3.   Interview, David Cortright and Max Watts with representatives of Avanguardia Operaia.

4.   Ibid. See also *Esercito e Popolo* (Milan), July 1975.

5.   Author Max Watts was in Udine during the election and with a team of assistants poll watched and counted votes at six electoral districts where soldiers in the region voted. Vote totals were then analyzed and compared with figures for civilian votes to give the relevant percentages.

6.   Interviews, Max Watts with several Italian soldiers, Venice, June 1976. See also *Quotidiano del Lavaratore* (daily newspaper of Avanguardia Operaia), May 26, 1976.

7.   *Newsfront International* (New York) 175 (February 14, 1976), based on articles in *Quotidiano del Lavaratore* and *Lotta Continua*.

8.   Ibid.

9.   Interview, Max Watts with Marcello Bettin et al.

10.   Ibid.

11.   Ibid.

Chapter 13

1.   Based on interviews, Max Watts with Miguel Durin and other representatives of the Union of Democratic Soldiers, Malmö, Sweden,

March 1979 and Putten, Holland, November 1979. The Spanish soldiers were in Sweden and Holland to attend the first and second conferences of the European Conference of Conscripts' Organization, ECCO. See Chapters 8 and 18.

2. Copies of *La Voz del Soldado* and other Spanish soldier newspapers in the files of Max Watts, Weichselstrasse 37, D 1000 Berlin 44.

3. Interviews, Max Watts with Miguel Durin et al.

4. Ibid.

5. Ibid.

6. Ibid.

Chapter 14

1. Our description of the Portuguese revolution is based on the following sources: Lawrence S. Graham and Harry M. Makler, eds., *Contemporary Portugal: The Revolution and Its Antecedents* (Austin: University of Texas Press, 1979); Robert Harvey, *Portugal: Birth of a Democracy* (London: Macmillan, 1978); Jane Kramer, "A Reporter at Large: The Portuguese Revolution", *The New Yorker*, December 15, 1975; Phil Mailer, *Portugal: The Impossible Revolution* (London: Solidarity Press, 1977); Douglas Porch, *The Portuguese Armed Forces and the Revolution* (Stanford, CA: Hoover Institution Press, 1977); *Portugal: Revolution and Backlash*, Special Report of the Institute for the Study of Conflict, London, 1975; Christine and Malte Rauch, directors, *Viva Portugal*, a film, 1975; and R. A. H. Robinson, *Contemporary Portugal: A History* (London: Allen and Unwin, 1979). The authors also benefited greatly from interviews, Max Watts with Father Cesare Bertulli, Kaiserslautern, West Germany, June 1973. (Father Bertulli was a White Father priest expelled from Mozambique in 1971 for "anti-Portuguese" activities who testified at the trial of Pvt. Larry Johnson; see Chapter 2.)

2. Interview, Max Watts with Captain Matos Gomes, Heidelberg, October 1975.

3. Our description of soldier activities based on Interviews, Max Watts with SUV soldiers Antonio and Fernandez, Hanau, West Germany, December 1975 and January 1976. (The soldiers had just fled Portugal following the crackdown against the left there and did not wish to reveal their last names.)

4. See *Viva Portugal* (film).

5. Phil Mailer, p. 222; Robert Harvey, p. 50.

6. Interviews, Max Watts with Antonio and Fernandez.

7. Ibid.

8. Ibid.

9. Ibid.

10. Ibid.
11. Ibid.

Chapter 15

1. For general sources on the Allende period and the September 1973 putsch, see Gary MacEoin, *Chile: The Struggle for Dignity* (London: Coventure Press, 1975); Ian Roxbourough, Philip O'Brien, and Jackie Roddick (assisted by Michael Gonzalez), *Chile: The State and the Revolution* (London: Macmillan, 1977); and Armando Uribe, *The Black Book of American Intervention in Chile* (Boston: Beacon Press, 1975).

2. Ian Roxbourough et al., *Chile*, p. 193.

3. Interview, Max Watts with Chilean Petty Officer Hernandez, Putten, Holland, November 1979. Hernandez, who was in Putten attending the European Congress of Conscripts' Organization second conference (see Chapter 18), was stationed in Valparaiso at the time and personally participated in the described events.

4. Ibid.

5. *New York Times*, August 9, 1973, p. 10.

6. Nathaniel Davis, *The Last Years of Salvador Allende* (New York: Cornell University Press, 1985), p. 185.

7. Reported in Davis, *Last Years*.

8. *New York Times*, August 11, 1973, p. 8.

Chapter 16

1. See, for example, *New York Times*, February 7, 1979, p. 1.

2. Personal letter to authors' research assistant from *Newsweek* reporter Elaine Sciolino, August 9, 1979; Sciolino was in Iran covering the story of the revolution during the time of the described events.

3. *New York Times*, December 15, 1978, p. 1.

4. *Los Angeles Times*, December 15, 1978.

5. Ibid. See also *Washington Post*, December 14, 1978.

6. *New York Times*, February 7, 1979, p. 6.

7. *New York Times*, February 10, 1979, p. 8.

8. *Washington Post*, February 11, 1979, p. 13.

9. *New York Times*, February 11, 1979, p. 1.

10. *New York Times*, February 12, 1979, p. 1.

11. Interview, Max Watts with Sergeant George Long, Paris, 1967.

Chapter 17

1. For an account of these events see Alfred McCoy, Marian Wilkinson, and Gwen Robinson, "The Last Days of Marcos," *The National Times* (Sydney), October 5, 1986, pp. 25-28, and October 12, 1986, pp. 25-27.

2. Ibid.; Interviews, Max Watts with Luis Jalandoni, international representative of the National Democratic Front of the Philippines, Sydney, 1985 and 1986.

3. McCoy, Wilkinson, and Robinson, "Last Days"; interview, Max Watts with Carlotta McIntosh, correspondent for ABC (Australian Broadcasting Corporation) News in Manila, Sydney, 1986.

Chapter 18

1. Author Max Watts personally participated in the first and second ECCO conferences in Malmö, Sweden (March 1979) and Putten, Holland (November 1979). The ECCO *Newssheet* has been published continuously since 1979 and can be obtained by writing to VVDM at Postbus 85031, 3508 AA Utrecht, The Netherlands.

2. "ECCO-4 Conference Report, Denmark, June, 1982," Utrecht: VVDM, 1982, p. 17.

3. *ECCO Newssheet*, no. 4 (July/August 1986): p. 3.

4. Based on interviews, David Cortright with officials of VVDM and ECCO, Utrecht, The Netherlands, August 1984,; and David Cortright with Jan Coolen, Eindhoven, The Netherlands, August 1984. Also based on reports in *ECCO Newssheet*, no. 3 (March 1984) and no. 4 (June 1984) and reports in *ECCO Bulletin* no. 1 (March 1984) and no. 2 (June 1984).

5. Interview, David Cortright with Guido Janjagers, then head of the Belgian VVDM, Leuven, Belgium, May 1975.

Chapter 19

1. "Investigation of Attempts to Subvert the United States Armed Forces," *Hearings Before the Committee on Internal Security, House of Representatives*, 92d Cong., 1st and 2d sess. (three volumes).

2. See Marshall McLuhan, *Understanding Media* (New York: McGraw-Hill, 1964), and Zbigniew Brzezinski, *Between Two Ages: America's Role in the Technetronic Age* (New York: Viking Press, 1970).

3. Ronald Inglehart, *The Silent Revolution: Changing Values and Political Styles Among Western Publics* (Princeton, N.J.: Princeton University Press, 1977).

4. Thomas R. Rochon, *Mobilizing for Peace: The Antinuclear Movements in Western Europe* (Princeton: Princeton University Press, 1988), pp. 35-37.

5. Harold Sheppard and Neal Herrick, *Where Have All The Robots Gone: Worker Dissatisfaction in the 70's* (New York: The Free Press, 1972).

6. Herbert Marcuse, *Counter-Revolution and Revolt* (Boston: Beacon Press, 1972), p. 18.

7. Herbert Marcuse, *An Essay on Liberation* (Boston: Beacon Press, 1969), p. 5.

Bibliography

Books

Addlestone, David. *Military Discharge Upgrading*. Washington, D.C.: National Veterans Law Center, 1982.

Altwies, James E. *Why Would the Military Unionize?* Maxwell Air Force Base, Alabama: Air Command and Staff College, 1976.

America's Volunteers. Washington D.C.: Office of the Assistant Secretary of Defense, Manpower and Reserve Affairs, 1978.

Armanski, Gerhard, Peter Ramin, and Georg Richter, eds. *Rührt Euch! Über den Antimilitaristischen Kampf in der Bundeswehr*. West Berlin: Rotboch Verlag, 1976.

Aronowitz, Stanley. *False Promises: The Shaping of American Working Class Consciousness*. New York: McGraw-Hill, 1973.

Bertrand, Jean Pierre. *Les Soldats Seront Troubadours*. Paris: Presses D'Aujourd'hui, 1979.

Binkin, Martin, et al. *Where Does the Marine Corps Go From Here?* Washington, D.C.: The Brookings Institution, 1976.

Bowman, William, Roger Little, and G. Thomas Sicilia, eds. *The Volunteer Force After A Decade*. Washington, D.C.: Pergamon-Brassey's, 1986.

Burton, Anthony. *The Destruction of Loyalty: An Examination of the Threat of Propaganda and Subversion Against the Armed Forces of the West*. London: Foreign Affairs Research Institute, 1976.

Carew, Anthony. *The Lower Decks of the Royal Navy, 1900-39: The Invergordon Mutiny in Perspective*. Manchester, England: University of Manchester Press, 1981.

Cincinnatus. *Self Destruction: The Disintegration and Decay of the U.S. Army During the Vietnam War*. New York and London: W. W. Norton, 1981.

Cockerill, A. W. *Sons of the Brave: The Story of Boy Soldiers*. London: Leo

Cooper, 1984.

Coffey, Kenneth. *Strategic Implications of the All Volunteer Force.* Chapel Hill: University of North Carolina Press, 1979.

Cohen, Eliot A. *Citizens and Soldiers: The Dilemmas of Military Service.* Ithaca, N.Y.: Cornell University Press, 1985.

Cortright, David. *Soldiers in Revolt: The American Military Today.* New York: Anchor/Doubleday, 1975.

_____. *Unions in the Military.* Washington, D.C.: American Enterprise Institute, 1977.

Cortright, David, Max Watts, et al. *Widerstand in der U.S. Armee: GI Bewegung in den siebzieger Jahren.* West Berlin: Harald Kater Verlag, 1986.

Crozier, Michael J., Samuel P. Huntington, and Joji Watanuki. *The Crisis of Democracy.* New York: New York University Press, 1975.

Doorn, Jacques Van. *The Soldier and Social Change.* Beverly Hills, Calif.: Sage Publications, 1975.

Fields, Rona M. *The Portuguese Revolution and the Armed Forces Movement.* New York: Praeger Publishers, 1975.

Gardner, Fred. *Unlawful Concert: An Account of the Presidio Mutiny Case.* New York: Viking Press, 1970.

Gottlieb, David. *Babes in Arms: Youth in the Army.* Beverly Hills, Calif.: Sage Publications, 1980.

Grabler, Ronald V. *Military Unions: An Analysis of Unionization in Norway and Germany as it Relates to the United States.* Wright-Patterson Air Force Base, Ohio: U.S. Air Force Institute of Technology, 1971.

Hackel, Erwin. *Military Manpower and Political Purpose.* London: International Institute for Strategic Studies, 1970.

Harries-Jenkins, Gwyn, ed. *The Military and the Problem of Legitimacy.* Beverly Hills, Calif.: Sage Publications, 1976.

Hasek, Jaroslav. *The Good Soldier Schweik.* New York: Frederick Ungar Publishing, 1930. Reprint. 1962.

Holm, Jeanne. *Women in the Military: The Unfinished Revolution.* Novato, Calif.: Presidio Press, 1982.

Inglehart, Ronald. *The Silent Revolution: Changing Values and Political Styles Among Western Publics.* Princeton: Princeton University Press, 1977.

Janowitz, Morris. *The U.S. Forces and the Zero Draft.* London: International Institute for Strategic Studies, 1973.

_____. *Sociology and the Military Establishment.* 3d ed. Beverly Hills, Calif.: Sage Publications, 1974.

Johnston, Jerome, and Gerald Bachman. *Young Men and Military Service.* Ann Arbor, Mich.: Institute for Social Research, 1972.

Karsten, Peter. *Soldiers and Society: The Effects of Military Service and War on American Life.* Westport, Conn.: Greenwood Press, 1978.

Keeley, John B., ed. *The All-Volunteer Force and American Society.* Charlottesville: University of Virginia Press, 1978.

Krendel, Ezra, and Bernard Samoff, eds. *Unionizing the Armed Forces*. Philadelphia: University of Pennsylvania Press, 1977.

MacEoin, Gary. *Chile: The Struggle for Dignity*. London:Coventure Press, 1975.

Mailer, Phil. *Portugal: The Impossible Revolution*. London: Solidarity Press, 1977.

Marcuse, Herbert. *An Essay on Liberation*. Boston: Beacon Press, 1969.

_____. *Counter-Revolution and Revolt*. Boston: Beacon Press, 1972.

McArdle, Stephen J. *Analysis of Unionization Trends in Relation to U.S. Armed Forces*. Washington, D.C.: Industrial College of the Armed Forces, 1976.

Mockaitis, Joseph P., and Donald Johnson. *An Analysis of Military Unionization in Austria, Denmark and Sweden*. Wright-Patterson Air Force Base, Ohio: U.S. Air Force Institute of Technology, 1972.

Moskos, Charles, and Frank R. Wood, eds. *The Military: More Than Just a Job?* Washington, D.C.: Pergamon-Brassey's, 1988.

Olson, Howard C., and R. William Rae. *Determination of the Potential for Dissidence in the U.S. Army*. Technical Paper RAC-TP-410. McLean, Va: Research Analysis Corporation, 1971.

Olson, Howard C., R. William Rae, and Stephen B. Forman. *Future Impact of Dissident Elements Within the Army*. Technical Paper RAC-TP-441. McLean, Va: Research Analysis Corporation, 1972.

Pomorin, Jurgen. *Rührt Euch Kameraden: Tagebuch eines Wehrpflichtigen* Dortmund: Weltkreis Verlag, 1975.

Porch, Douglas. *The Portuguese Armed Forces and the Revolution*. Stanford, Calif.: Hoover Institution Press, 1977.

Recruiting for the Armed Forces of the 1970s. London: Royal United Service Institution, 1970.

Report of the Committee on Boy Entrants and Young Servicemen. London: H. M. Stationary Office, 1970.

Report of the President's Commission on an All Volunteer Force. London: Collier-Macmillan, 1970.

Richard, Denis, and Elisabeth Carriere, eds. *Le Proces du Draguignan*. Paris: Editions du Rocher, 1975.

Rivkin, Robert, and Barton Stichman. *The Rights of Military Personnel: The Basic ACLU Guide for Military Personnel*. Rev. ed. New York: Avon Books, 1977.

Rochon, Thomas R. *Mobilizing for Peace: The Anti-nuclear Movements In Western Europe*. Princeton: Princeton University Press, 1988.

Rothstein, Andrew. *The Soldiers' Strikes of 1919*. London: The Journeyman Press, 1985.

Roxbourough, Ian, Philip O'Brien, and Jackie Roddick. *Chile: The State and* the Revolution. London: Macmillan, 1977.

Rustad, Michael. Women in Khaki: The American Enlisted Woman. New York: Praeger Publishers, 1982.

Sabrosky, Alan. Blue-Collar Soldiers? Unionization and the U.S. Military. Philadelphia, Pa: Foreign Policy Research Institute, 1977.

Scowcroft, Brent, ed. Military Service in the United States. Englewood Cliffs, NJ: Prentice-Hall, 1982.

Segal, David R. Recruiting for Uncle Sam: Citizenship and Military Manpower Policy. Lawrence: University Press of Kansas, 1989.

Segal, David R., and H. Wallace Sinaiko, eds. Life in the Rank and File: Enlisted Men and Women in the Armed Forces of the United States, Australia, Canada and the United Kingdom. Washington, D.C.: Pergamon-Brassey's, 1986.

Soldaten en Kernwapens. Utrecht, Holland: VVDM, 1980.

Stanton, Shelby. The Rise and Fall of an American Army. Novato, Calif.: Presidio Press, 1985.

Stapp, Andy. Up Against the Brass. New York: Simon &Schuster, 1970.

Stieber, Jack. Public Employee Unionism: Structure, Policy. Washington, D.C.: The Brookings Institution, 1973.

Stockwell, John. In Search of Enemies. New York: Norton, 1978.

Taylor, William, Roger Arango, and Robert Lockwood, eds. Military Unions: U.S. Trends and Issues. Beverly Hills, Calif.: Sage Publications, 1977.

Touraine, Alain. The Post-Industrial Society. New York: Random House, 1971.

Unionization of the Armed Forces. Hearings Before the Committee on Armed Services, United States Senate, 95th Cong., 1st sess., on S. 274 and S. 997. Washington, D.C., 1977

Vagts, Alfred. A History of Militarism. New York: The Free Press, 1967.

Walden, Eric. The Goose Step is Verboten. New York: Free Press of Glencoe, 1964.

Waterhouse, Larry, and Mariann Wizard. Turning the Guns Around. New York: Delta, 1971.

Watts, Max. U.S. Army Europe: Von der Desertion zum Widerstand in der Kaserne, oder wie die U-Bahn zur RITA fuhr. West Berlin: Harald Kater Verlag, 1989.

Westmoreland, William C. A Soldier Reports. Garden City, N.Y.: Doubleday and Company, 1976.

Woddis, Jack. Armies and Politics. New York: International Publishers, 1977.

Wool, Harold. The Military Specialist. Baltimore: The Johns Hopkins University Press, 1968.

Young, Ken. Civil Liberties and Service Recruitment: The Plight of Reluctant

Servicemen. London: National Council for Civil Liberties, 1970.

Articles

"The Black Soldier." Special Issue. *Black Scholar* (November1970).

Buck, James. "The Japanese Self Defense Force." *Naval War College Review* 26 (January-February 1974).

Clarity, James F. "Military Unions Stir Paris Alarm." *New York Times* (November 30, 1975).

Cook, Don. "Unions in European Armies on Increase." *Los Angeles Times* (November 17, 1976).

Cortright, David. "A Look at Dutch Military Union." *Air Force Times* 36 (September 3, 1975).

————. "The Union Wants to Join You." *The Nation* (February 21, 1976).

Cortright, David, and Boykin Reynolds. "Armed Forces Union Runs Into Many Snags." *Federal Times* (December 24, 1975).

Dietz, Peter J., and J. F. Stone. "The British All-Volunteer Army." *Armed Forces and Society* 1 (Winter 1975).

Dodd, Norman. "Volunteer Recruiting in Great Britain." *Military Review* 53 (June 1973).

Drumm, Robert H. "The Air Force Man and the Cultural Value Gap." *Air University Review* 19 (May-June 1968).

Ensign, Todd, and Michael Uhl. "Soldiers as Workers." *Progressive* 40 (April 1976).

Fleckenstein, Bernhard. "The Military and Labor Union Organizations in Germany." *Aus Politik Und Zeitgeschichte* (May 22, 1976).

Goldman, Nancy. "Women in NATO Armed Forces." *Military Review* 54 (October 1974).

Hitchens, Christopher. "Barrack Room Rumblings." *New Statesman* (March 22, 1974).

Janowitz, Morris, and Charles Moskos. "Five Years of the All-Volunteer Force: 1973-1978." *Armed Forces and Society* 5 (Winter 1979).

Jones, Bradley K. "The Gravity of Administrative Discharge: A Legal and Empirical Evaluation." *Military Law Review* (Winter 1973).

Manley, T. Roger, Charles W. McNichols, and G. C. Saul Young. "Attitudes of Active Duty U.S. Air Force Personnel Toward Unionization." *Armed Forces and Society* 3 (Summer 1977).

Moskos, Charles. "Making the All-Volunteer Force Work: A National Service Approach." *Foreign Affairs* 60 (Fall 1981).

Murthy, P. A. Narasmha. "The Self Defence Forces of Japan." *Journal of the Institute for Defense Studies and Analyses* 4 (October 1971).

Rimland, Bernard, and Gerald E. Larson. "The Manpower Quality Decline:

An Ecological Perspective." *Armed Forces and Society* 8 (May 1981).

Schmemann, Serge. "In East German Army Ranks, A Headlong Farewell to Arms." *New York Times* (March 9, 1990).

Slavin, Peter. "The Cruelest Discrimination: Vets With Bad Discharge Papers." *Business and Society Review* (Summer 1975).

Teplyakov, Yuri. "The Other Face of War: Talks With Different Afghanistan Vets." *Moscow News* (September 17, 1989).

Tsypkin, Michael. "The Soviet Union: The Conscripts." *Bulletin of Atomic Scientists* 39 (May 9, 1983).

Van Doorn, Jacques. "The Decline of the Mass Army in the West: General Reflections." *Armed Forces and Society* 1 (Winter 1975).

Watts, Max. "Watergate on the Neckar." *Die Tageszeitung* (April 16, 1980).

Wilson, George C. "Ex-paratrooper Battles to Unionize 82d Airborne." *Washington Post* (March 26, 1977).

Wolpin, Miles. "Military Radicalism in Latin America." *Journal of Inter-American Studies and World Affairs* 23 (November 1981).

_____. "Socio-Political Radicalism and Military Professionalism in the Third World." *Comparative Politics* 15 (April 1983).

Acknowledgments

Many people contributed to the work of *Left Face* over its fifteen years of production. The most important contributions came from the more than 100 soldiers and recent veterans whose words and experiences make up the primary source material for the book. We acknowledge many of these people in the Notes. We cannot thank everyone, though, and apologize to those we may have overlooked.

We offer special thanks to Robert Borosage, who supported the initial work on the book as director of the Center for National Security Studies in the 1970s; to Robert K. Musil, fellow at the Center who assisted and encouraged the early writing; and to Michael Mawby, then an intern at the Center, who provided research assistance. Thanks also go to Phil Hill, Tom Conrad, and Boykin Reynolds for research and translation services. We acknowledge the encouragement of the late Clyde Webber and offer special thanks to Greg Kenefick and Al Kaplan of the AFGE. Special thanks also go to Tom Doran, and to Todd Ensign and Michael Uhl of Citizen Soldier. Kathy Gilberd from the Military Law Task Force of the National Lawyers Guild was helpful as well.

We are deeply indebted to Dave Harris and Dieter Brunn, who assembled and maintain the GI archive in Berlin and who contributed greatly to the writing and research of this book. We thank Ben Dankbaar, formerly with the BVD in Holland, for extensive assistance and support and also acknowledge the contributions of Johan Leestemaker and many other Dutch colleagues from BVD and VVDM. Important contributions were also made by Robert Rivkin, Patrick Silberstein, John Michael MacDougal, and Adam Keller.

Special thanks go to colleagues at SANE in Washington who helped with production, typing, editing, and research for the book, especially Beth Baker, Duane Shank, Charlie Kraybill, Ellie Zogran, and John Schloerb.

Barbara Budgett prepared the final production text.

Our greatest debt is to those who supported us personally during this long endeavor: to Patricia Cortright, and to the children Michael and Catherine Cortright; to June L. V. and Rosie K.; and to Karen Jacob. Without the support and understanding of our family and loved ones, this work would not have been possible.

Index

About the Authors

DAVID CORTRIGHT is a visiting fellow at the Institute for International Peace Studies at the University of Notre Dame. His previous publications include *Soldiers in Revolt,* as well as numerous articles on peace and military resistance issues that have appeared in newspapers and national journals.

MAX WATTS presently lives in Annandale, Australia, where he studies and writes about the evolution of socialist countries, applied Marxism, and rank-and-file soldier resistance movements. He has authored numerous articles in Australian, Asian, American, and European journals and newspapers.